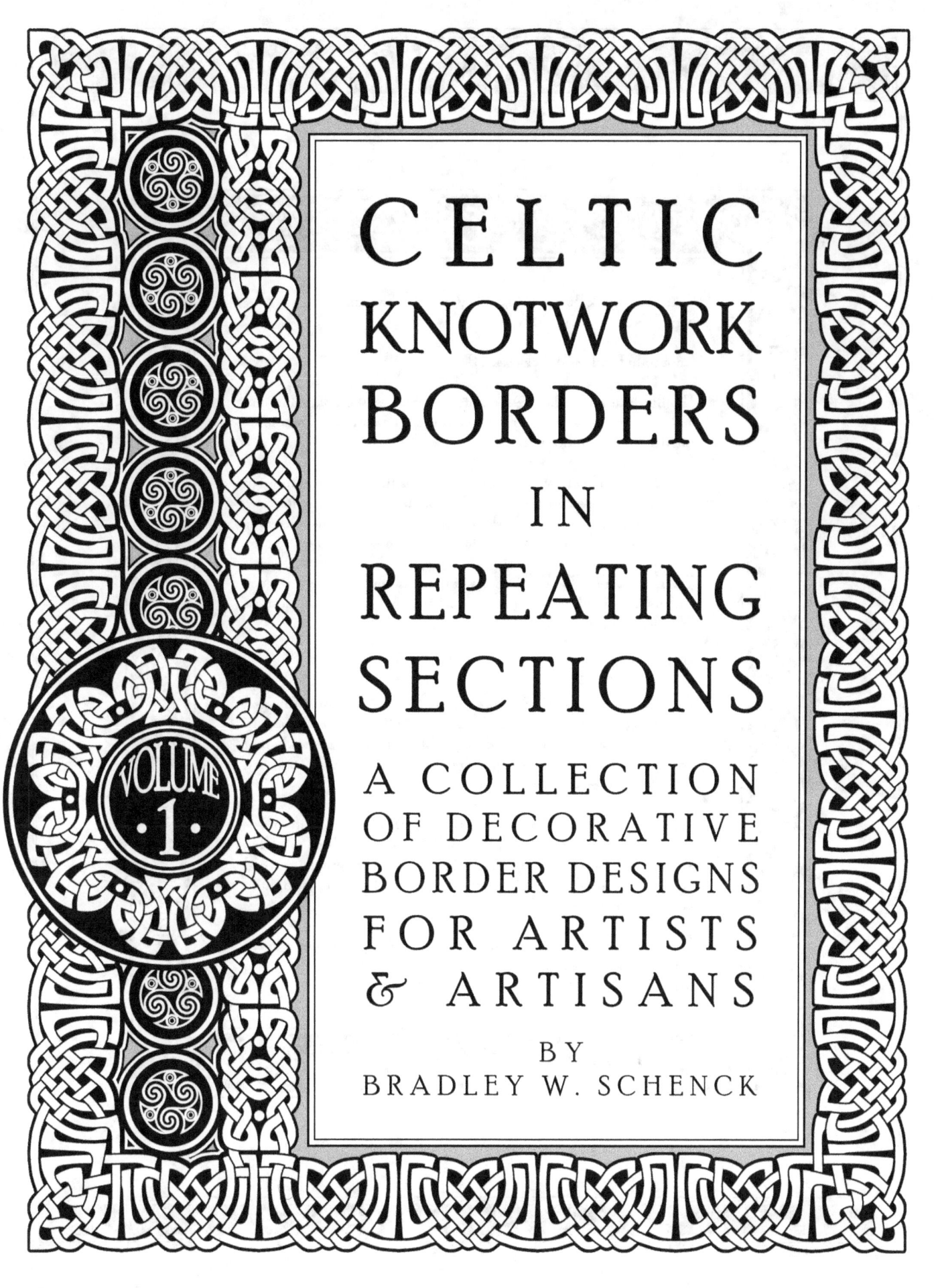

CELTIC
KNOTWORK
BORDERS
IN
REPEATING
SECTIONS

A COLLECTION
OF DECORATIVE
BORDER DESIGNS
FOR ARTISTS
& ARTISANS

BY
BRADLEY W. SCHENCK

VOLUME
·1·

The fine print

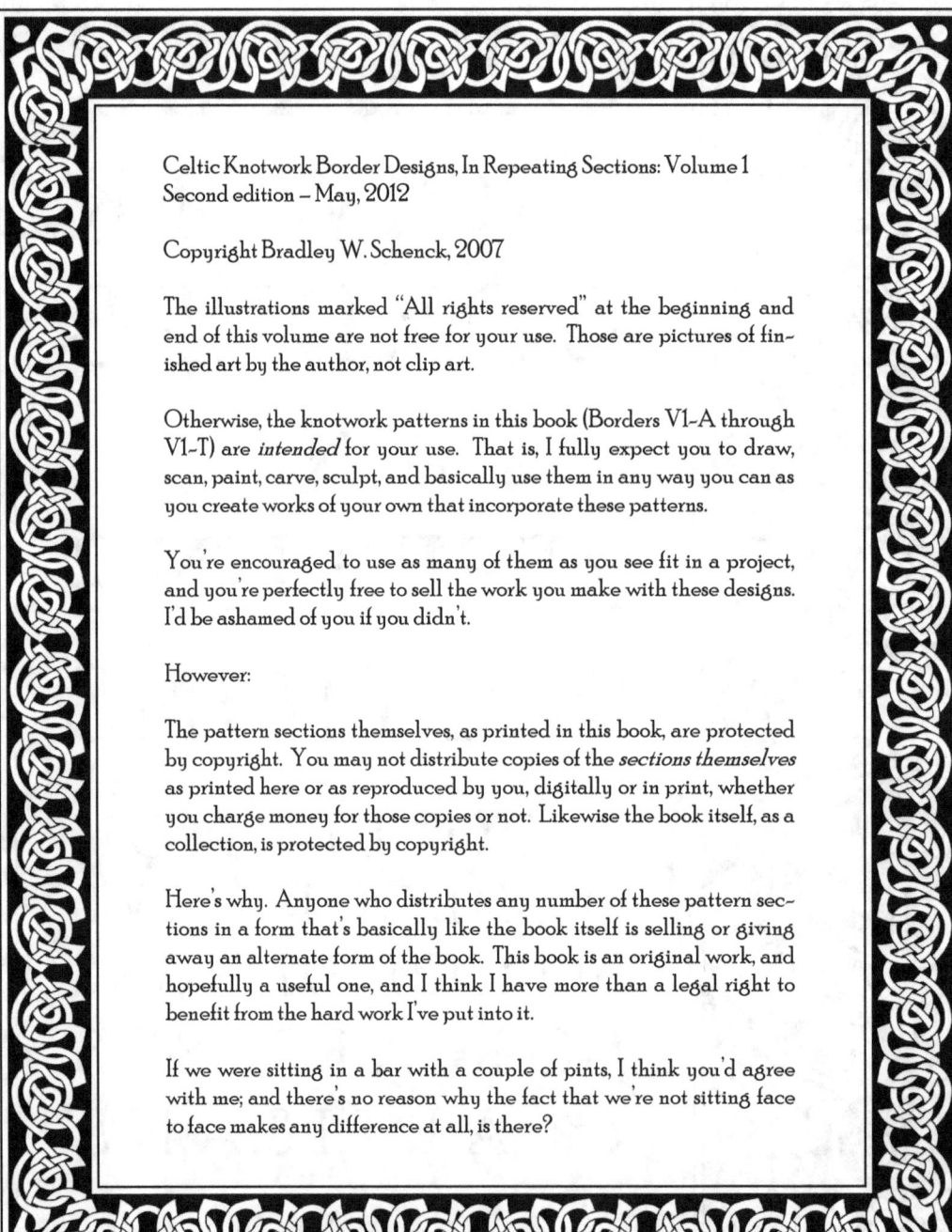

Celtic Knotwork Border Designs, In Repeating Sections: Volume 1
Second edition – May, 2012

The illustrations marked "All rights reserved" at the beginning and end of this volume are not free for your use. Those are pictures of finished art by the author, not clip art.

Otherwise, the knotwork patterns in this book (Borders V1-A through V1-T) are *intended* for your use. That is, I fully expect you to draw, scan, paint, carve, sculpt, and basically use them in any way you can as you create works of your own that incorporate these patterns.

You're encouraged to use as many of them as you see fit in a project, and you're perfectly free to sell the work you make with these designs. I'd be ashamed of you if you didn't.

However:

The pattern sections themselves, as printed in this book, are protected by copyright. You may not distribute copies of the *sections themselves* as printed here or as reproduced by you, digitally or in print, whether you charge money for those copies or not. Likewise the book itself, as a collection, is protected by copyright.

Here's why. Anyone who distributes any number of these pattern sections in a form that's basically like the book itself is selling or giving away an alternate form of the book. This book is an original work, and hopefully a useful one, and I think I have more than a legal right to benefit from the hard work I've put into it.

If we were sitting in a bar with a couple of pints, I think you'd agree with me; and there's no reason why the fact that we're not sitting face to face makes any difference at all, is there?

Table of contents

Introduction 1

How to use these designs 4

The three rules of Celtic knotwork 4

Using the straight border sections 5

Using the circle border sections 7

Pattern sizes & scaling 8

Non-digital scaling 8

Digital scaling 9

Using the borders in computer graphics 9

What about works on paper, wood, or cloth? 11

The big picture 13

Metric & arc conversions 14

Border V1-A 15

Border V1-B 20

Border V1-C 24

Border V1-D 28

Border V1-E 33

Border V1-F 36

Border V1-G 39

Border V1-H 42

Border V1-I 47

Border V1-J 52

Border V1-K 55

Border V1-L 59

Border V1-M 64

Border V1-N 69

Border V1-O 73

Border V1-P 76

Border V1-Q 79

Border V1-R 83

Border V1-S 87

Border V1-T 90

About the Author 95

Biography 96

The author's web sites 97

Introduction

It's possible that there has never been a better time for artists and craftspeople who want to incorporate Celtic knotwork patterns into their work. Not only are there plenty of examples to stumble across in everyday life – from book covers on the shelf, to tattoos walking down the street – but there are a large number of books available on the subject, and they're easier than ever to find, thanks to the World Wide Web.

When I began to get the idea of designing a volume of patterns myself I had to wonder why on Earth one more book ought to exist. It didn't seem to be enough to offer a series of designs that were original and unique, although these are; the field's simply too wide for that alone to matter. I think I found the answer when I thought about what all those books were, and how they address what an artist needs and wants.

As I see it, books of Celtic knotwork designs fall into two types.

The first type, like George Bain's "Celtic Art: the Methods of Construction" – that venerable reprint that got me started in the first place – is a collection, usually of traditional patterns, that have been deconstructed into a system that the artist can use to recreate them by plotting them on a grid, on a series of dots, or with some other device that may or may not be similar to methods used by scribes and artists during the Middle Ages. Books like these are valuable tools for anyone who wants to understand how the patterns work, and wants to either build them up from scratch or understand how new patterns can be created.

The second type of Celtic knotwork reference is nothing more than a clip art collection – often line drawings based on period art, sometimes reprints of work that's fallen into the public domain. These designs can include repeating borders, but those are most often presented as complete borders that you're expected to copy as they are. This offers very little control over the size or shape of the border itself.

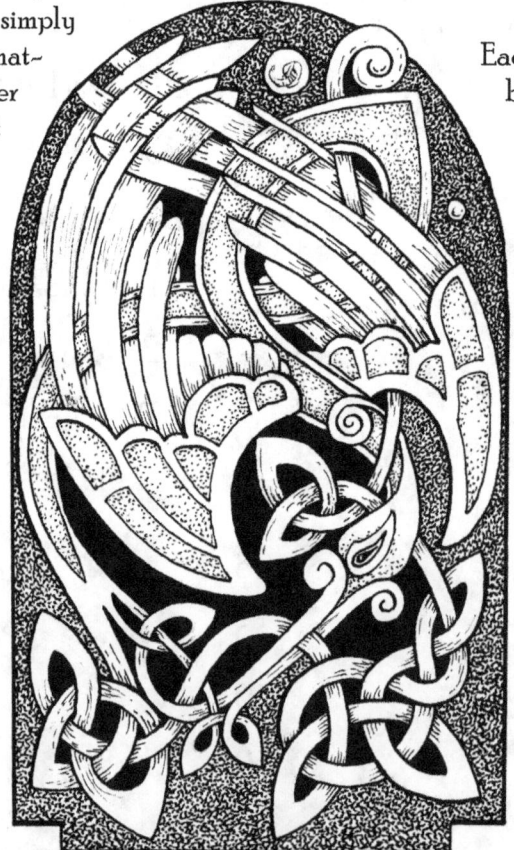

Interlaced bird design by the author, 1985
Note the splits in the tail and loose ends (page 4).

Each of those two types of books addresses a need. But neither one corresponds, exactly, to the way I work myself.

As I kept thinking about what a book like this one might be good for, I tried to come up with a presentation for the designs that would work, as much as possible, the way I do.

So what *do* I do, and how does this book encourage you to work that way?

To start with, I design the pattern itself. Over the years I've almost always done this on graph paper. Once I was making my art entirely on computers I sometimes plotted out a design in paint software, though I'd usually only do that with panel designs and designs meant to conform to an odd shape. The patterns in this book are the largest body of repeating designs I've ever done digitally from start to finish.

But whether I'm working digitally or on paper, there's no need to go through that first step more than once. I'm not a medieval scribe, after all. I'm an artist who came of age during the twentieth century ~ and by the time I discovered knotwork I was already using many tools and techniques that hadn't existed before modern times. Because I am an artist, and not an historian, I adapted those same tools to my knotwork designs.

So when I was carving or painting or dyeing, I'd work out the repeating sections of my patterns and then use those drawings to plot out an entire border on drafting vellum – that's an archival, non~yellowing tracing paper. When I was happy with the border I'd transfer the complete border design onto the surface I meant to put it on. This is just the way I handled my sketches of anything else.

When I'm working digitally I work out the re~peating sections of the design in one document, then copy and paste them into the document I'm painting the final piece in. It's more or less like moving little drawings around. There's plenty more I do after that: color, and lighting effects, and texture. Those more painterly steps, though, are done to the whole border as it's been laid out, not to the individual repeating sections.

In either case what I'm doing is keeping three steps separate.

Designing the pattern is the first step. Laying its parts out in a complete border is the second step. Painting or carving that compete border is the third step.

In each case I use the tools available to me to make the second step as simple as possible. The truly creative work is all in steps one and three.

And that's exactly how my work differs from that of a medieval scribe, isn't it? If I were a scribe working on an illuminated manuscript during the seventh century, my material would be a precious piece of parchment – the final work surface. I'd have no way to lay out a design on some other surface, preserving the parchment. Parchment can be translucent, but it's hardly transparent: and even if it were, I'd have no other material like modern drafting vellum on which to rough out my design.

A medieval scribe had no choice but to use a system ~ grid, dots, or otherwise ~ to lay out every repeat of his design on the final work surface. But it's a choice that *you* have.

Now, here's the thing about you. Following what you believe is a medieval technique for creating these designs may be exactly what you're about. That process may be part of the art, for you. If so, more power to you, and good luck.

But if you're a little more like me, what you're really after is that piece of art that's in your head and desperate to get out. Getting it out involves many creative steps – in fact, some would day that the work *is* those creative steps – but plotting out a repeating border is *not* a creative step. It's a task you'd like to simplify so that you can get on with it.

So here's my book. It's the best approach I've been able to come up with for helping you simplify what I called step two, up above – that mechanical task of plotting out the repeats of some specific Celtic knotwork borders.

What I am giving you is a collection of original knotwork border designs that you can adapt to your own work, whether that work's on paper, canvas, wood, or any other material, or even if it's entirely digital in nature. Every one of these repeating borders is presented in several sizes – including arcs for circular borders with different numbers of repeats around a full circle. Half of the designs also include complementary "inner border" designs that branch out from the outer border, with T-sections to connect the two and crosspieces so that the inner borders can also cross.

I'm giving you some instructions and ideas for how those parts can be combined, like puzzle pieces, to build out your own complete borders in just about any size your project needs. If those sizes aren't enough, I'll show you how you can scale the sections in this book to the size that you do need.

To my way of thinking this is a type of book that doesn't already exist, and I hope it's useful to you.

What it won't do is to teach you how to design your own knotwork borders. I hope you'll see what I've done and maybe pick up a thing or two – but like I said at the beginning, there are many books out there that will help you make a start on creating original designs. I recommend that, and them!

Bradley W. Schenck
February, 2007

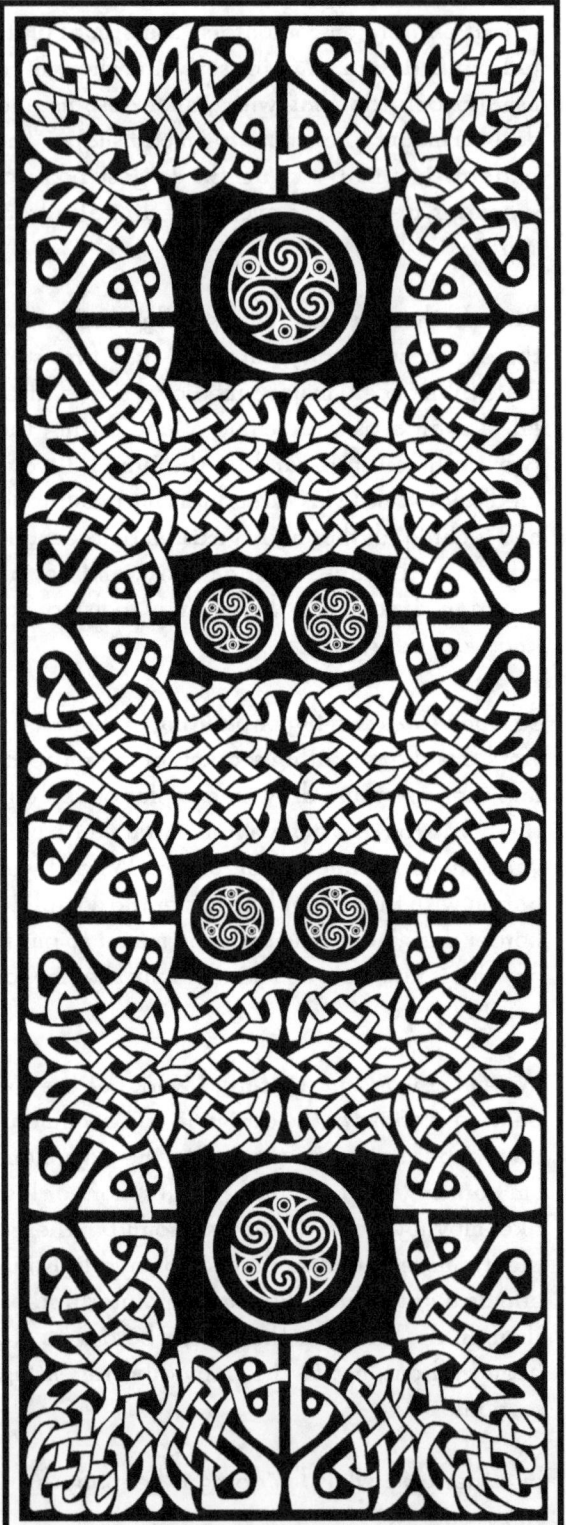

The three rules of Celtic knotwork

Now for the most part, because you'll be using patterns I've designed for you, you won't have to worry about these. But in order to understand how to use the border sections it'll be a great help to you if you keep the rules in mind.

1. As you follow the band (or bands) of the pattern, they *must* pass alternately over and under in the same way that a simple basket (or tabby) weave does. If a band passes over another part of the pattern it must pass *under* the next part of the pattern it meets.
2. There should be no loose ends in the pattern; every part of the pattern should be a continuous loop
3. In addition, most of us believe that in its ideal form a knotwork pattern should be composed of only one band, with no other bands or rings in the design.

Where do these rules come from? Well, we sort of made them up. But not really.

Back in the seventh century and beyond, as this style of decoration appeared and found its home in illuminated manuscripts, on standing stones, in jewelry designs, and elsewhere, no one was writing about what they were doing. Writing itself, especially in book form, was quite rare – and the books themselves were unbelievably expensive to produce (by hand, of course). We had no printing presses in the western world at that time.

So if we want to understand what these medieval artists were trying to do we have to look at what they did, and then think about what we're looking at.

The three rules I wrote above are our best guess about what was important to these artists. You shouldn't assume that every historical knotwork pattern adheres to the rules; many break them. We believe that they're rules because on the whole, this seems to be the ideal the artists were trying for

Did they ever break the rules on purpose? Yes, I think they did. In forms of knotwork that show animals or plants we sometimes see loose ends in the designs – in places like the ends of tails, or claws, or wings, for example. There are cases where those loose ends turn into abstract bands of patternwork; but there are also cases where the ends seem to have been left there deliberately to better show the shape of the animal or plant.

We may see similar broken rules in the over-and-under weave of the pattern in these pictures of animals, and sometimes this seems to be the result of those loose ends of tails, wings, or other shapes. Leaving those ends loose just makes it impossible to resolve the over-and-under pattern without errors.

And there are even many cases in which abstract border designs break the rules, especially the third one – that is, they may be made up of more than one band, and sometimes even include pretty obvious "rings" within the design.

Today we believe that these three rules matter, and we think they mattered in medieval times as well. Now Celtic knotwork has been revived and reinterpreted before, and it doesn't always work just the same way – if you look at the Celtic Revival work from the early part of the twentieth century you'll be more likely to find some broken "rules", and also a unique tendency to make internal splits, like holes, in bands that may still respect the rules. (Other parts of the pattern obey the over-and-under rule as they weave through these holes.)

The patterns I've designed for this book all obey the first rule. However, half of these patterns include what I call "inner border" sections which tie into the main design- and in most of those cases I've relaxed the third rule. The resulting pattern, if it uses those inner border sections, is composed of more than one band. That may also be true of the ring borders based on those inner border sections.

But if you choose to hold strictly to the three rules you can do so with these designs, by avoiding the sections I've identified as being made up of more than one band. There's a "Structure" note at the introduction of each design that tells you when that's true.

There's one more reason you need to keep the first rule in mind as you assemble your own borders from my sections.

Using the straight border sections

Each of these designs is presented as a series of repeating sections, in several sizes. I've only shown each section, per size, once: but as you build up a border from those sections you'll need to *rotate* the sections as they go around the border.

For example:

You must never make a right corner by flipping, or mirroring, a left corner. The same goes for top and bottom corners.

You must never make a right side straight section by flipping, or mirroring, a left side straight section. The same goes for repeats along the top and bottom.

In short, you must always *rotate* a section to fit, and never flip it or mirror it.

Why? For a couple of reasons. Number one is the first rule I wrote above – because if you flip a section the over-and-under pattern of its weave will be broken where the mirrored section meets another section that has not been mirrored. Your pattern just won't line up as a proper knotwork design, and it'll look funny, too. The second reason is that as I've drawn the sections I've always made sure that they lined up properly, within about 1/300th of an inch, with all the other sections they may come into contact with. To the best of my ability I've made sure that this will always work as seamlessly as possible. So you should always rotate the sections as I'm showing here to take advantage of that.

By their nature these parts can be combined in all sorts of ways, Figure 1 shows. A single panel can be made with nothing but four corner sections rotated in 90 degree increments; a square or rectangular border can be laid out using just the corner section and the straight repeating section of an outer border, always rotating the pieces as they run from one side to the next. If you start adding in the inner border sections a large number of possibilities arise. You see some of these in Figure 1, and I've shown many more on the pages that introduce those designs that include inner borders.

It's helpful to think of the border sections as tiles. They're designed to meet up at their edges, and by rotating them you can make a

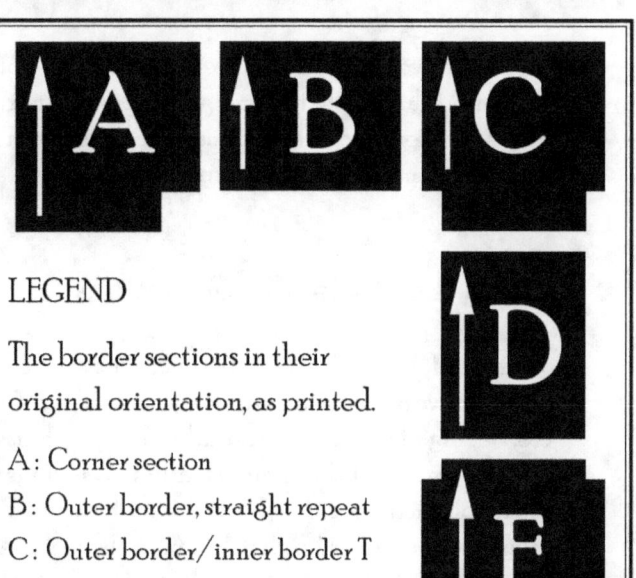

LEGEND

The border sections in their original orientation, as printed.

A: Corner section
B: Outer border, straight repeat
C: Outer border/inner border T
D: Inner border, straight repeat
E: Inner border, crosspiece

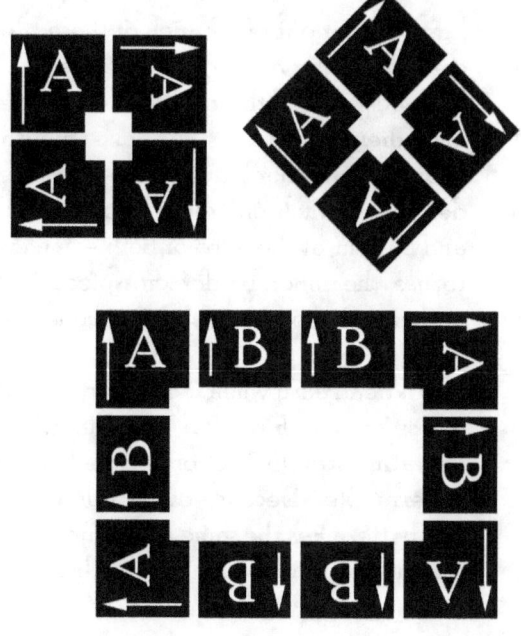

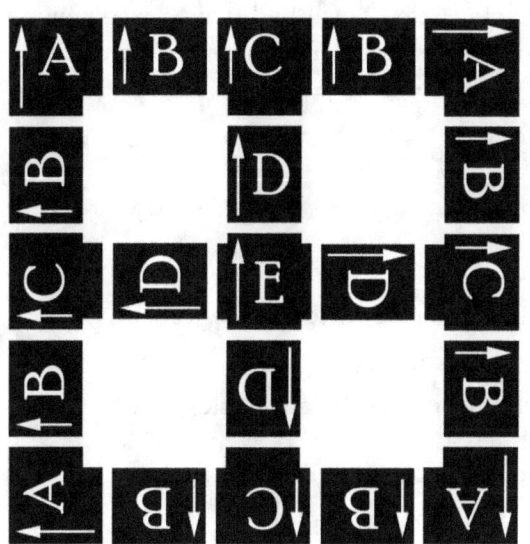

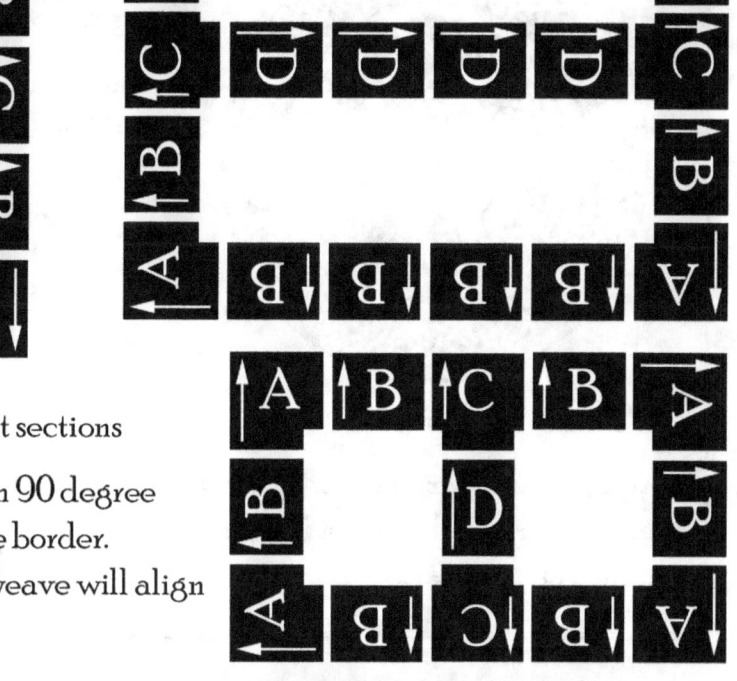

Figure 1: How to arrange the straight sections

Note that all sections are rotated in 90 degree increments as they pass around the border. This ensures that their edges and weave will align correctly.

large border out of a bunch of these tiles. Because the inner border/outer border T-sections intersect with both variations of the design – and they're always the same length as a straight outer border section – the inner borders can branch off from the outer at the top and bottom, at the sides, or both – you just need to use the inner border crosspiece to tie together the inner borders where they meet.

This is dead easy when it comes to those designs whose corners have the same length as their repeating straight sections – like Border V1-L, for example. Because every single section of this pattern has the same length you can create a complete border on a grid with that dimension.

I might have made your life simpler by conforming every pattern to that grid. It's just that in most cases I can make much more interesting

corners if I've allowed their length to vary. So you'll find that while the straight sections, inner border/outer border T sections, and crosspieces share the same length, the corners often don't.

Using the circle border sections

Each of these designs also includes one or more versions arranged as sections of a circle, or ring. Because almost all of the patterns are asymmetrical there are usually two facings of the outer border design, and sometimes two facings of the inner border design in those patterns that include an inner border.

The biggest differences between the circle sections are their number of repeats – that is, the number of times that the arc repeats around a complete circle. You'll find that a large number of repeats results in a narrow border, while

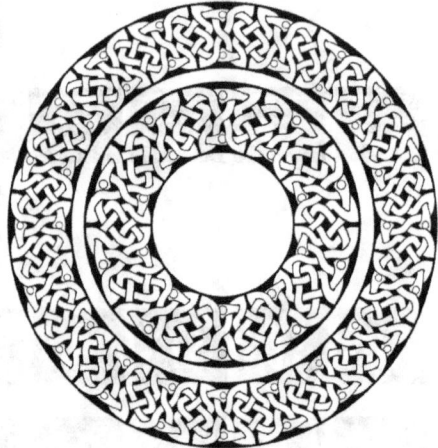

Figure 2: How to arrange the circle sections

Outer ring: 20 repeats
(each section is rotated 18 degrees)
Inner ring: 10 repeats
(each section is rotated 36 degrees)

Notice that the border is wider when the number of repeats is smaller.

At right, a diagram showing how the 10 repeat section is oriented as it's rotated 36 degrees in each of its repeats.

a small number of repeats gives you a proportionally wider border. So when you choose a circle section to use for your ring-shaped border you can choose whether you want it to be narrow or wide depending on the number of times it repeats.

I've given you many circle sizes on these pages. The idea, as it is with the straight sections, is that I have no idea what sort of project you have in mind – you may be creating a border to use on a printed page, but you might also be placing a border around your dining room table. So within the limits of space I've always tried to give you small and large sizes to choose from.

But however well I've managed that, you're still going to surprise me.

Pattern sizes and scaling

The sizes I've made for you are meant to be a good starter set, but that's all they can be. I've tried to make sure that from one design to another you'll have a good variety of sizes – so even without scaling the sections you should be able to find *some* size of *some* border that's about the size you're looking for. But when you find that you really like Border V1-M, and it's not printed in the size you want, you'll need to improvise. You'll need to either enlarge or reduce the pattern to the size you need.

The first, crucial, and probably really obvious thing is that when you do this you must scale all the sections you're going to use by the exact same amount. The easiest way to be sure of that is to scale them together at the same time.
You have several options for how you're going

to scale them. What it comes down to is whether you're able or willing to do that scaling on your computer.

Non-digital scaling

If you never do any graphics work on a computer, try these techniques:

1. Use the enlarging and reducing functions of a photocopier to scale the design – do the complete page or pages you want at the same time, if that's possible.
2. Trace the design onto translucent graph paper, and redraw the parts on graph paper at a larger or smaller size. You are truly old school if you go this way, but it's possible that if you're making a very, very large version of the design, it's the only way to go – unless you…
4. Use an opaque projector to blow the design up to a very large size. I've done this for a mural, and it can work just fine – but remember that it's very difficult to keep your projector and your drawing surface square to one another. You should draw a perfectly square outline on your paper to check the pattern and be prepared to sketch in some corrections to make it square. You're likely to run into trouble where the edges of the sections meet.

With any of these techniques you should remember that you don't need to enlarge or reduce an entire border. All you really need are the larger or smaller *sections*, as they appear in this book – once you have those you can trace or transfer them, as sections, onto your work surface.

Digital scaling

On the other hand, in this day and age many or most of you are able to scan, scale and print artwork on your computer. So long as the size of the sections you need is not larger than the paper you're able to print on, you can do that with a minimum of fuss.

Here are some things to remember if you're going to scan the borders:

1. Again, remember that all the sections you want should be scaled by the exact same amount, or they won't fit together any more.
2. For the very best results you should scan the sections at a high resolution even if you're going to print them small.
3. Regardless of the resolution you're scanning at, you can print the sections at any size you like through your software's features. For example, in Photoshop™ you can change the DPI of an image *without scaling the image itself* – the new "dots per inch" setting will cause the exact same image to print at a different size. (You do this in the Image menu, under "Image Size", by unchecking "Resample Image" and changing the value in "Resolution".)

In addition, you can physically scale the parts – remembering to do them all together – by leaving "Resample Image" checked and changing the Pixel Dimensions or Document Size. In order to scale several scanned images by the same amount, you should scale by percentage rather than the number of pixels or size in inches.

Now if you're only using your computer to scale the pattern, in order to print it out and lay out your border on paper, that's about all you need to worry about. Print out the border sections in their new sizes and lay out a border (see below for more on that).

But if you're going to do the design itself on your computer for a digital image there are a couple of other things to consider.

Using the borders in computer graphics

First, congratulations! In the long run you've got a great set of tools to work with and – provided you work in layers and save often – you're never going to spoil the piece you're working on. Tell that to a *watercolorist*, if you're heartless, and bored.

Second, watch out! It's almost impossible to get a scanned image lined up exactly square in your image. And if it's not exactly square within the image, you're about to lay out a border that isn't square either.

To get around this, you ought to start by scanning the image at the highest resolution you can manage. This will be important because you're going to need to rotate it, – at least slightly – in order to square things up. If you start with a low res image, then rotating it by anything other than 90 degrees is going to degrade its quality. (Why? Because pixels are square. You can rotate them 90 degrees without changing them – they're just squares, now facing a different way – but anything else will make them just a little fuzzier and less precise.)

This is another reason why you should scan all the sections you want together. If you rotate them to square them up you want to be sure that you're rotating them all by the exact same amount, to make sure they continue to fit properly.

If you're using Photoshop™, there's a trick I use to get things square. This should also work with other graphics software if it has floating "palettes" or tool panels – provided those palettes always float above your artwork.

Zoom in to a comfortable size, one where you'll still be able to rotate the image. Drag a floating palette over the image and scale that palette, if you can, to be at least as wide as the image you're going to rotate. Move the palette near with the top, bottom, or either side of your image.

Because the palette is perfectly square on the screen, and because it's floating above your work, it's a ruler you can use as you rotate your image to square it up.

You will probably find that you'll need to make slight corrections where the sections meet. You can do this in black and white, and use the corrected sections to lay out the complete border.

Once you have the sections squared up it's also a good idea to lay out the border at the largest size you can manage. Don't scale it till all the

pieces are merged together and you won't be manipulating them again. This way you only scale the border once, and you'll prevent it from getting any fuzzier or less precise than you want.

Circles are a little more complicated, or may be, depending on your software. You don't have to worry whether your scanned circle section is square unless that matters to you – the trick this time is to rotate all the sections by the exact same (and correct) amount.

In versions of Photoshop™ through 5.5, you can do this under the Edit menu (Transform/Transform Numeric). From Photoshop™ 6 on, the same thing is possible in the Options bar at the top of the screen, where you enter the number of degrees to rotate next to a small degrees/angle icon. In either case you enter the number of degrees you want, including negative numbers to rotate counterclockwise.

Anyway, what you want is simple enough – if a circle section repeats 10 times, you want to rotate it 36 degrees for each section; if it repeats 15 times, it's a 24 degree rotation. This is simple calculator work, but I'm including a table of measurements for that and for metric conversions so you should be able to look it up there, in Figure 3.

Remember that rotating an image by anything other than 90 degrees degrades its quality slightly. Work at the highest resolution you can manage, to minimize that, and try rotating half your sections clockwise, and the other half counter-clockwise, based on the original section. Once you've got a third or one half the sections rotated you can merge them all together and finish up by rotating those large, merged groups.

Because scanning, scaling, and rotating the sections may give you imprecise edges, check the areas where the sections join. You may need to do a little retouching there.

All done? Well, yes and no. Once you've followed these steps you'll have a black-and-white digital border – but that may be just the beginning. If you plan to use the border in color, try this: take that black-and white border layout and (in Photoshop™ or a comparable program) set its Layer Properties to "Multiply". Now create a new layer *under* that layer, and start painting on that new layer in color. What you'll see is the black outlines of your border showing over the painting, while the white areas of the border are transparent. Texture and paint that color layer as you please; try adding light effects to it. You can emphasize the three-dimensional quality of the knotwork's weave by airbrushing shadowed areas on an "underlapping" band, or airbrushing highlights on an "overlapping" one. Or both. You'll get the idea.

One thing you should never forget is that layers are your friend. Use separate layers for every separate thing you do – but do yourself a favor, and remember to give them descriptive names. You'll be glad you did.

At one point when I was working on my "Triskelion Mandala" I found that Photoshop™ would no longer let me create a new layer. This may depend on the memory in your system; that time, I think I had seventy layers in the one image.

Finally, I'm the first to admit that if you want to use these images in computer graphics what

you really need is a digital resource, so you'll never have to scan the patterns or worry about whether or not they're *really* square. As I write this I am thinking about doing just that – with both black and white and full color versions of the designs – but I have no idea when or if that may happen. You can always find out what I've been up to lately if you follow the links I'll provide near the end of the book.

What about works on paper, wood, or cloth?

Regardless of whether or not you've scaled the patterns – or even *how* you've scaled them – you may intend to use them in wood carvings, paintings, on signs, or in a batik or fabric painting project. So what you'll need to know is how to use these border sections to lay out the design on a physical object, whether it's a piece of paper, or anything else.

By the time I started using knotwork design in my own work I'd been painting for several years, so I had my own ways of working out a design and getting it onto my work surface. You may have ways of your own, and they're probably as good or better than mine. So what follows is just an explanation of the way I do it, in case you may want to try your hand at it my way.

I'm a big believer in drafting vellum. It's not really *vellum*, of course, which is parchment – drafting vellum is a 100% rag tracing paper that doesn't yellow or grow brittle with age. I've got drawings that are over 25 years old that are still flexible and useful. Drafting vellum is the bee's knees.

How to use these designs

I started using it because when I was working with watercolor I wanted to preserve my work surface so it'd be undamaged by my scribbling and erasures. If I worked out my sketches on a less precious surface, my paper would be in perfect shape when I started to paint; and if anything undoable went wrong I would still have my original drawing, so I could start again.

When working with drafting vellum you can use several layers, because you can see through one to the next. This made it perfect for me when I began to use Celtic borders around my paintings.

I'd use one main sheet for the border, and on that sheet I'd rule out the square lines that would contain the border. If I wasn't sure of its exact dimensions I'd just draw two square sides (in a corner) and add the other two once all of my repeats were drawn. Because I'd drawn a single straight and a single corner section of the pattern on another sheet of paper I would slip those under my vellum and trace them in place. When one section was done, I'd slide the original section over so that I could trace the next section, and so on, until my one sheet of drafting vellum held the whole border.

When working on cloth or wood or other materials I'd do the exact same thing – to start, I'd lay out the pattern on drafting vellum. It's only when I was satisfied with it that I wanted it on my work surface.

Once the pattern's completely drawn on the vellum you need to transfer it to your surface. There are plenty of options for transfer paper – most people use a kind of graphite paper you can find in art supply stores. But because graphite paper is messy, and only available in certain sizes, I've always made my own.

What I do is to take a sheet of (was there any doubt?) drafting vellum, and smear one side of it with a Conte crayon – a black crayon for work on light surfaces, or a white crayon for work on dark wood or other dark materials. Conte crayon is a slightly waxy crayon that isn't as messy as graphite. You just tape your drawing to the work surface and slide the transfer paper between them (crayon side down), and trace over the drawing through the transfer paper. The dark or light Conte crayon will transfer the design to your surface.

One sheet of this stuff lasts for years, which might be why they don't sell it. When it finally starts to get faint you can "recharge" it with Conte crayon again.

This has worked for me on all sorts of materials. It's not messy, and the crayon is faint and erases easily afterwards. Where necessary you can sketch lightly over it with pencil.

For borders, you can even cheat a bit – once you've got two corners and two sides of a rectangular border on your vellum you can transfer that much, then rotate the drawing 180 degrees to transfer the other half. But in order to keep things lined up just right I usually do the whole thing.

And if you're plotting out a circle design the principle is just the same – on your sheet of drafting vellum, draw a circle of the correct diameter and then trace the circle sections of the border in place. You can also skip the big drawing – just draw the circle itself directly on your workpiece, and transfer the sections into place one by one. I like having the big drawing, myself.

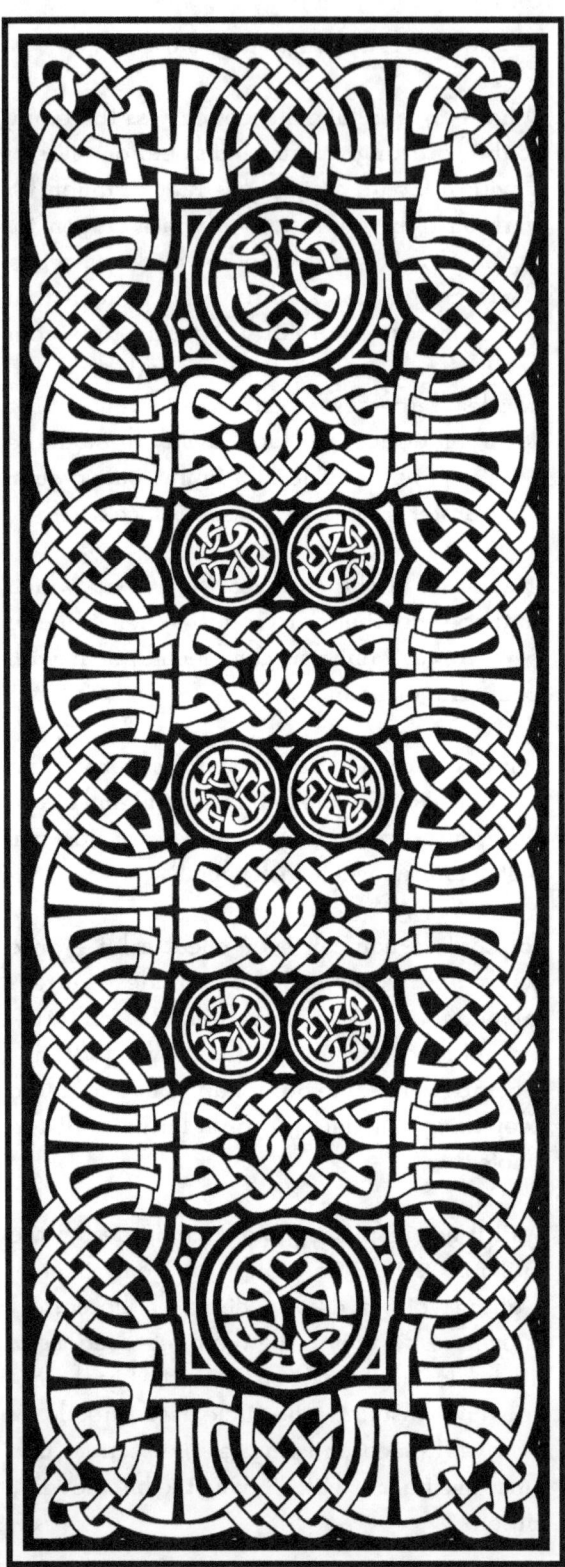

The big picture

I mentioned in the Introduction that when I conceived this book, it was based on the way I work – and now you can see how that is. When I was working on paper, wood, leather, or other materials, I'd work in just this way: design only the sections of a border pattern, scale them if necessary, and assemble them on a sheet of drafting vellum. Only when that was worked out to my satisfaction would I transfer the design to my final surface.

Since I've been working digitally the same basic idea has held true – even more so, I think. I design a pattern on paper or in my paint software, again just doing each section once. Then I copy and paste the repeats into place to form a complete border design. The repetitive, mechanical task of laying out the border is done pretty quickly and easily – so that I can start painting, texturing, adding lighting effects, and concentrating on all the other far more creative parts of the work as quickly as I can.

What I think one should avoid is trying to eliminate those steps, too. It would be a pretty simple matter to perform those painterly steps on the sections alone, and then piece the painted sections together into a border. But every piece of the border would then be exactly the same – you'd have to avoid texturing that didn't repeat seamlessly, you'd have no effects of light that spanned the entire border, and your work would end up looking mass produced and without life. That's not the end result I think we should be after, is it?

Digital tools make it easy to perform mechanical tasks that would otherwise be tedious. They shouldn't be used to remove the artistry from the art.

Metric & Arc Conversions

3/4"	19 mm		16"	40.64 cm
1"	25.4 mm		17"	43.18 cm
1 1/4"	31.75 mm		18"	45.72 cm
1 1/2"	38.1 mm		19"	48.26 cm
1 3/4"	44.45 mm		20"	50.8 cm
2"	50.8 mm		21"	53.34 cm
2 1/4"	57.15 mm		22"	55.88 cm
2 1/2"	63.5 mm		23"	58.42 cm
2 3/4"	69.85 mm		24"	60.96 cm
3"	76.2 mm		25"	63.5 cm
3 1/2"	88.9 mm		30"	76.2 cm
4"	10.16 cm			
4 1/4"	10.795 cm			
4 1/2"	11.43 cm			
5"	12.7 cm			
5 1/2"	13.97 cm			
6"	15.24 cm			
6 1/4"	15.875 cm			
6 1/2"	16.51 cm			
6 5/8"	16.827 cm			
7"	17.78 cm			
7 1/2"	19.05 cm			
8"	20.32 cm			
9"	22.86 cm			
9 1/2"	24.13 cm			
10"	25.4 cm			
11"	27.94 cm			
12"	30.48 cm			
12 1/2"	31.75 cm			
13"	33.02 cm			
14"	35.56 cm			
15"	38.1 cm			

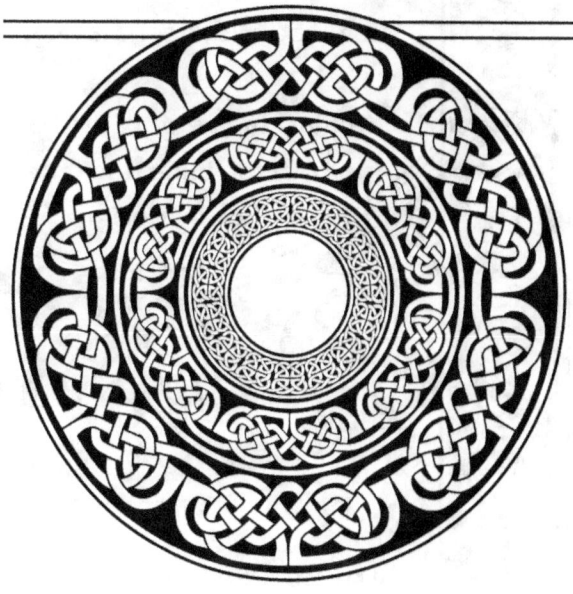

6 repeats around a circle: 60 degree arc

10 repeats around a circle: 36 degree arc

12 repeats around a circle: 30 degree arc

15 repeats around a circle: 24 degree arc

20 repeats around a circle: 18 degree arc

Figure 3: Metric and arc conversions

Border V1-A

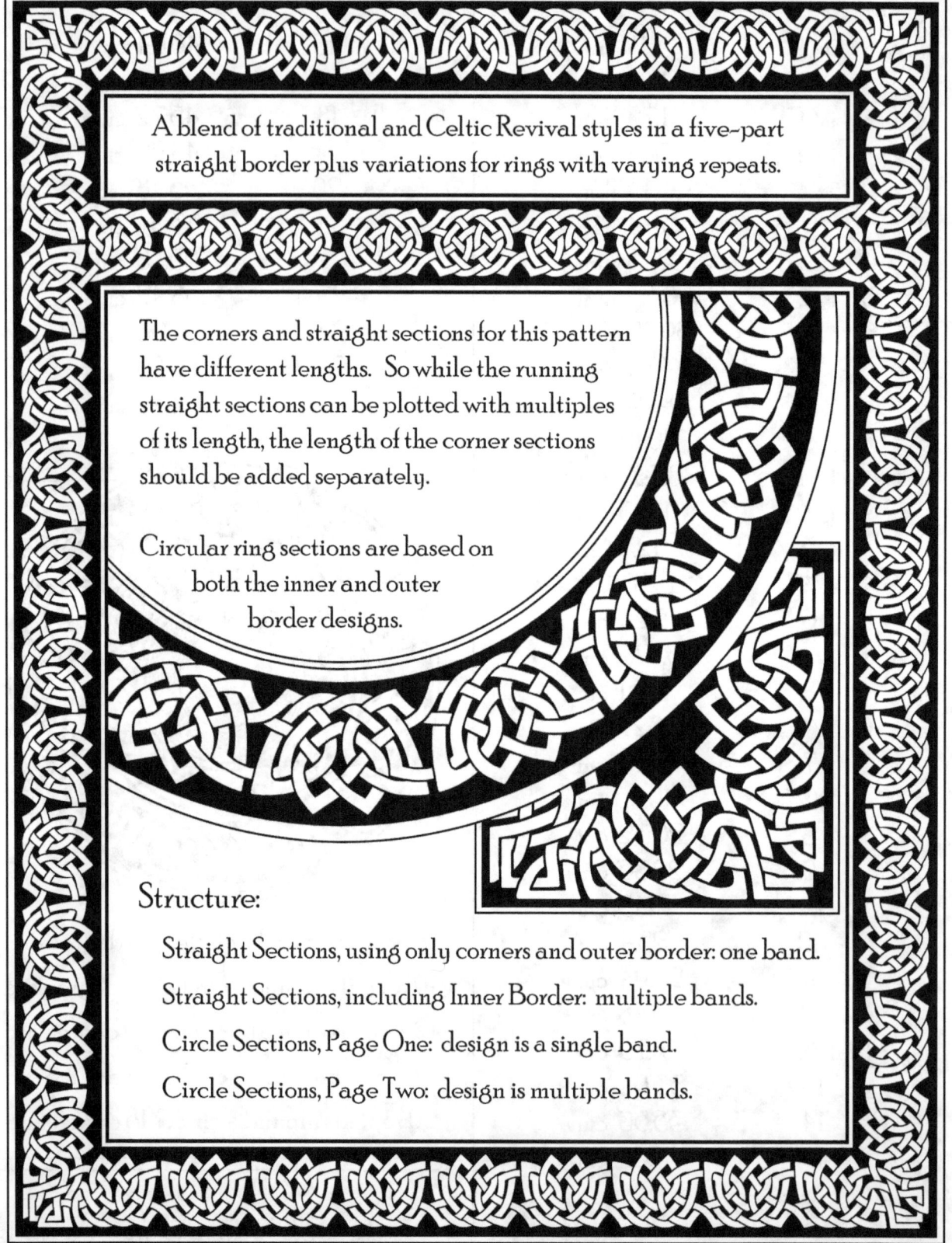

A blend of traditional and Celtic Revival styles in a five-part straight border plus variations for rings with varying repeats.

The corners and straight sections for this pattern have different lengths. So while the running straight sections can be plotted with multiples of its length, the length of the corner sections should be added separately.

Circular ring sections are based on both the inner and outer border designs.

Structure:

Straight Sections, using only corners and outer border: one band.

Straight Sections, including Inner Border: multiple bands.

Circle Sections, Page One: design is a single band.

Circle Sections, Page Two: design is multiple bands.

1 1/2" 1 1/2"

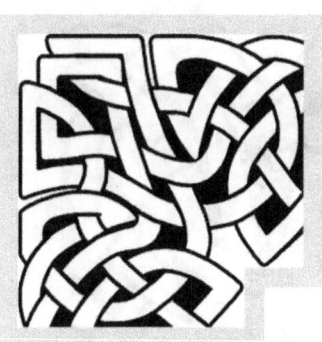

Corner Section

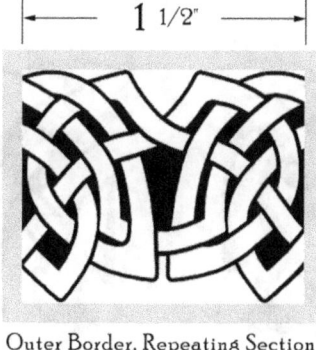

Outer Border, Repeating Section

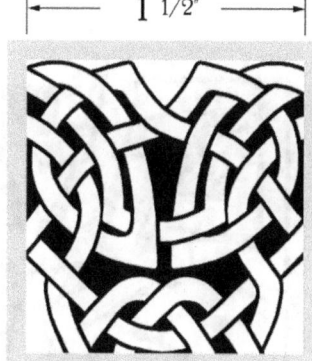

Outer Border / Inner Border T

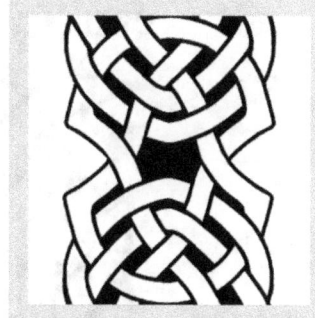

Inner Border, Repeating Section

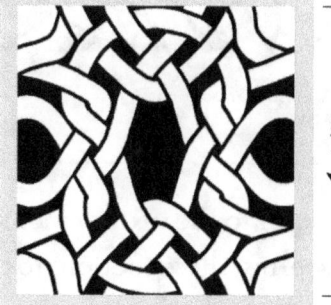

1 1/2"

Inner Border, Crosspiece

As with all the designs, rotate these five sections to make all the parts you need for a complete border.

The dimensions will help you to plot out the repeats ~ but you should remember that corners and the inner/outer T's are longer than the others.

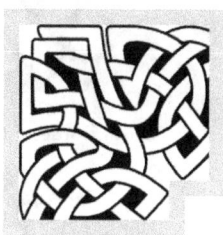

1" 1"

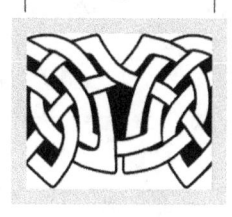

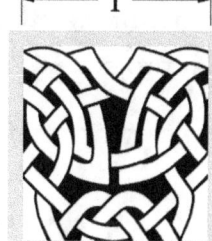

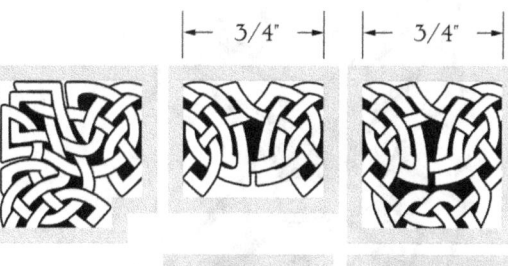

3/4" 3/4"

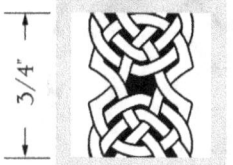

3/4"

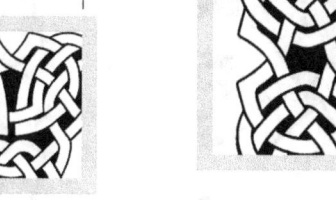

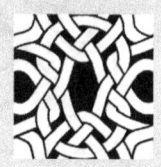

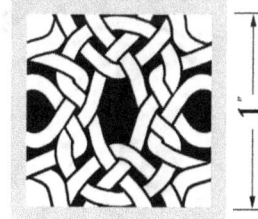

1"

Remember that these sections should always be rotated, not mirrored ~ if you flip them, the pattern will not line up properly!

2 1/4"

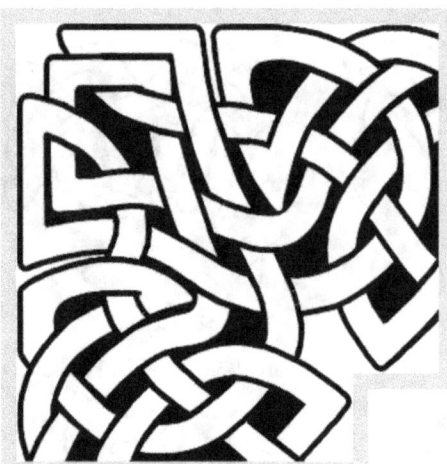

Corner Section

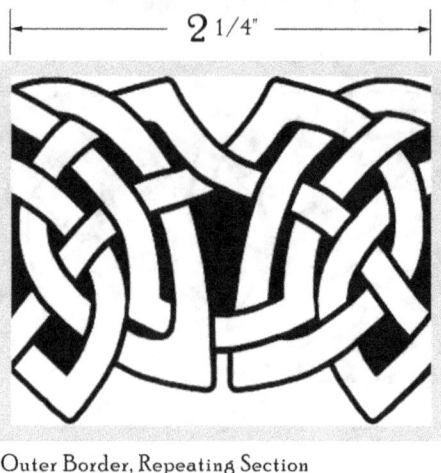

Outer Border, Repeating Section

Refer to the text for ideas about scaling these sections to other sizes, as well as tips on laying out your border with repeats to the length and width you need for your project.

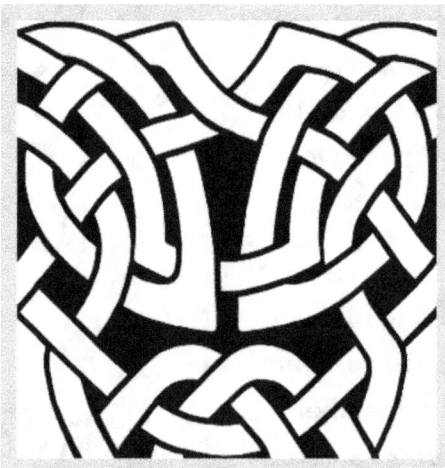

Outer Border / Inner Border T

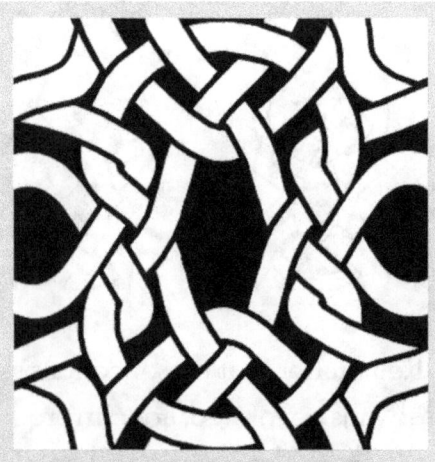

Inner Border, Crosspiece

2 1/4"

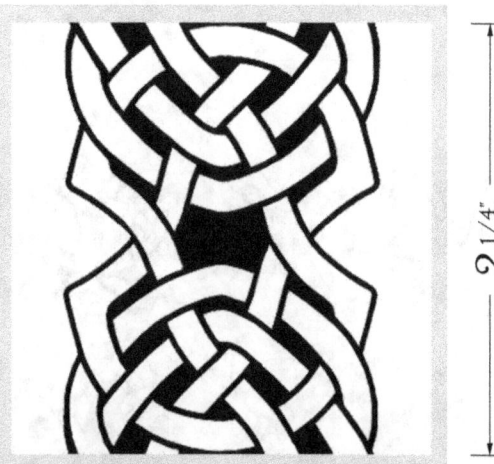

Inner Border, Repeating Section

2 1/4"

2 1/4"

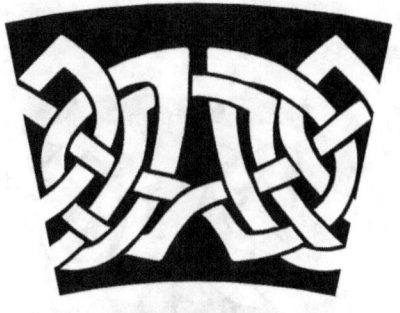

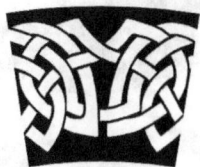 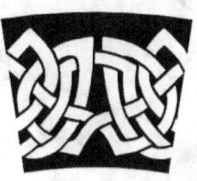

Each repeats 20 times around a
6 5/8" circle (outside diameter)

The measurements
for outside diameter
match the outer
black arc of each
section.

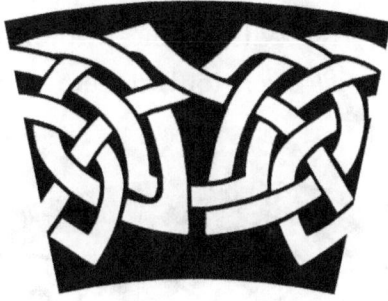

Each repeats 15 times around a
10" circle (outside diameter)

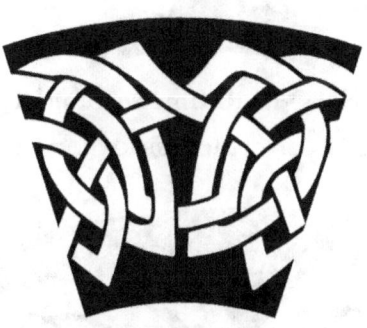

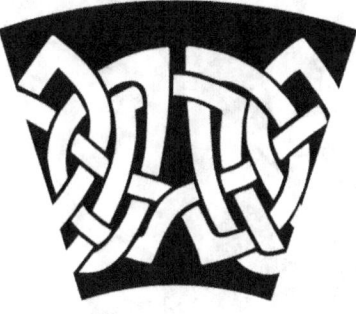

Each repeats 10 times around a
6 1/4" circle (outside diameter)

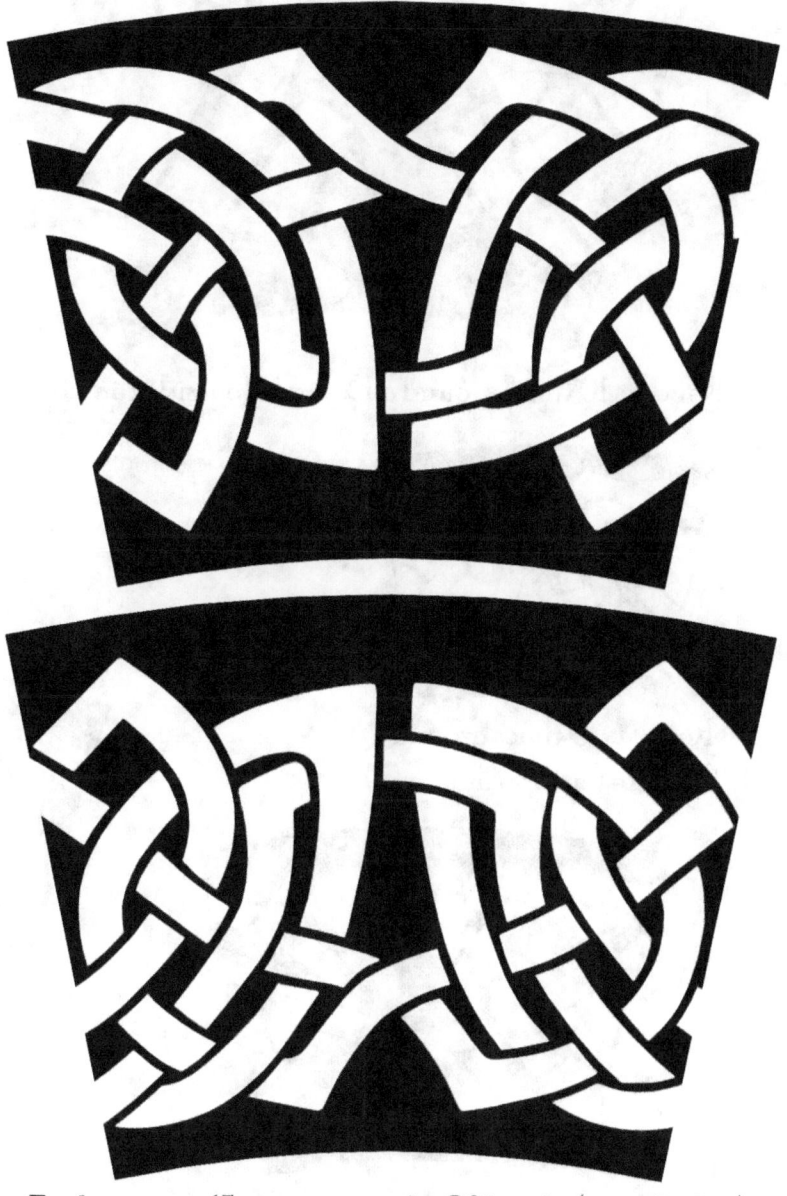

Each repeats 15 times around a 20" circle (outside dia.)

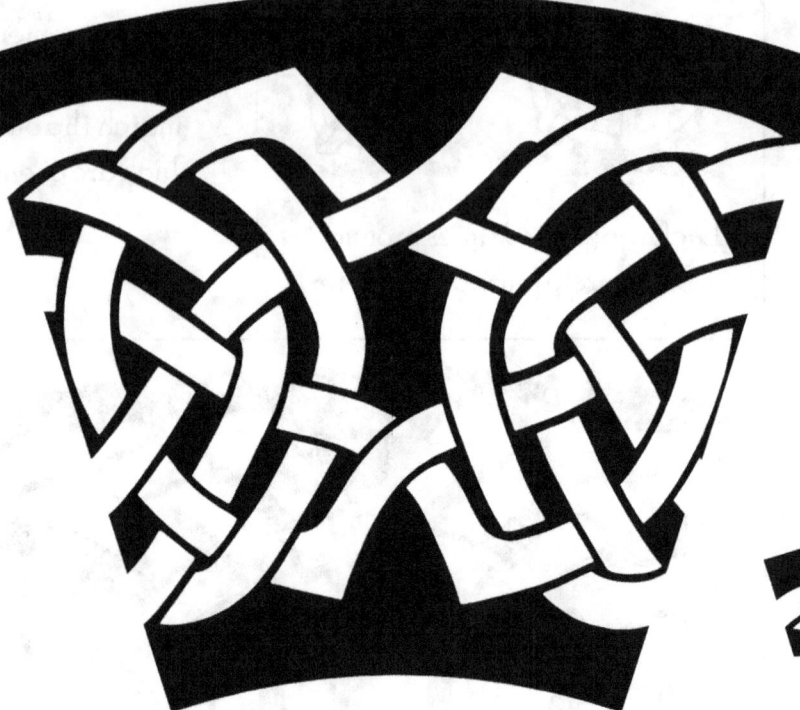

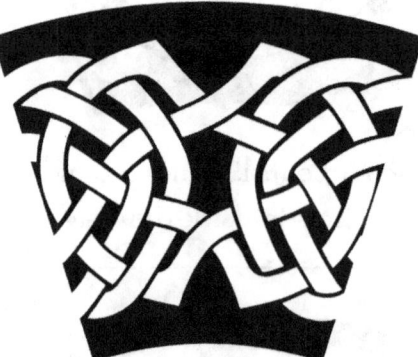

Repeats 20 times around a 10" circle (outside diameter)

Repeats 10 times around a 15" circle (outside diameter)

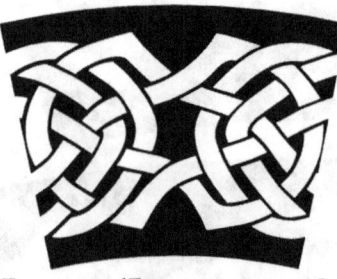

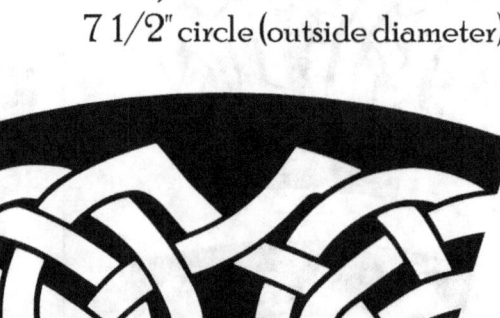

Repeats 10 times around a 7 1/2" circle (outside diameter)

Repeats 15 times around a 9" circle (outside diameter)

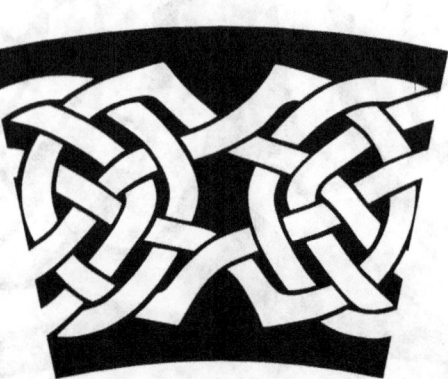

Repeats 15 times around a 12" circle (outside diameter)

Repeats 10 times around a 10" circle (outside diameter)

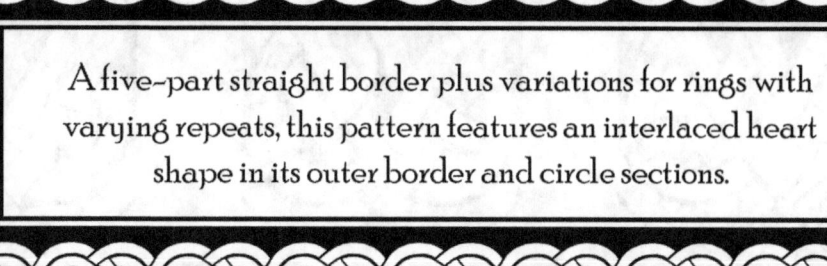

A five-part straight border plus variations for rings with varying repeats, this pattern features an interlaced heart shape in its outer border and circle sections.

Like the previous pattern, this one is built on multiples of the length of its straight section – except for the corners, which are a different size.

The straight outer border and all the inner border sections may be laid out on a grid of the sections' size, but the corners are slightly longer.

Structure:

Straight Sections, using only corners and outer border: one band.

Straight Sections, including Inner Border: multiple bands.

Circle Sections: design is a single band.

1 1/2"

1 1/2"

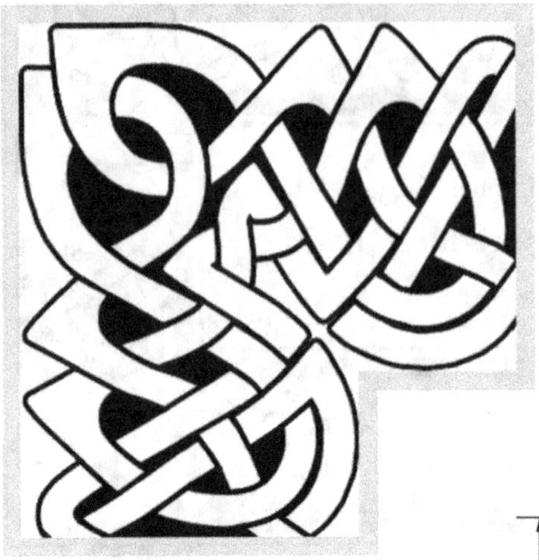

Corner Section

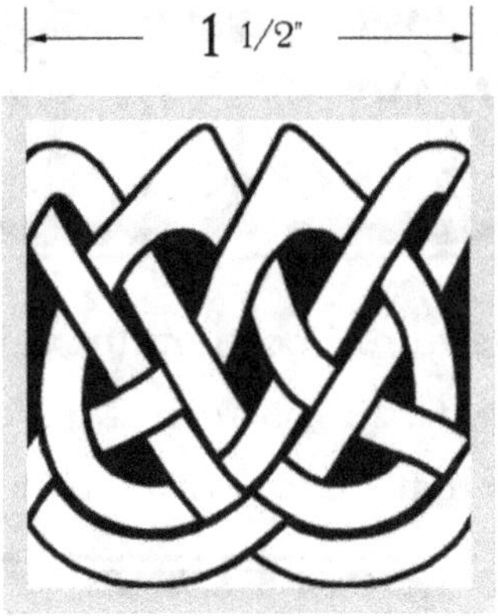

Outer Border, Repeating Section

1 1/2"

1 1/2"

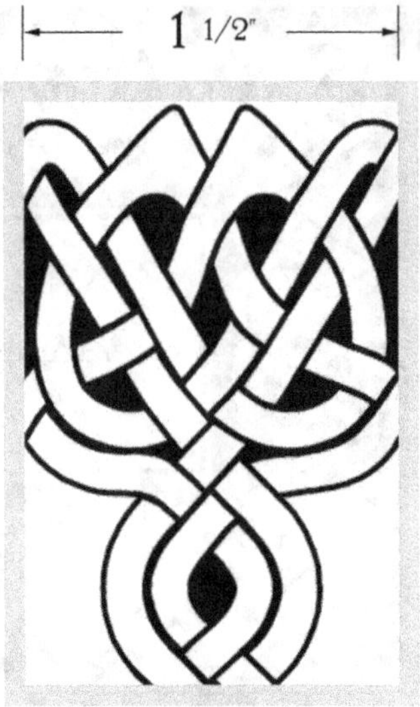

Outer Border / Inner Border T

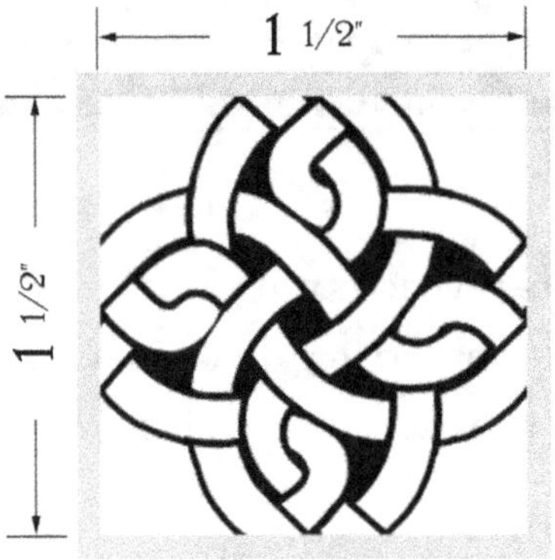

Inner Border, Crosspiece

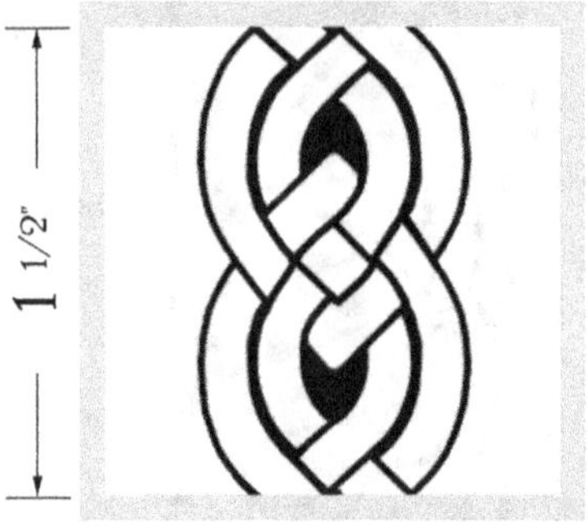

1 1/2"

These five sections can be repeated (or tiled) and rotated to construct a complete border.

By rotating them in 90 degree increments you'll have all the pieces you need. Always rotate ~ never flip or mirror!

Inner Border, Repeating Section

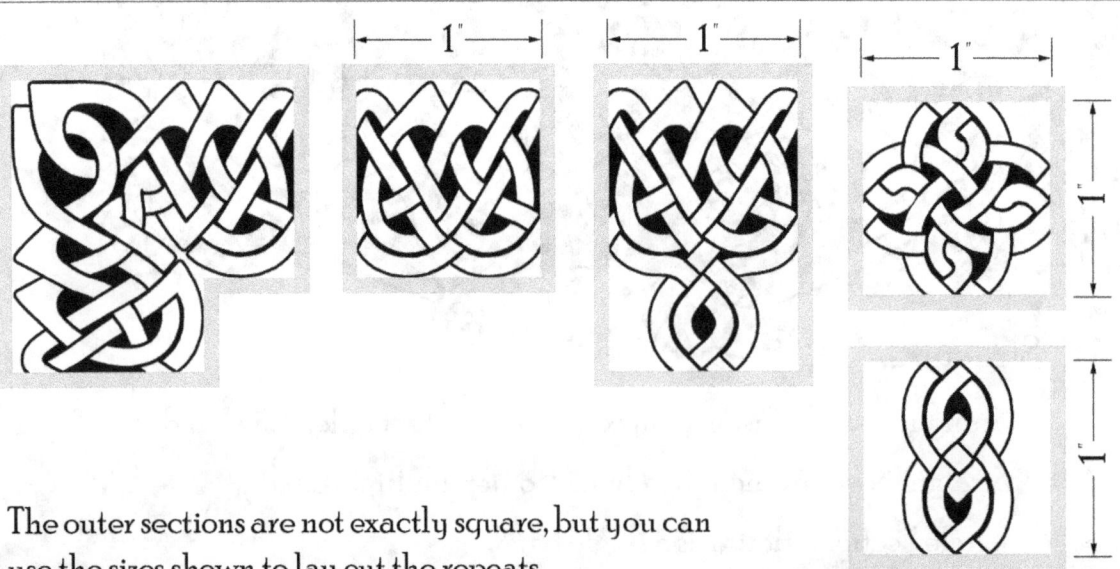

1"

1"

1"

1"

1"

The outer sections are not exactly square, but you can use the sizes shown to lay out the repeats.

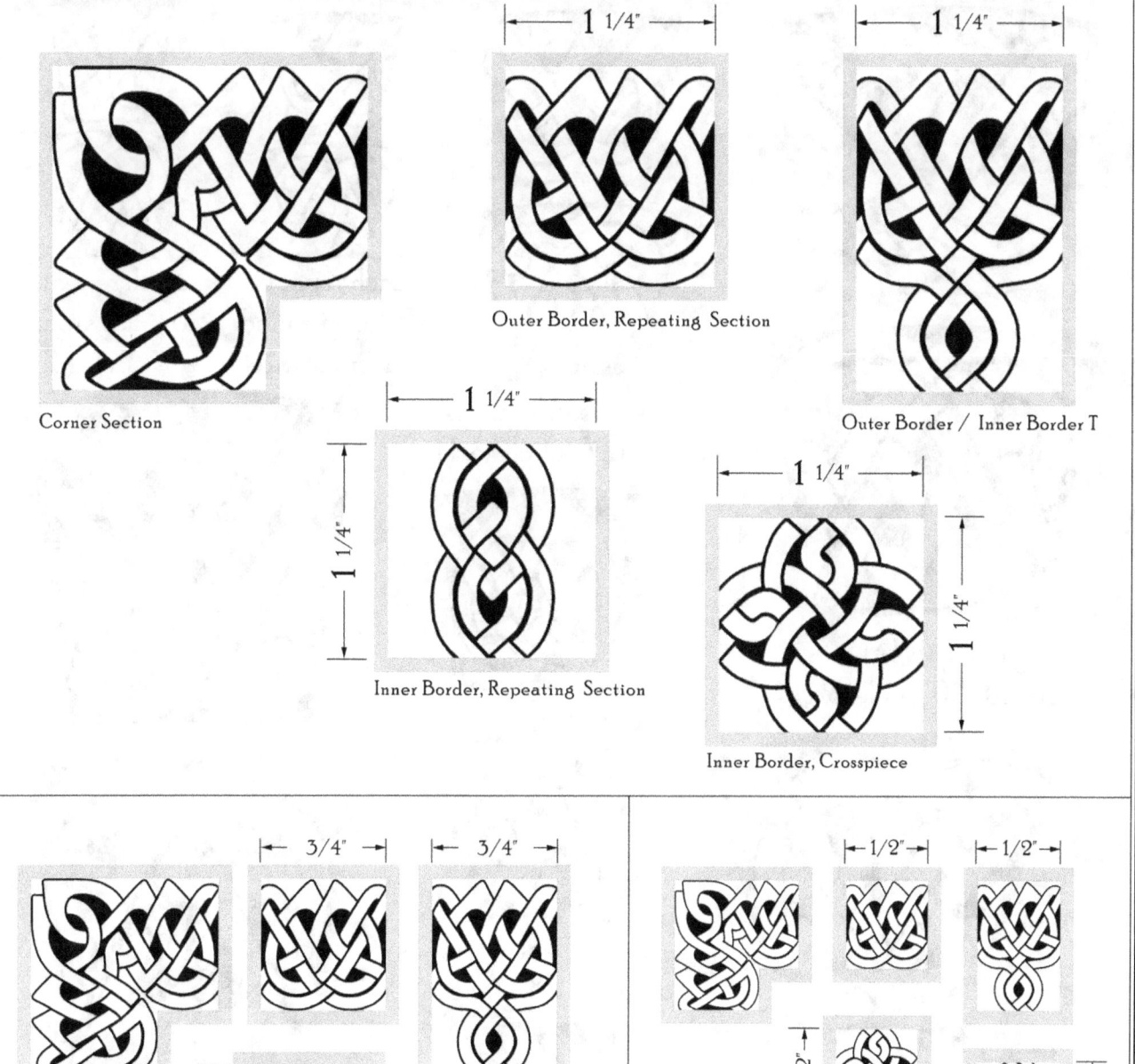

1 1/4"

1 1/4"

Corner Section

Outer Border, Repeating Section

Outer Border / Inner Border T

1 1/4"

1 1/4"

Inner Border, Repeating Section

1 1/4"

1 1/4"

Inner Border, Crosspiece

3/4"

3/4"

3/4"

3/4"

3/4"

1/2"

1/2"

1/2"

1/2"

1/2"

On these two pages, there are a total of five sizes of the design's sections. This is for your convenience ~ but remember that you have ways to scale them to the size that you need.

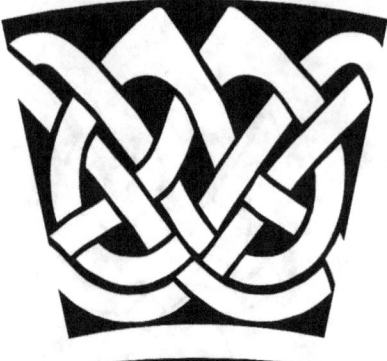

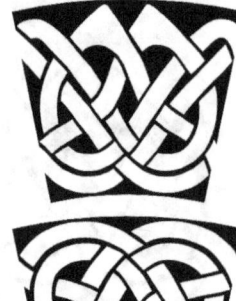

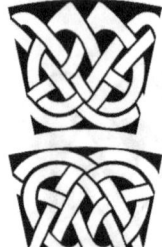

Each repeats
15 times around
a 4" circle (o.d.)

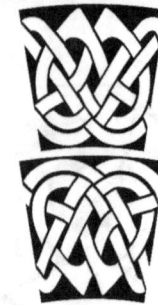

Each repeats
20 times around
a 5" circle (o.d.)

Each repeats 15 times
around a 6" circle (o.d.)

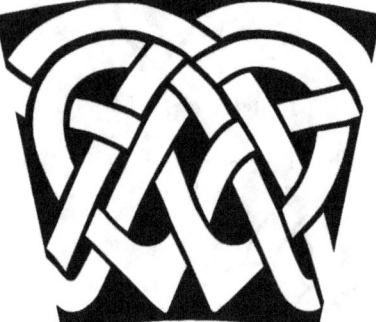

Each repeats 15 times
around a 10" circle (o.d.)

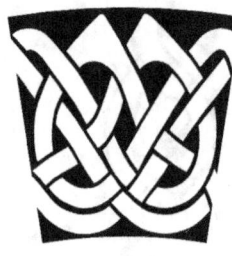

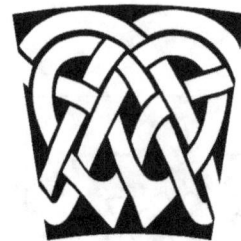

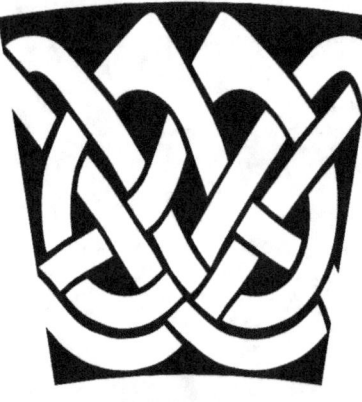

Each repeats 20 times
around an 8" circle (o.d.)

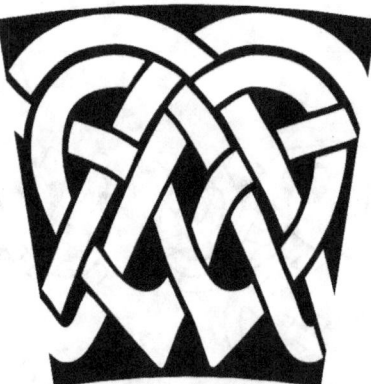

Each repeats 20 times
around a 13" circle (o.d.)

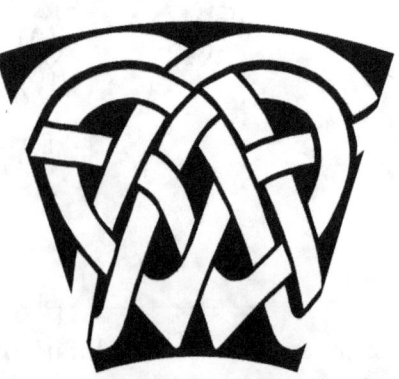

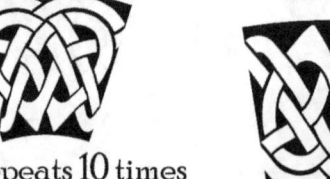

Each repeats 10 times
around a 3" circle (o.d.)

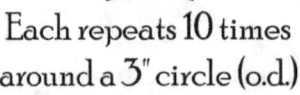

Each repeats 20 times
around a 6" circle (o.d.)

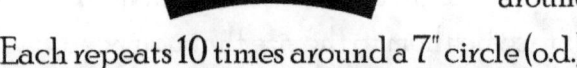

Each repeats 10 times around a 7" circle (o.d.)

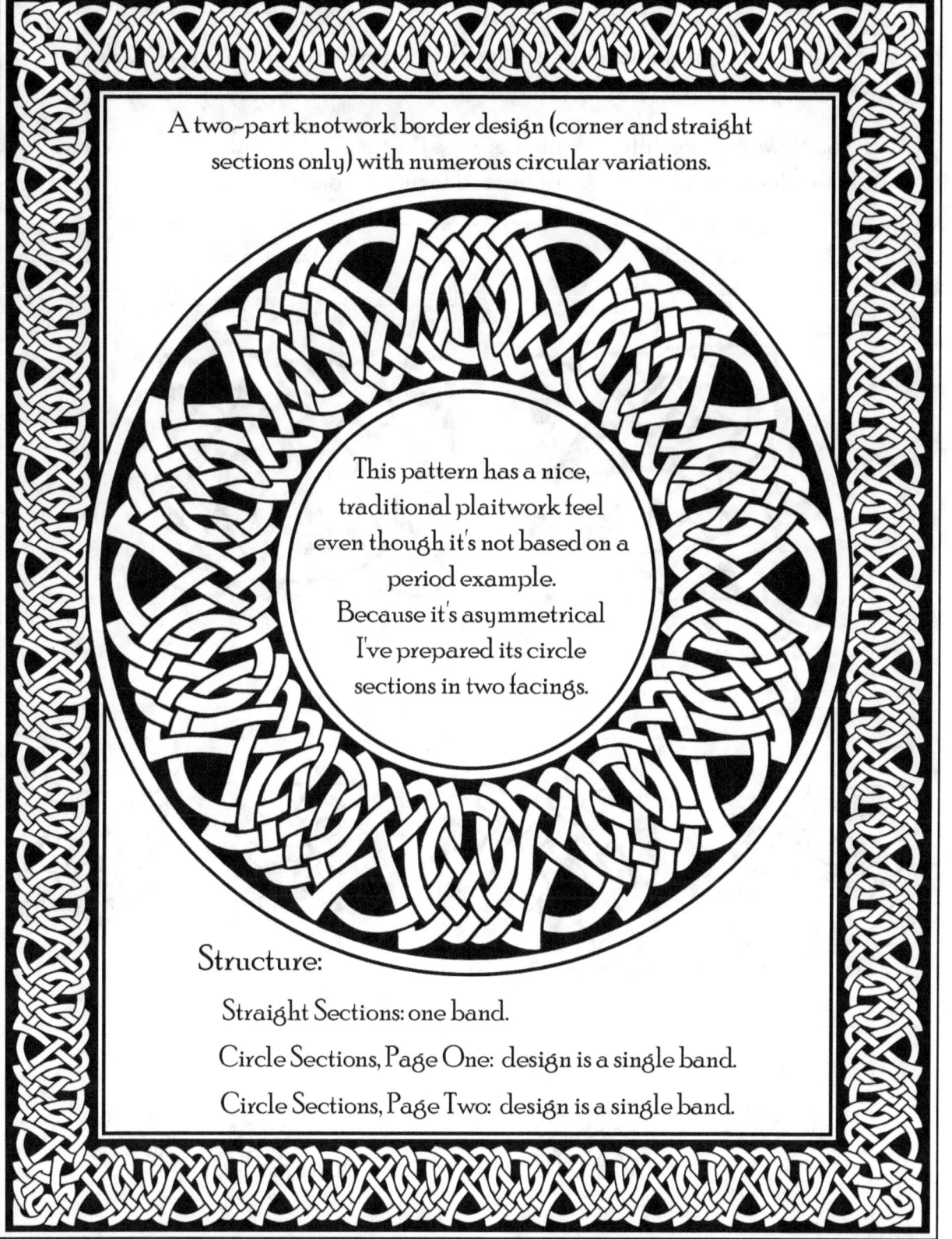

A two-part knotwork border design (corner and straight sections only) with numerous circular variations.

This pattern has a nice, traditional plaitwork feel even though it's not based on a period example. Because it's asymmetrical I've prepared its circle sections in two facings.

Structure:

Straight Sections: one band.

Circle Sections, Page One: design is a single band.

Circle Sections, Page Two: design is a single band.

Border V1-C ~ straight sections

Because this design has no separate inner border, an entire square or rectangular frame can be made by rotating just these two parts in 90 degree increments.

Although we see five different sizes here, see the text for ideas about how you can scale the design to whatever size you need for your project.

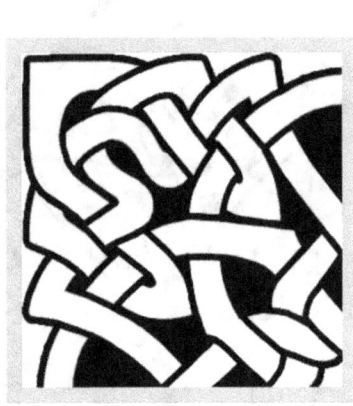

Corner Section

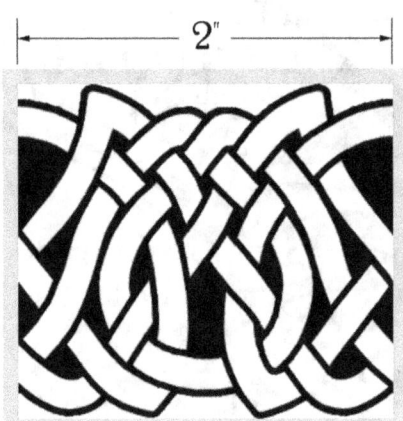

Repeating Section

2"

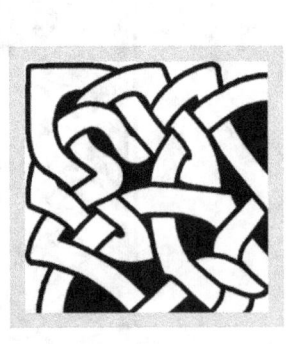

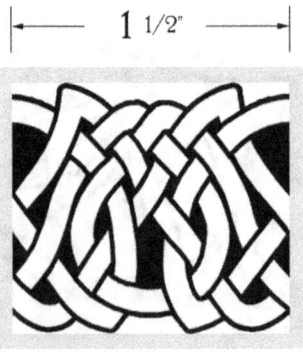

1 1/2"

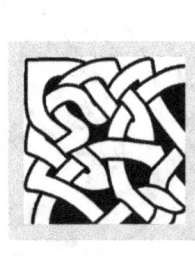

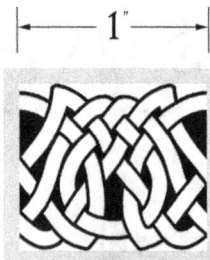

1"

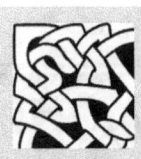

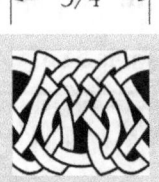

3/4"

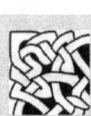

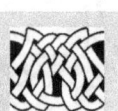

1/2"

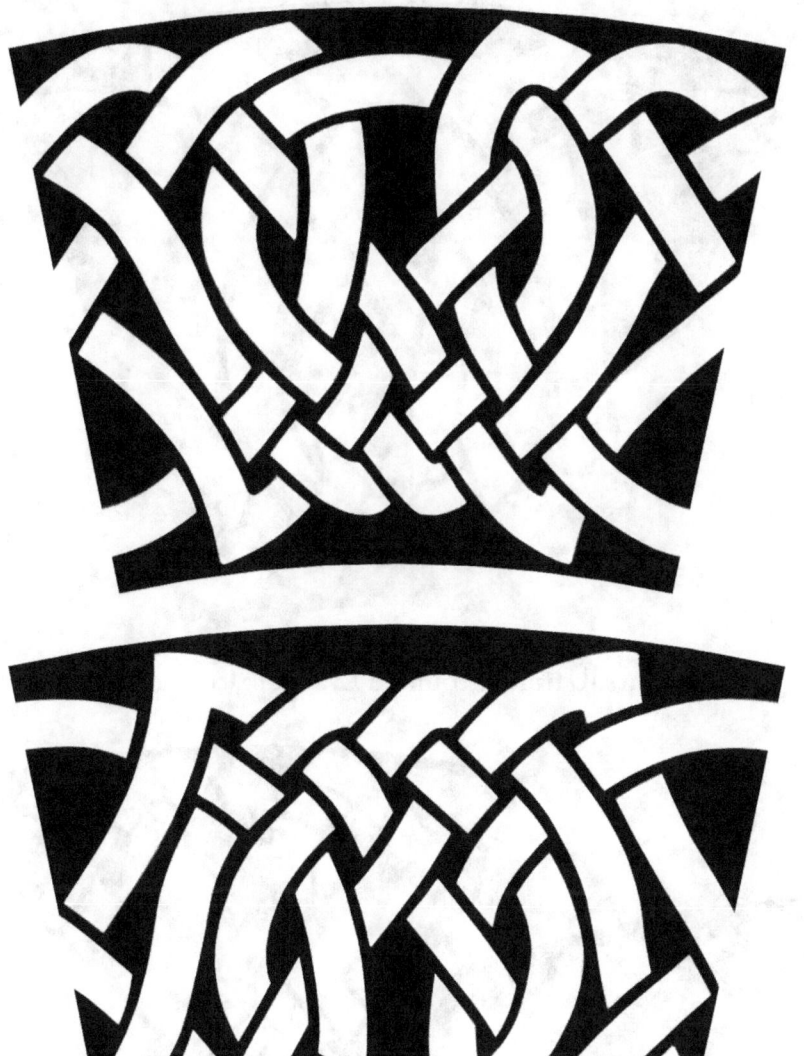

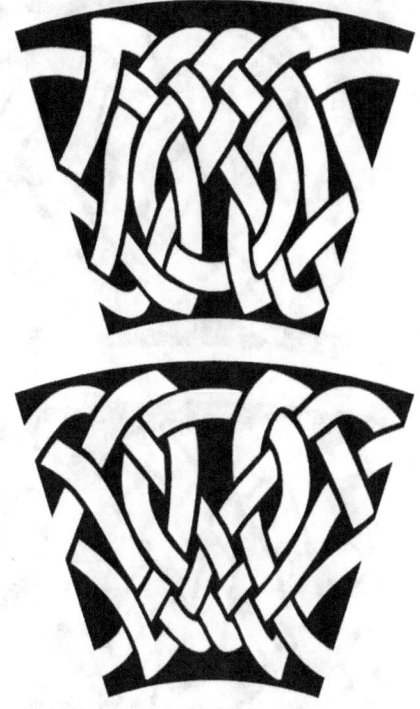

Each repeats 10 times around a 7" circle (outside dia.)

Each repeats 15 times around a 20" circle (outside dia.)

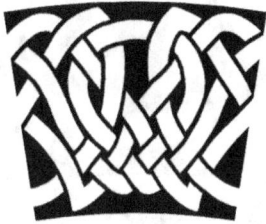 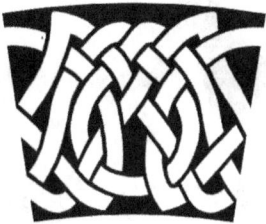

Each repeats 20 times around a 9" circle (outside dia.)

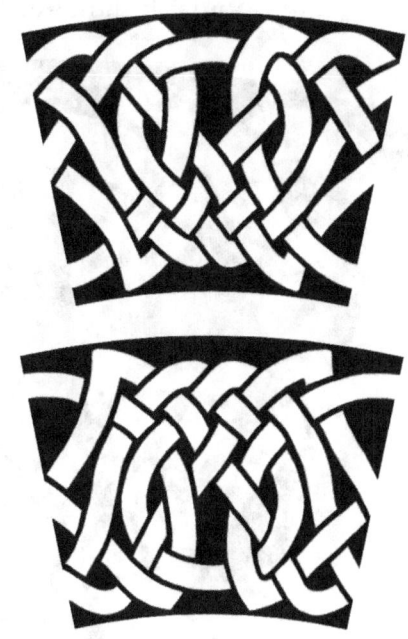

Each repeats 15 times around a 10" circle (outside dia.)

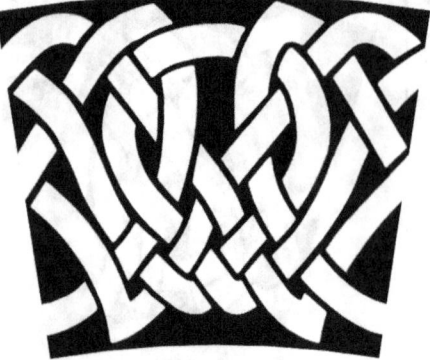

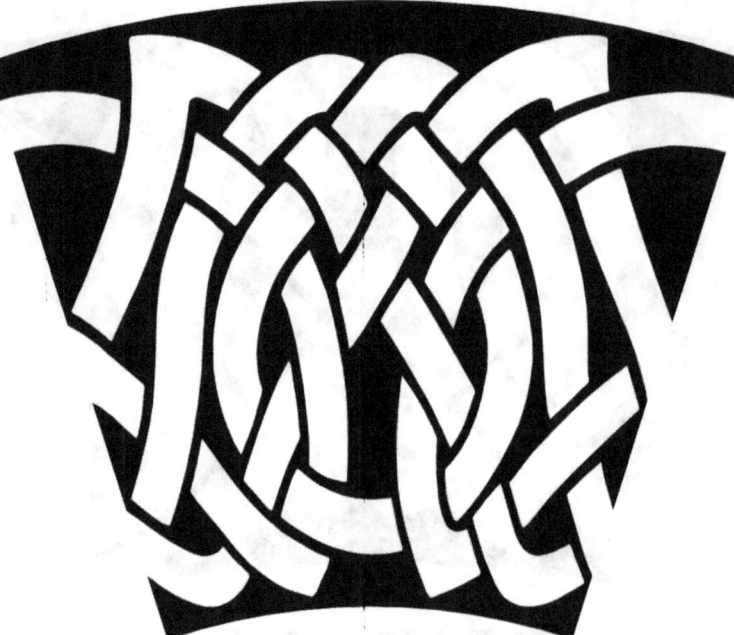

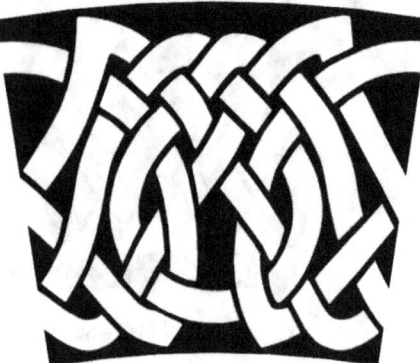

Repeats 10 times around a 12″ circle (outside dia.)

Each repeats 20 times around a 15″ circle (outside diameter)

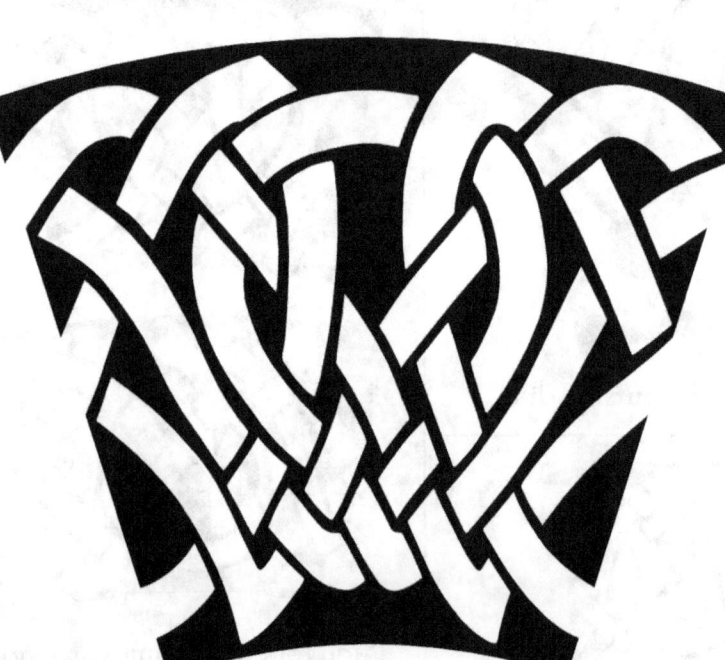

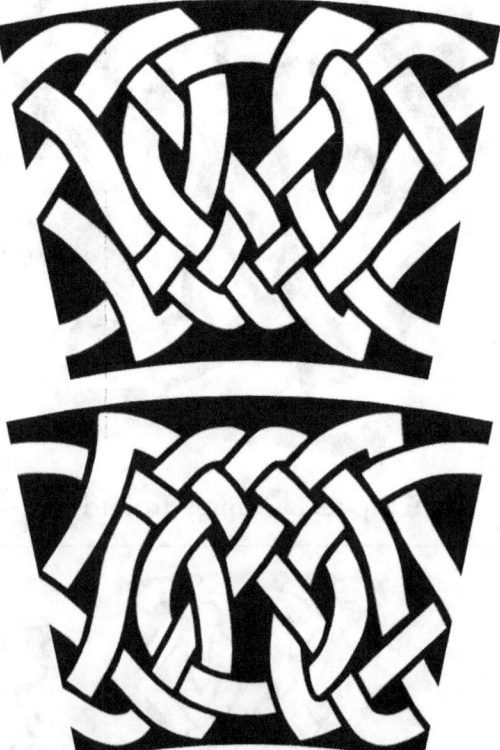

Repeats 10 times around a 12″ circle (outside dia.)

Each repeats 15 times around a 13″ circle (outside diameter)

Border V1-D

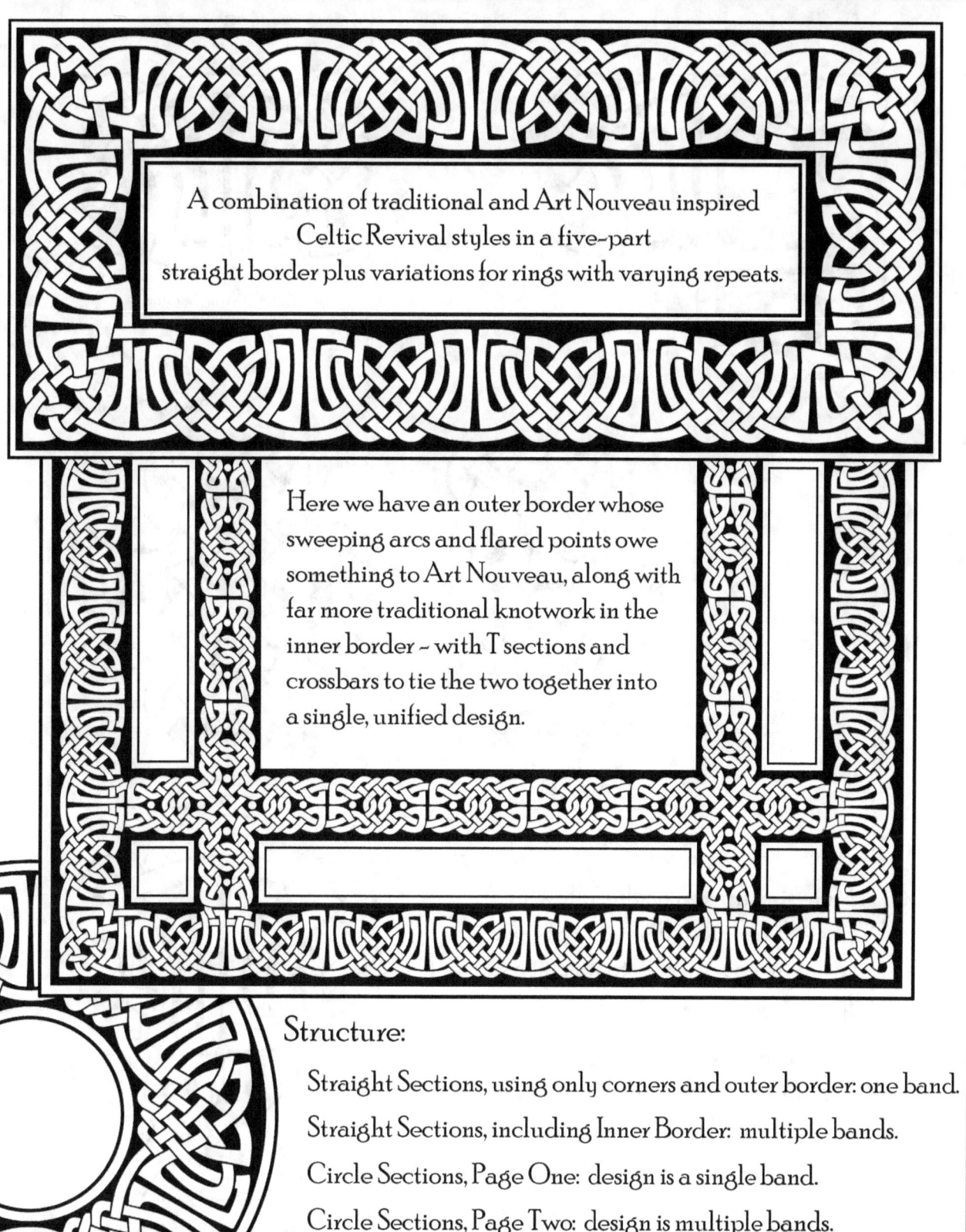

A combination of traditional and Art Nouveau inspired Celtic Revival styles in a five-part straight border plus variations for rings with varying repeats.

Here we have an outer border whose sweeping arcs and flared points owe something to Art Nouveau, along with far more traditional knotwork in the inner border ~ with T sections and crossbars to tie the two together into a single, unified design.

Structure:

Straight Sections, using only corners and outer border: one band.

Straight Sections, including Inner Border: multiple bands.

Circle Sections, Page One: design is a single band.

Circle Sections, Page Two: design is multiple bands.

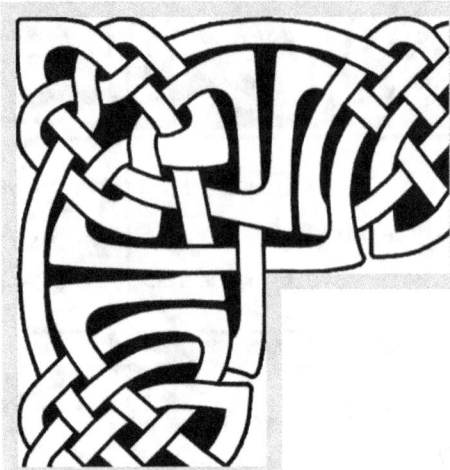

Corner Section

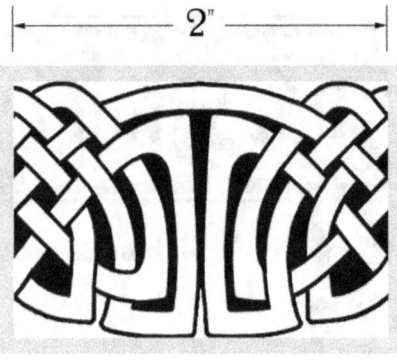

Outer Border, Repeating Section

Inner Border, Crosspiece

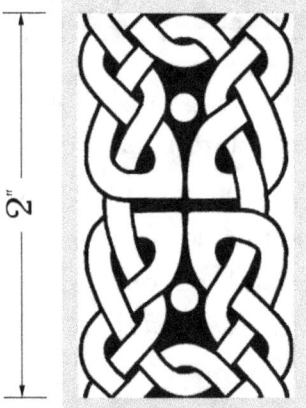

Inner Border,
Repeating Section

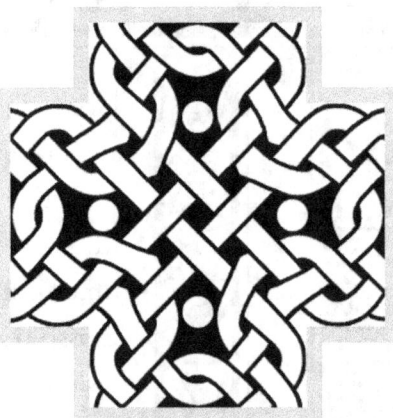

More sizes appear on the following page. Remember that you have ways to create your own custom sizes to suit your project.

This pattern is a handsome blend of traditional and Celtic Revival styles, and it's a good choice for larger treatments.

Outer Border /Inner Border T

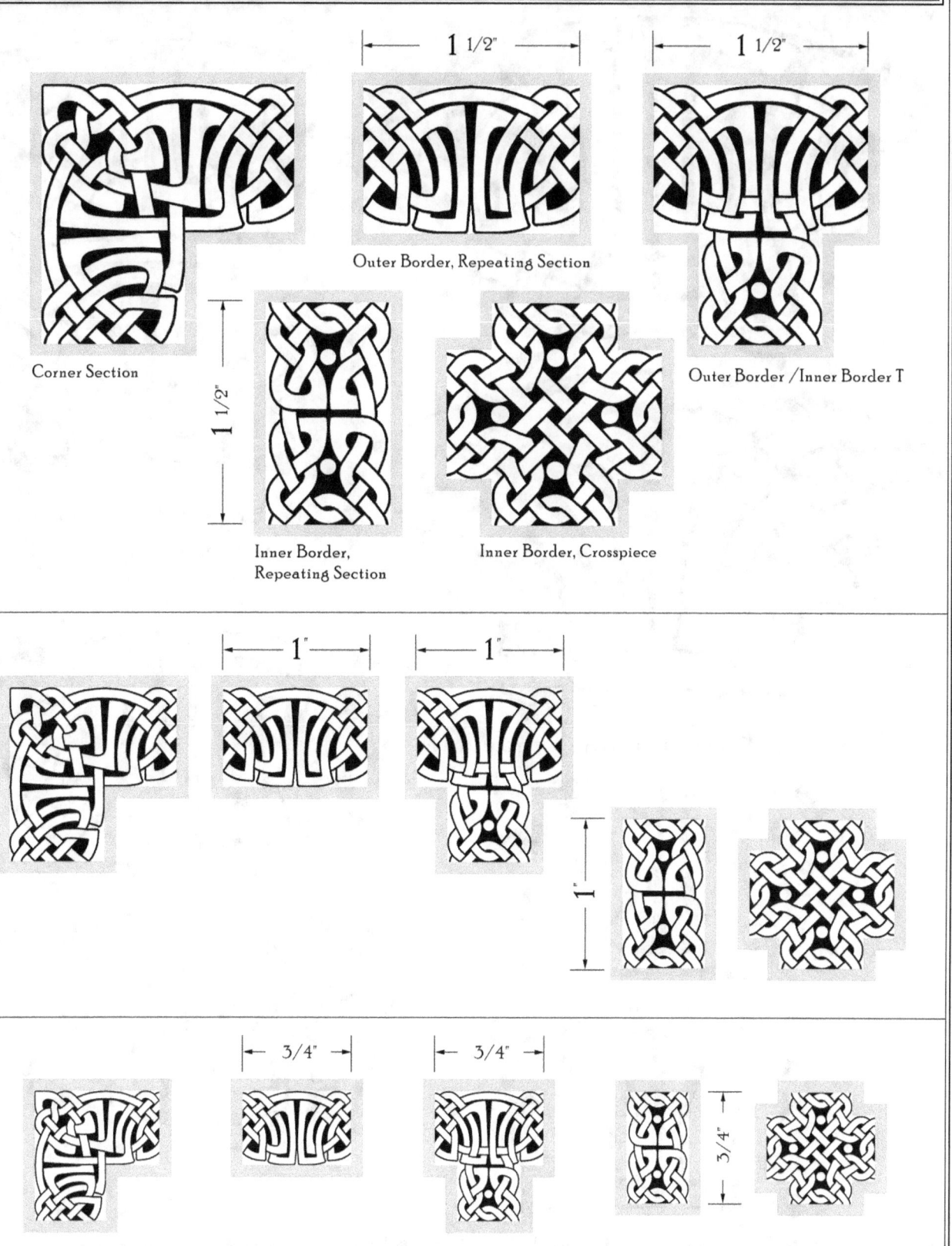

1 1/2"

1 1/2"

Corner Section

Outer Border, Repeating Section

Outer Border /Inner Border T

1 1/2"

Inner Border,
Repeating Section

Inner Border, Crosspiece

1"

1"

1"

3/4"

3/4"

3/4"

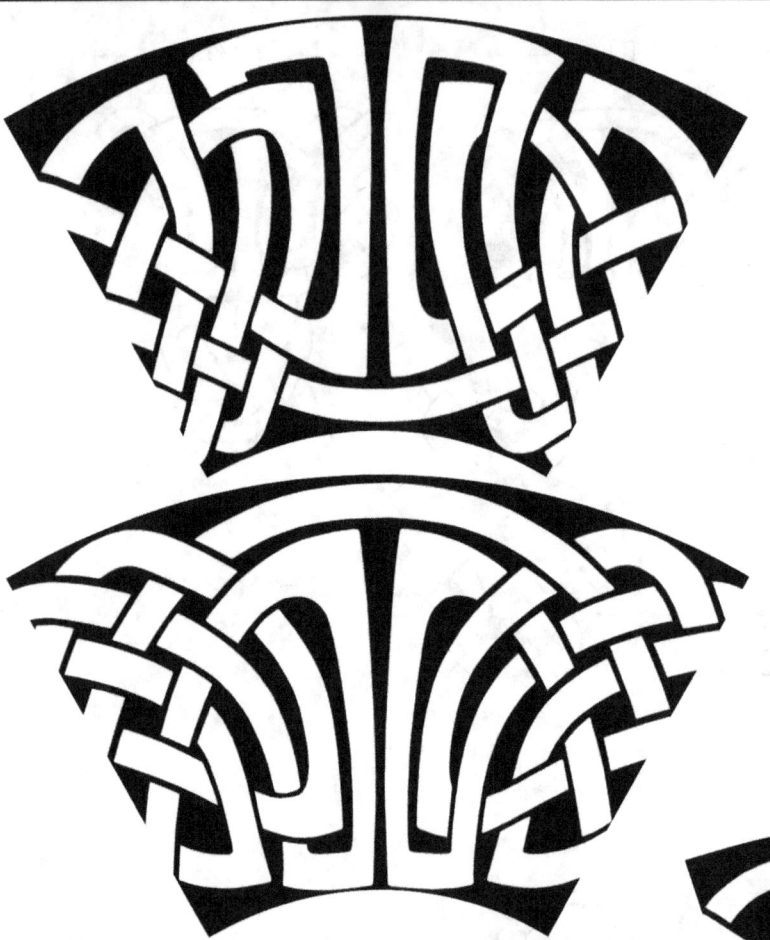

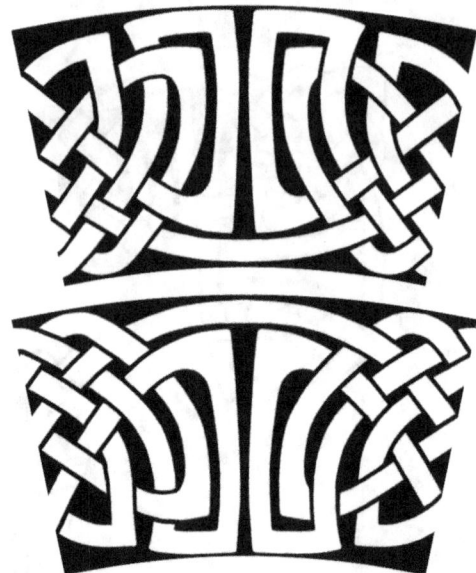

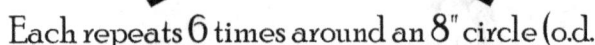

Each repeats 6 times around an 8" circle (o.d.)

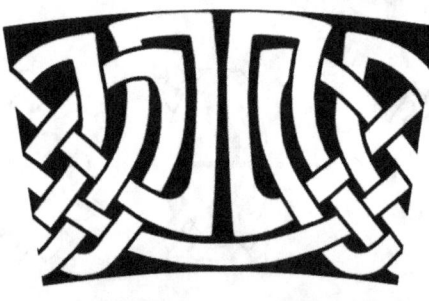

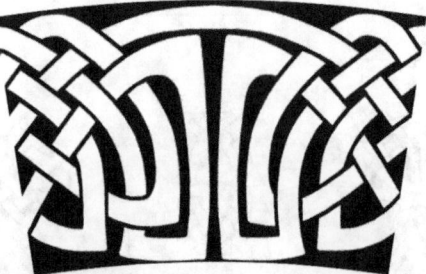

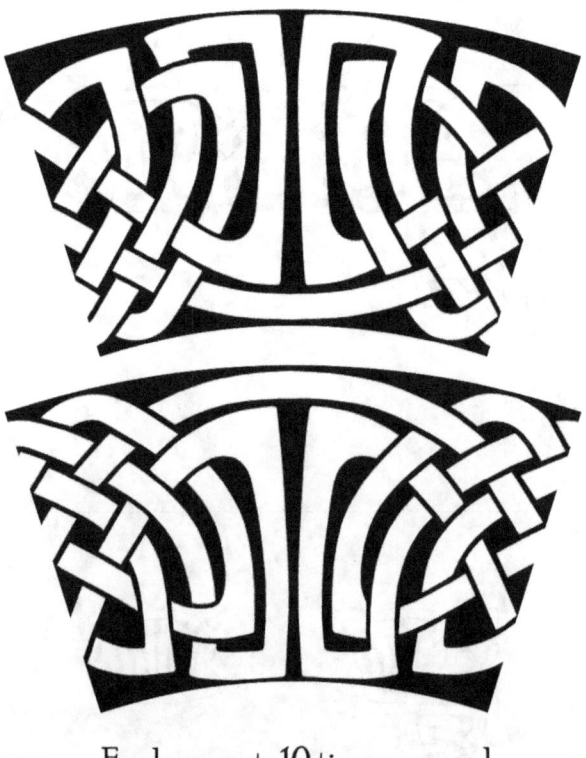

Each repeats 20 times around a 15" circle (outside dia.)

Each repeats 10 times around
a 10" circle (outside dia.)

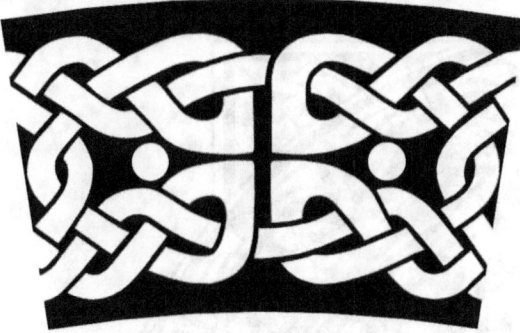

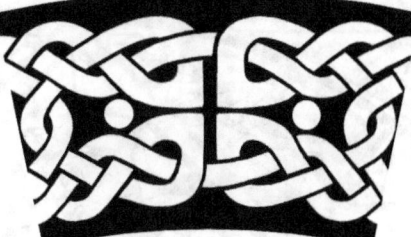

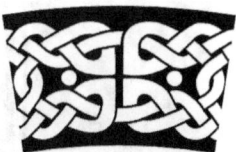

20 repeats around an 18" circle (o.d.)

15 repeats around an 11" circle (o.d.)

20 repeats around an 8" circle (o.d.)

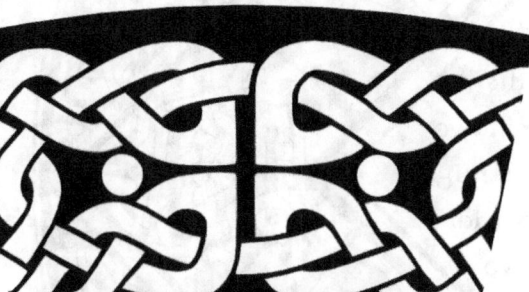

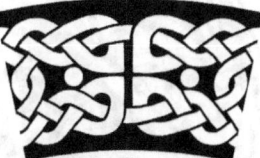

15 repeats around a 7" circle (o.d.)

15 repeats around a 15" circle (o.d.)

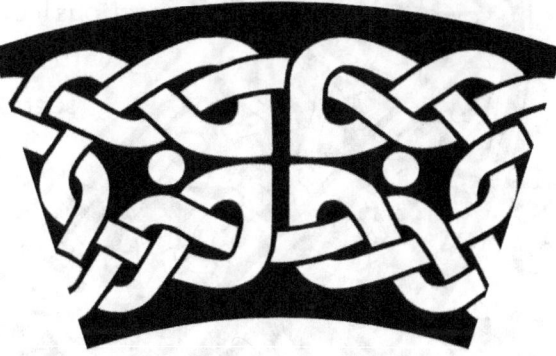

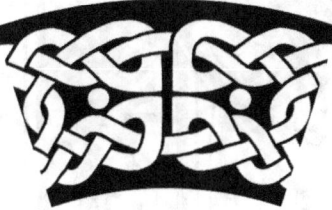

10 repeats around a 10" circle (outside dia.)

10 repeats around a 6" circle (outside dia.)

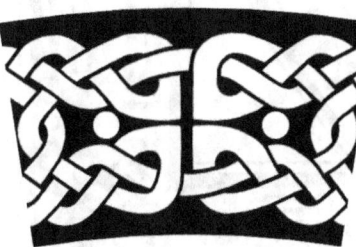

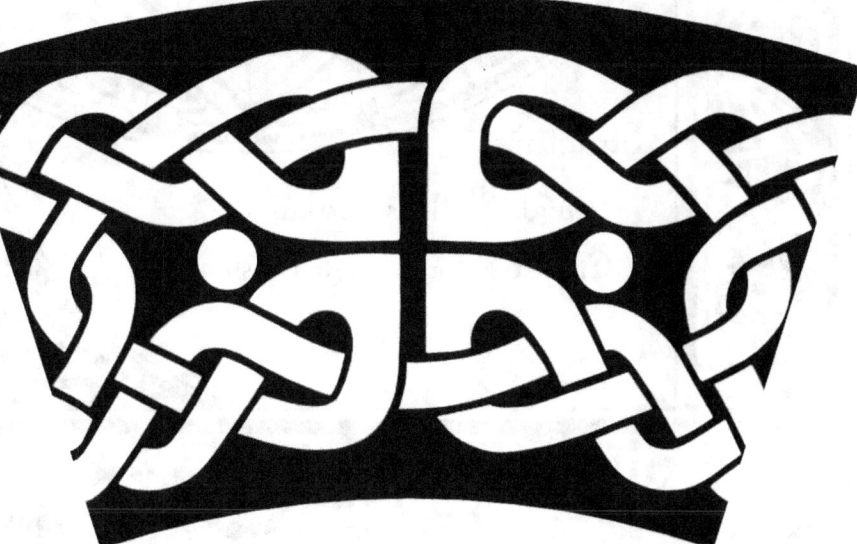

20 repeats around a 13" circle (o.d.)

Repeats 10 times around a 16" circle (outside dia.)

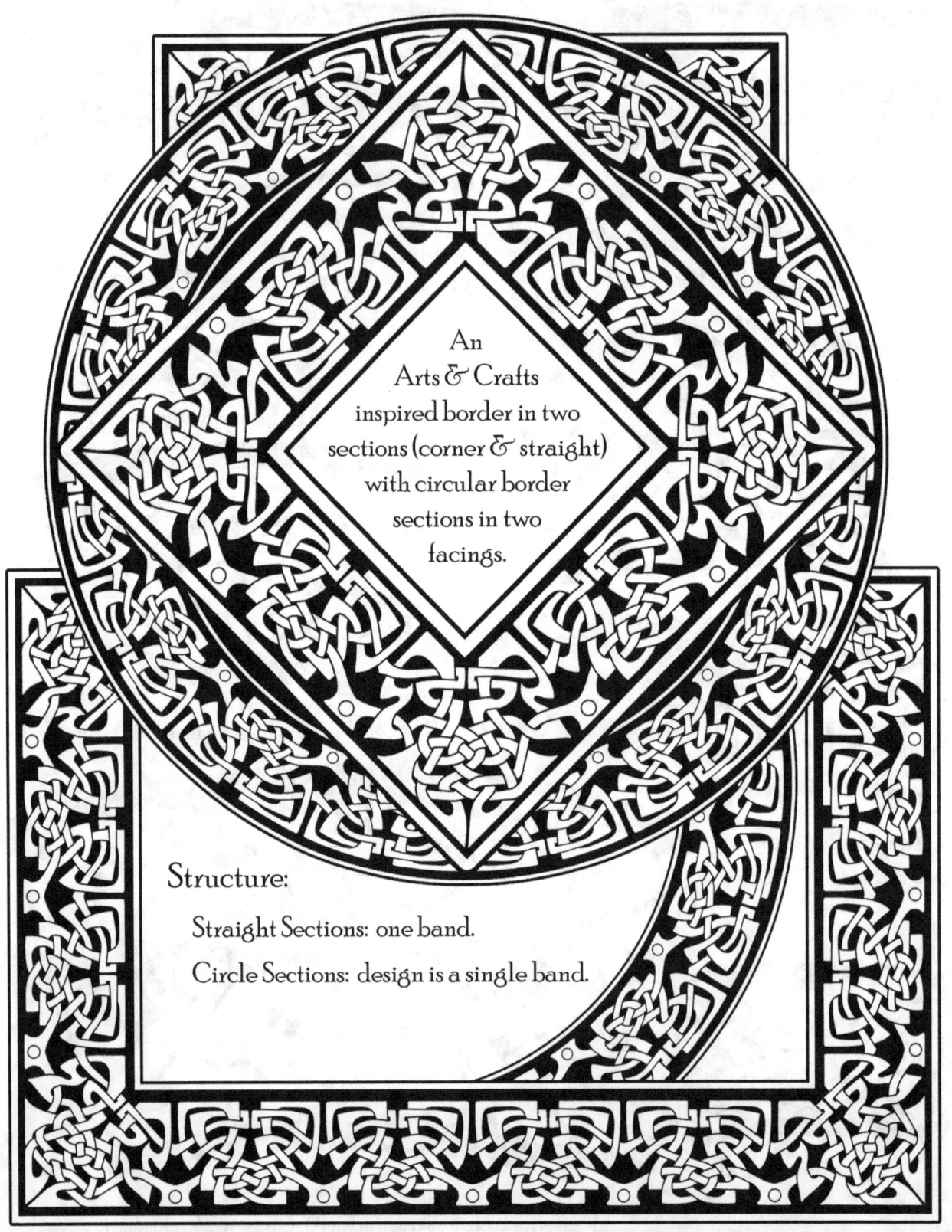

An
Arts & Crafts
inspired border in two
sections (corner & straight)
with circular border
sections in two
facings.

Structure:

Straight Sections: one band.

Circle Sections: design is a single band.

Border V1-E ~ straight sections

Because this design has no separate inner border, an entire square or rectangular frame can be made by rotating just these two parts in 90 degree increments.

Although we see five different sizes here, see the text for ideas about how you can scale the design to whatever size you need for your project.

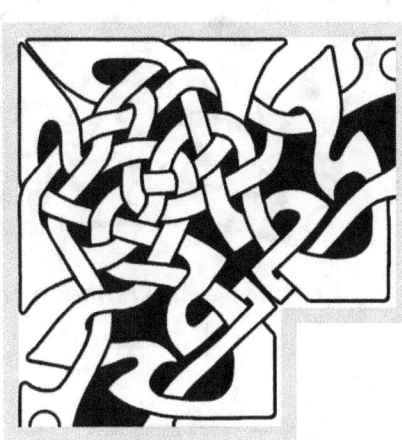

Corner Section

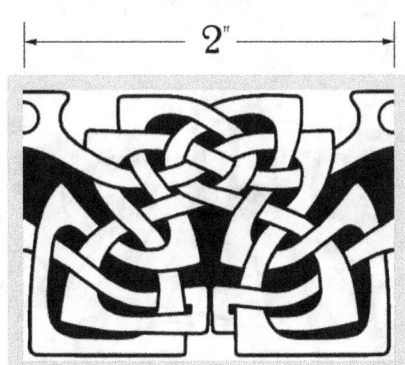

2"

Repeating Section

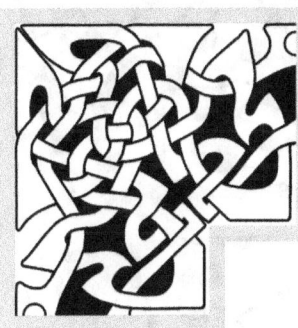 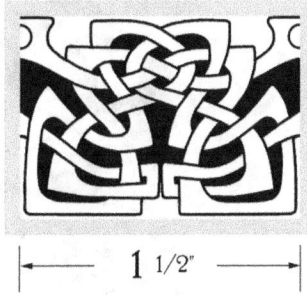

1 1/2"

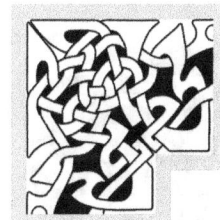 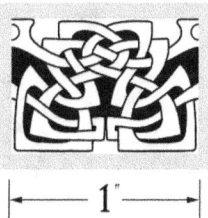

1"

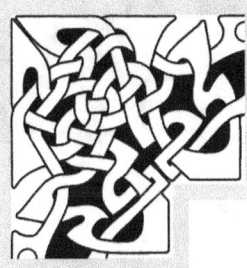 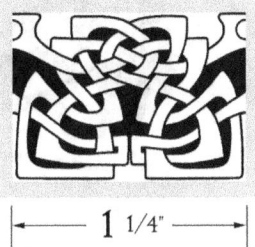

1 1/4"

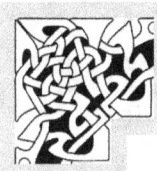 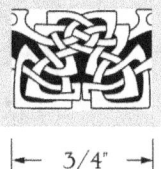

3/4"

34

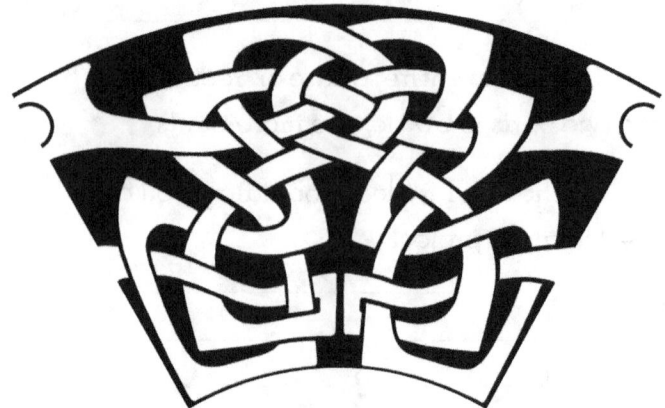

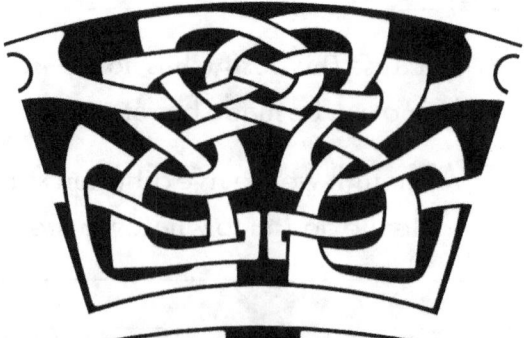

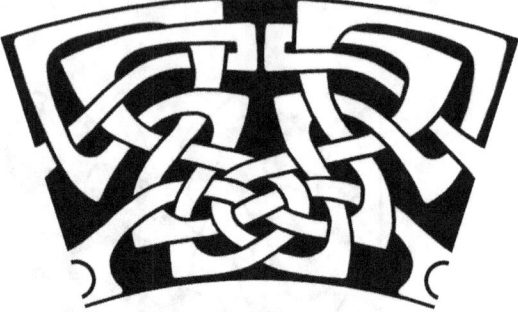

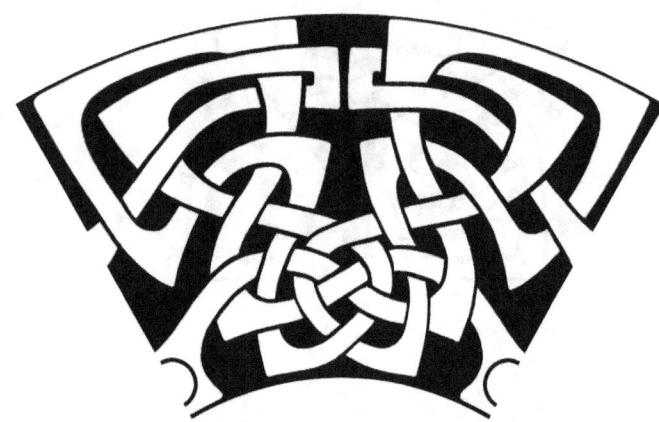

Each repeats 10 times around
a 9" circle (o.d.)

Each repeats 6 times around
a 7" circle (o.d.)

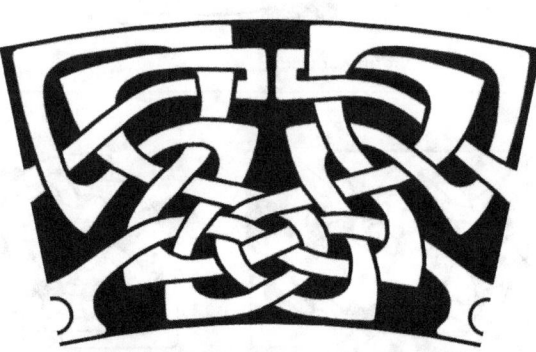

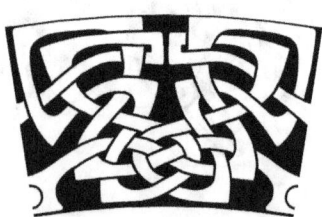

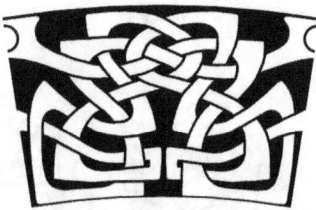

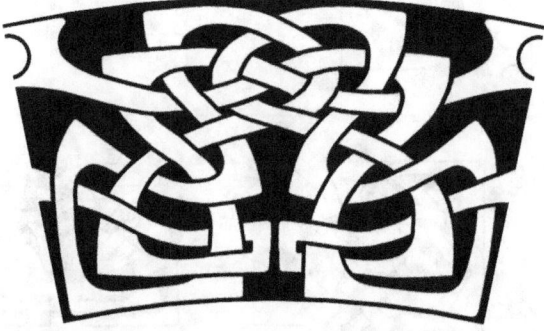

Each repeats 20 times around
an 11" circle (o.d.)

Each repeats 15 times around
a 14" circle (o.d.)

Border V1-F

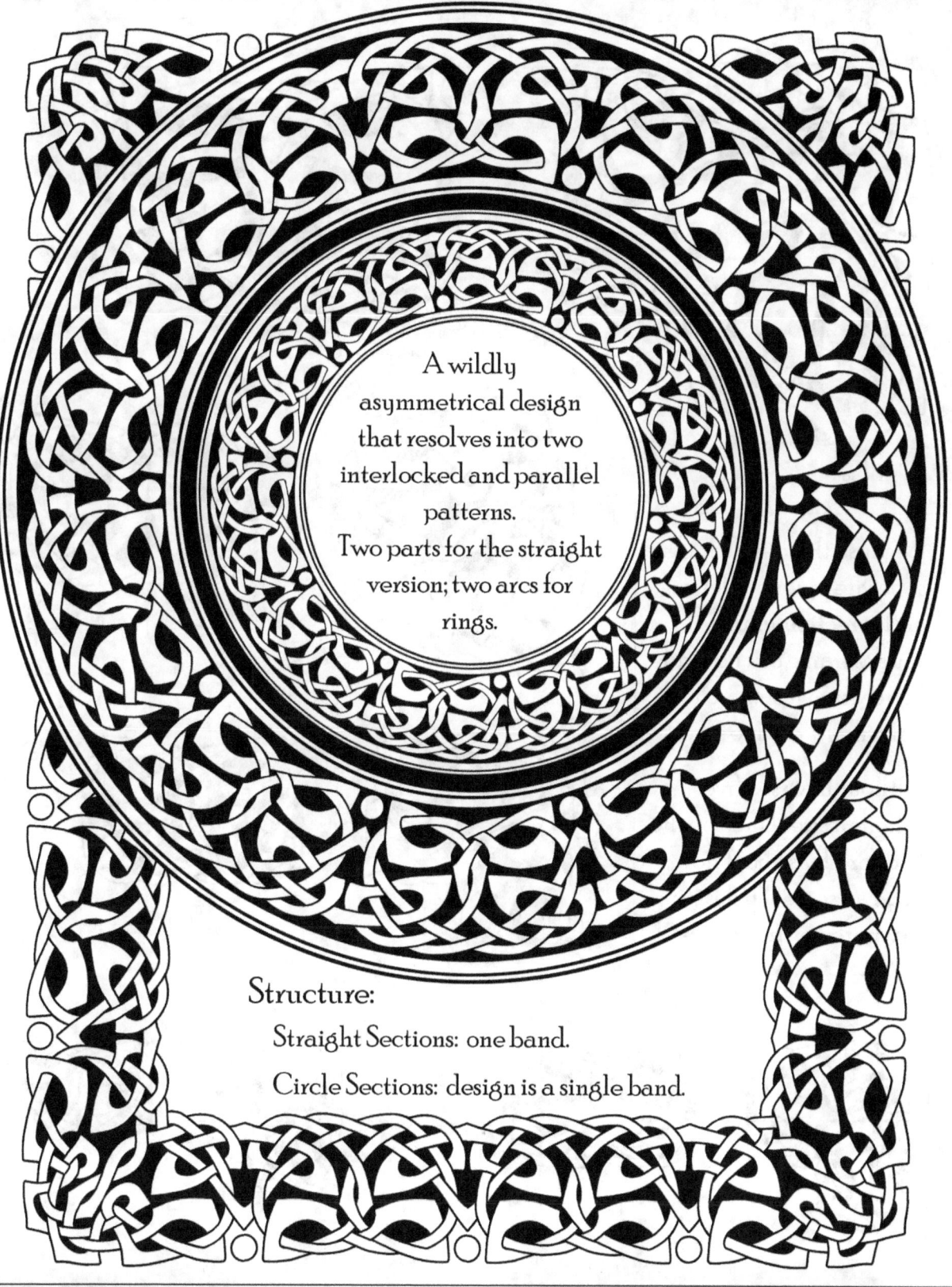

A wildly asymmetrical design that resolves into two interlocked and parallel patterns.
Two parts for the straight version; two arcs for rings.

Structure:

Straight Sections: one band.

Circle Sections: design is a single band.

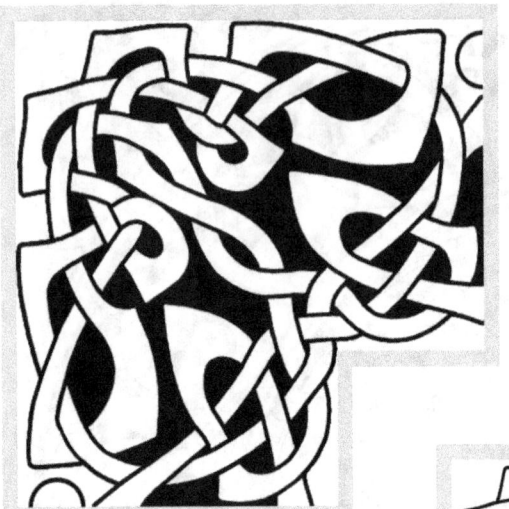

Corner Section

2 1/2"

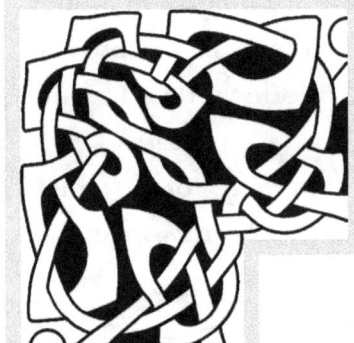

Repeating Section

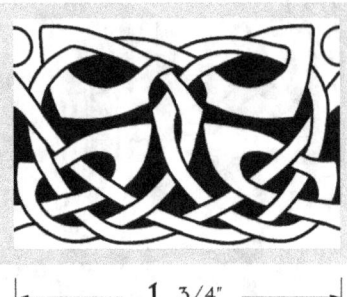

1 3/4"

Because this design has no separate inner border, an entire rectangular or square frame can be made by rotating just these two parts in 90 degree steps.

Although we see five different sizes here, see the text for ideas about how you can scale the design to whatever size you need.

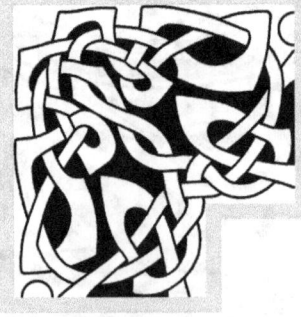

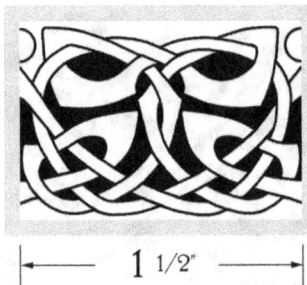

1 1/2"

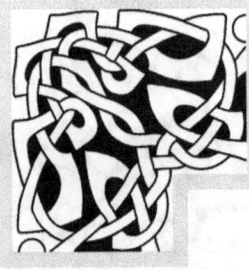

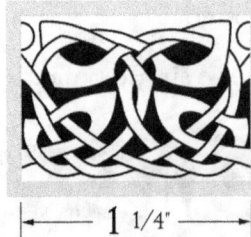

1 1/4"

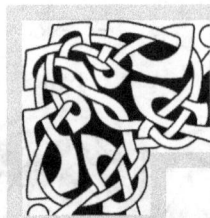

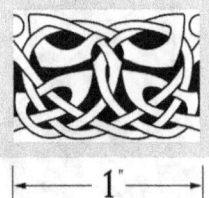

1"

Border V1-F ~ circle sections

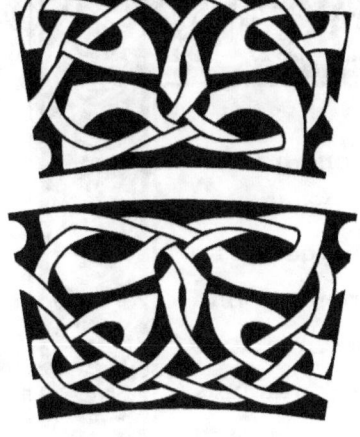

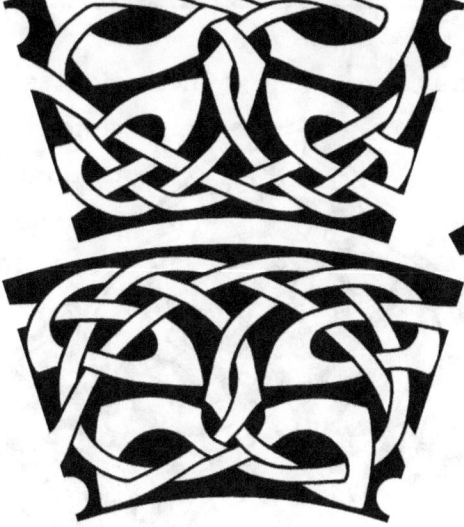

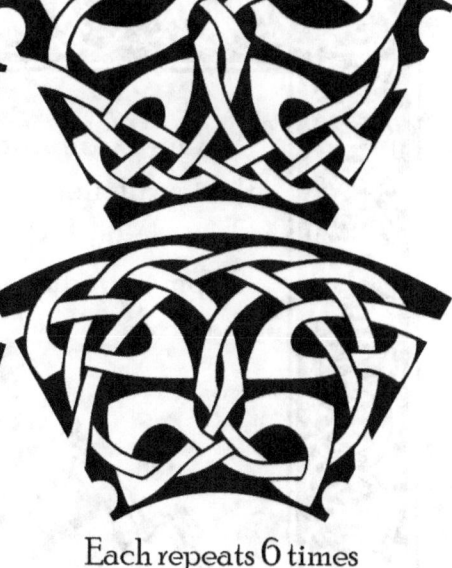

Each repeats 20 times
around a 12" circle (o.d.)

Each repeats 10 times
around an 8" circle (o.d.)

Each repeats 6 times
around a 5" circle (o.d.)

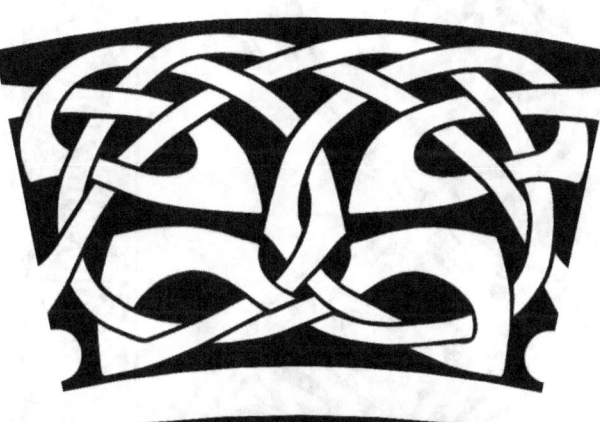

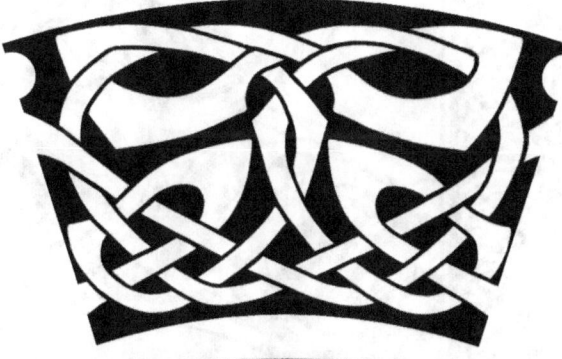

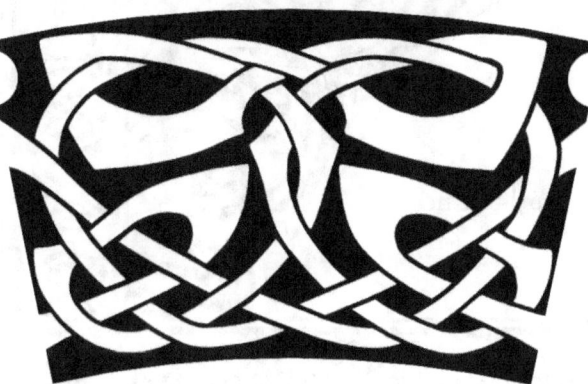

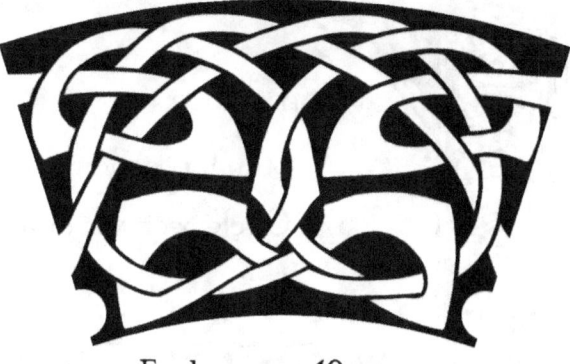

Each repeats 15 times around a 16" circle (o.d.)

Each repeats 10 times
around a 10" circle (o.d.)

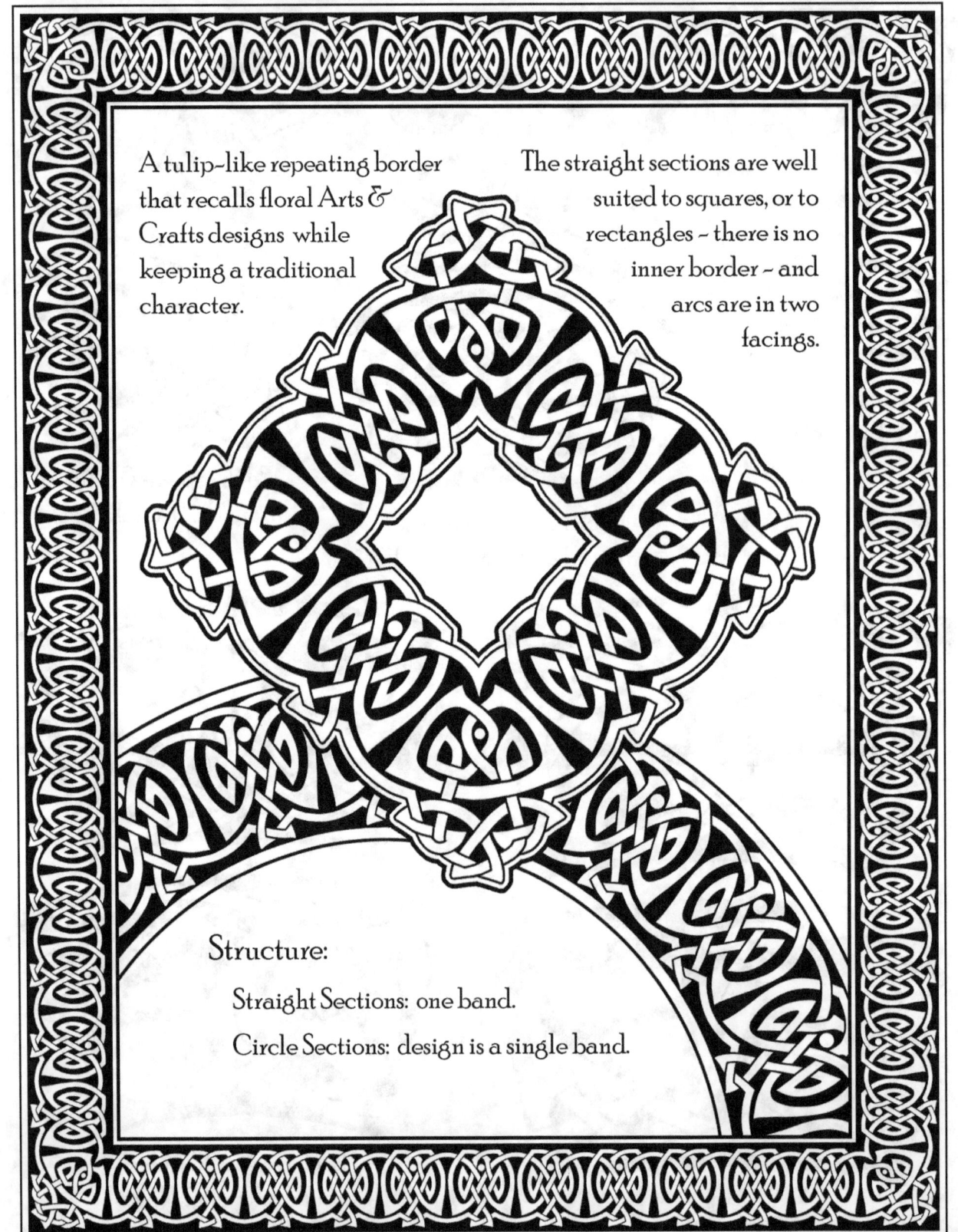

A tulip-like repeating border that recalls floral Arts & Crafts designs while keeping a traditional character.

The straight sections are well suited to squares, or to rectangles ~ there is no inner border ~ and arcs are in two facings.

Structure:

Straight Sections: one band.

Circle Sections: design is a single band.

1 3/4"

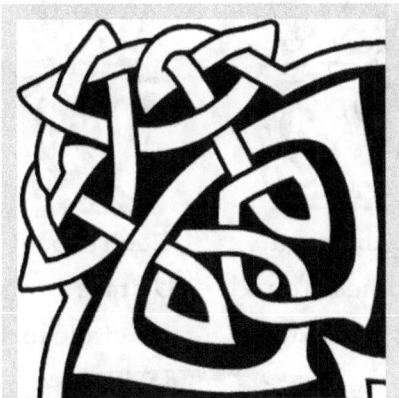

Corner Section

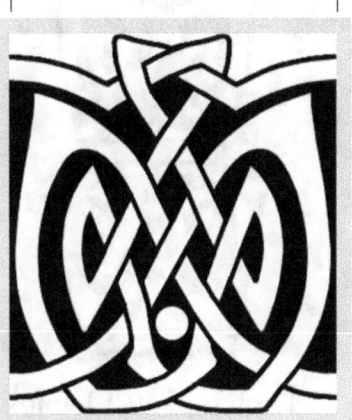

Repeating Section

Because this design has no separate inner border, an entire rectangular or square frame can be made by rotating just these two parts in 90 degree steps.

Although we see five different sizes here, see the text for ideas about how you can scale the design to whatever size you need.

1 1/2"

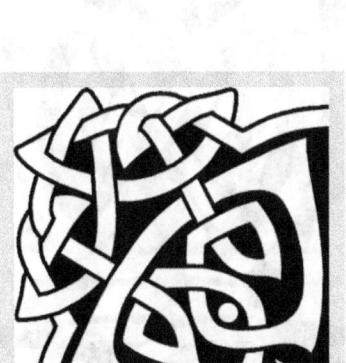

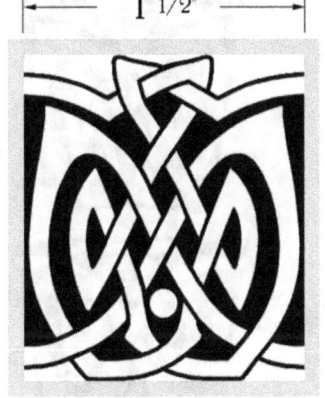

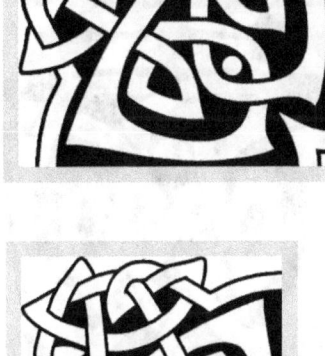

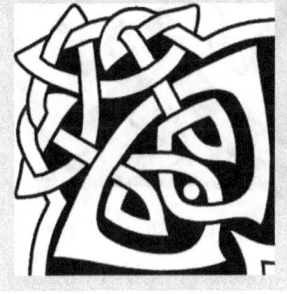

1"

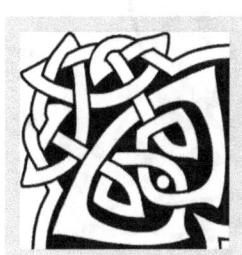

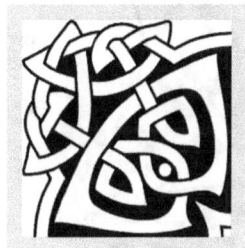

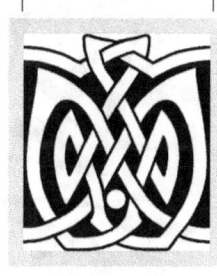

1 1/4"

3/4"

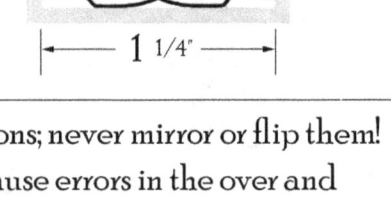

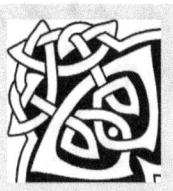

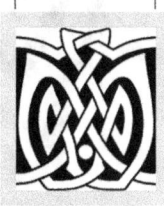

Always rotate the sections; never mirror or flip them! Flipping sections will cause errors in the over and under sequence of the pattern's weave.

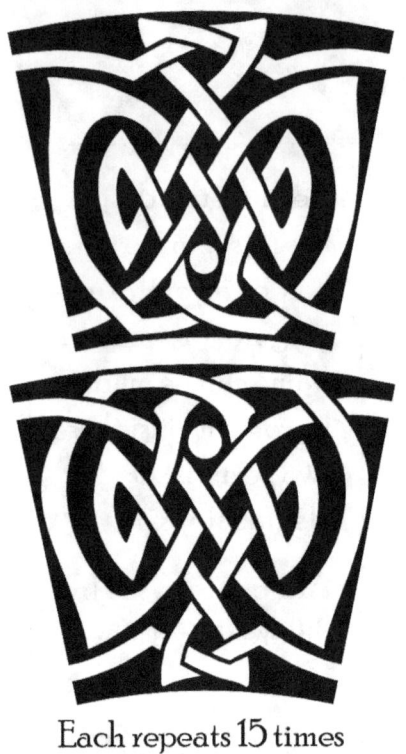

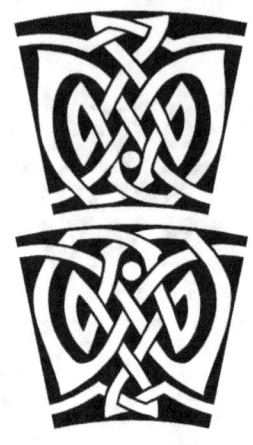

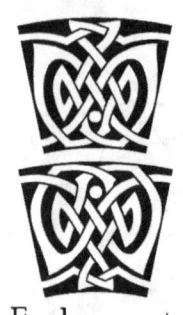

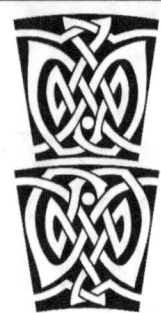

Each repeats
15 times around
a 4" circle (o.d.)

Each repeats
20 times around
a 5" circle (o.d.)

Each repeats 15 times
around a 6" circle (o.d.)

Each repeats 15 times
around a 10" circle (o.d.)

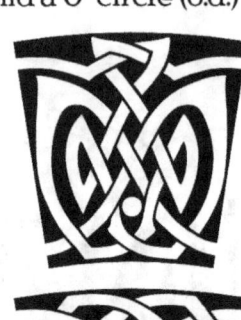

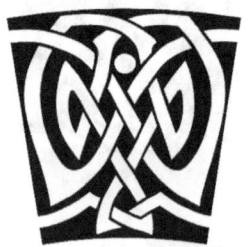

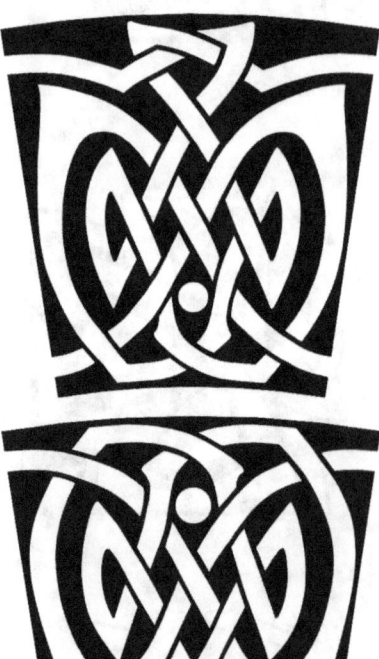

Each repeats 20 times
around an 8" circle (o.d.)

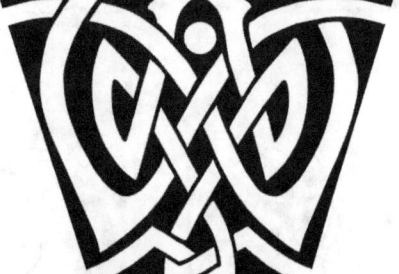

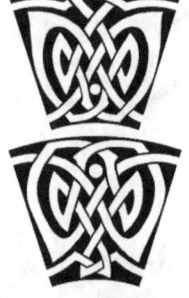

Each repeats 10 times
around a 3" circle (o.d.)

Each repeats 20 times
around a 13" circle (o.d.)

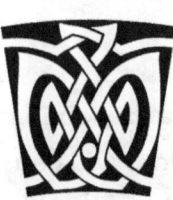

Each repeats 20 times
around a 6" circle (o.d.)

Each repeats 10 times around a 7" circle (o.d.)

Border V1-H

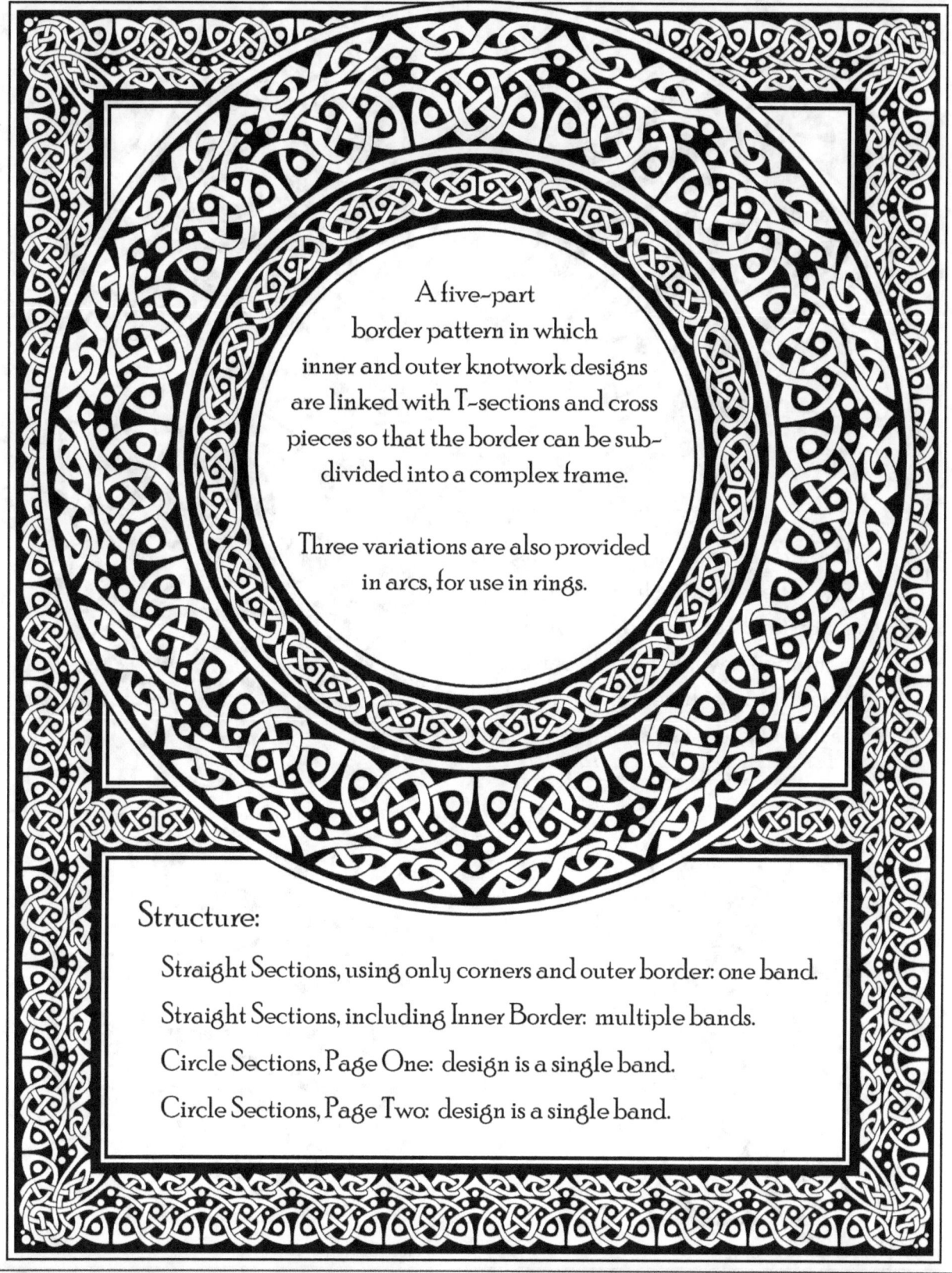

A five~part
border pattern in which
inner and outer knotwork designs
are linked with T~sections and cross
pieces so that the border can be sub~
divided into a complex frame.

Three variations are also provided
in arcs, for use in rings.

Structure:

Straight Sections, using only corners and outer border: one band.

Straight Sections, including Inner Border: multiple bands.

Circle Sections, Page One: design is a single band.

Circle Sections, Page Two: design is a single band.

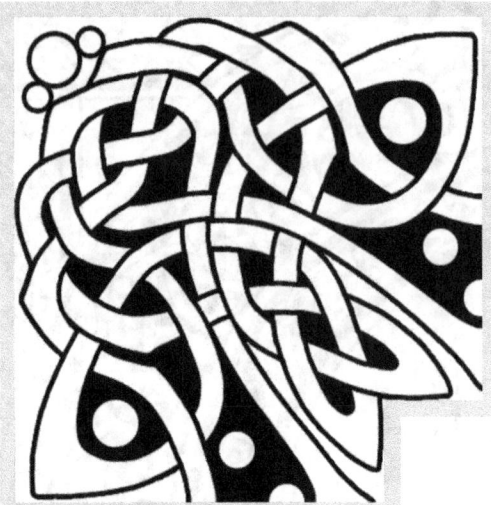

Corner Section

2 1/2"

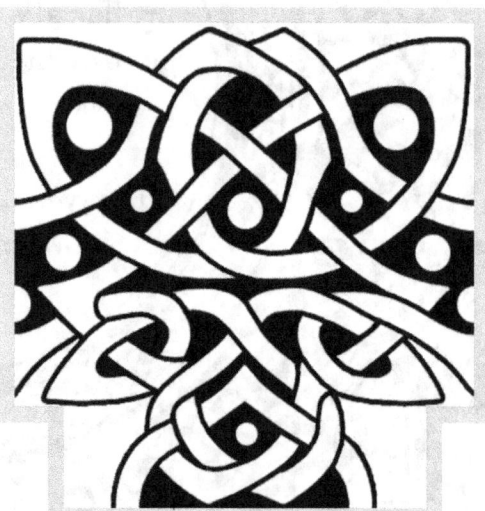

Outer Border, Repeating Section

More sizes appear on the following page. The repeating Inner Border section has been moved to fit; in this orientation it would go between the Outer Border / Inner Border T and the Inner Border Crosspiece.

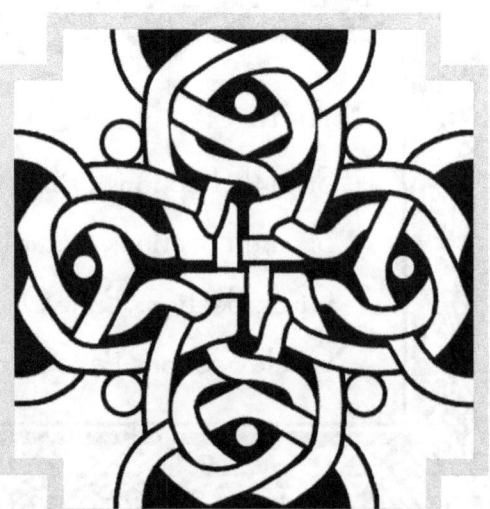

Outer Border / Inner Border T

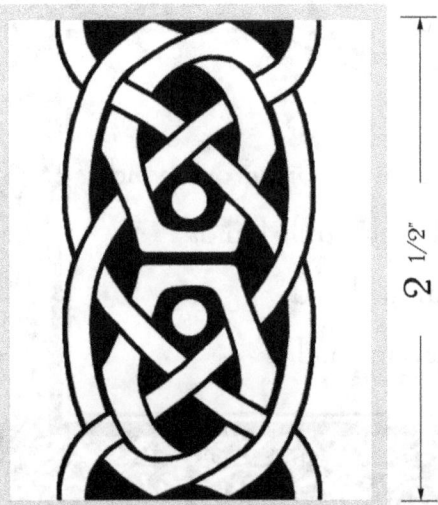

2 1/2"

Inner Border, Repeating Section

Inner Border, Crosspiece

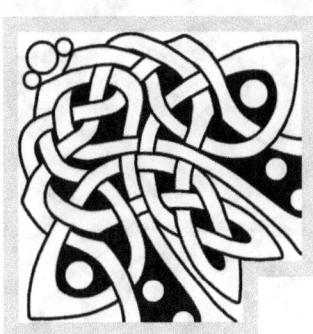

Corner Section

1 1/2"

Outer Border, Repeating Section

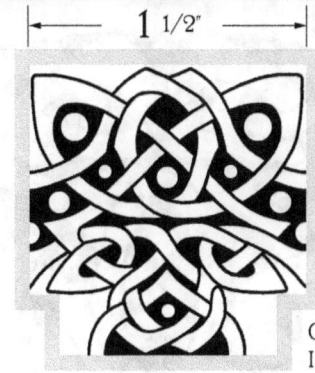

1 1/2"

Outer Border /
Inner Border T

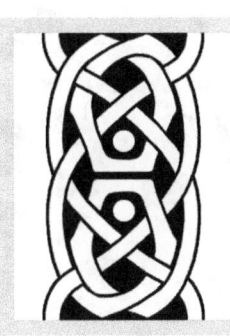

1 1/2"

Inner Border, Repeating Section

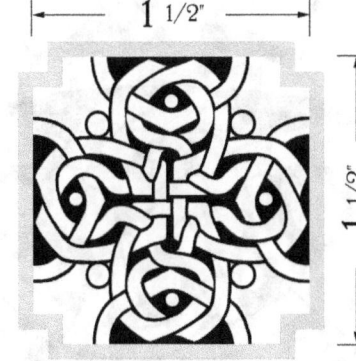

1 1/2"

1 1/2"

Inner Border, Crosspiece

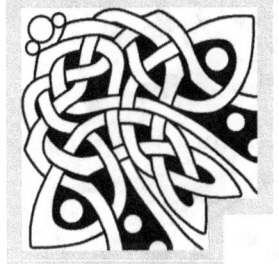

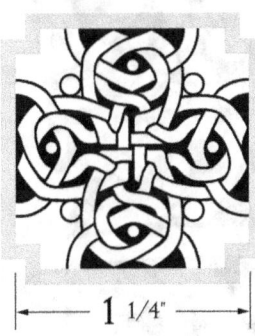

1 1/4"

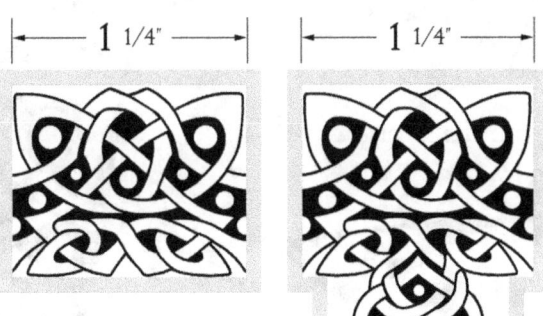

1 1/4"

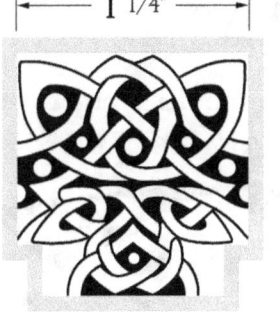

1 1/4"

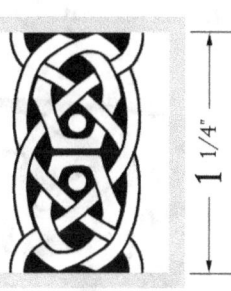

1 1/4"

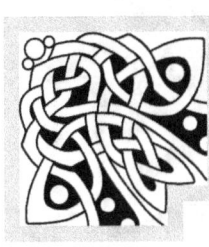

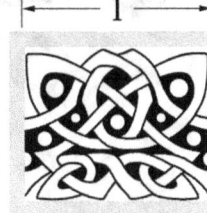

1"

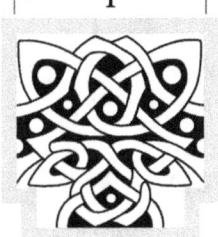

1"

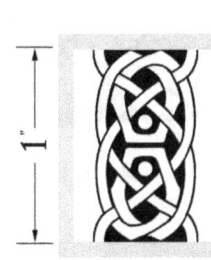

1"

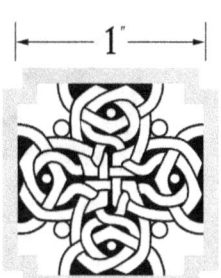

1"

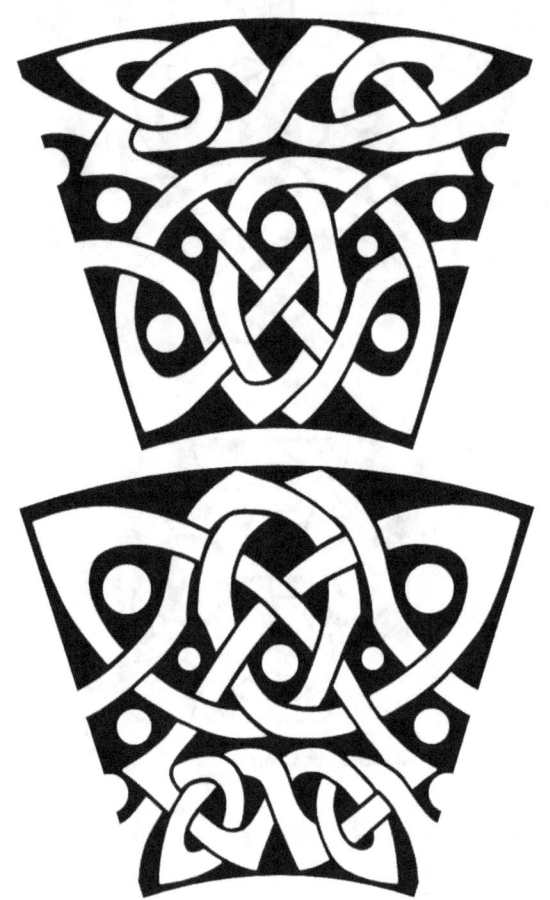

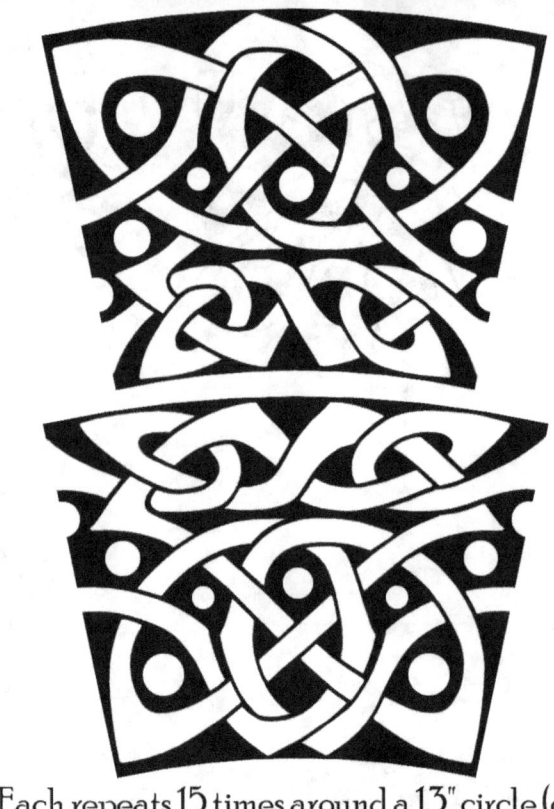

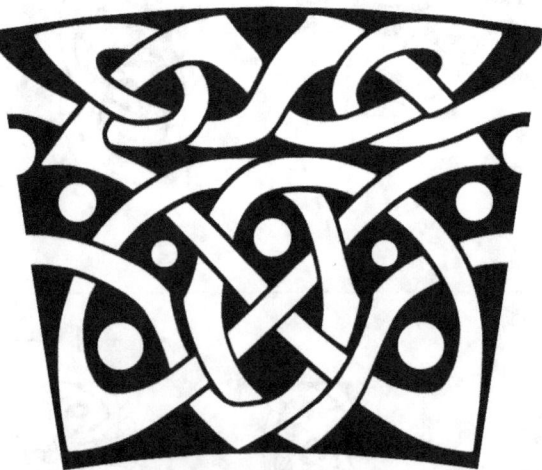

Each repeats 15 times around a 13" circle (o.d.)

Each repeats 10 times around a 9" circle (o.d.)

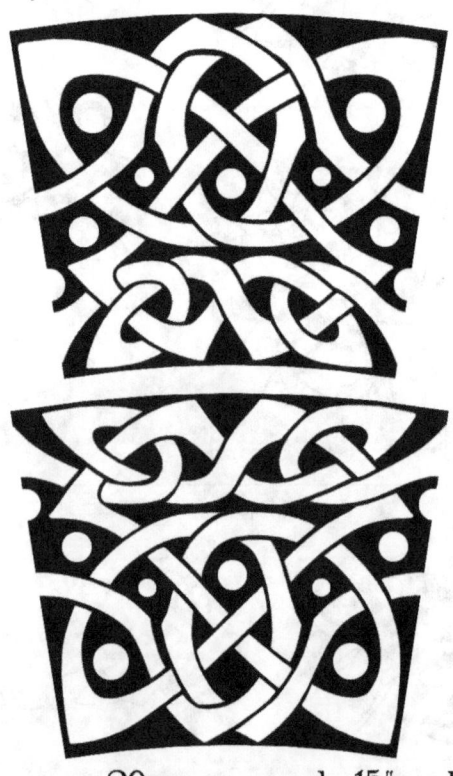

Repeats 20 times around a 19" circle (o.d.)

Each repeats 20 times around a 15" circle (o.d.)

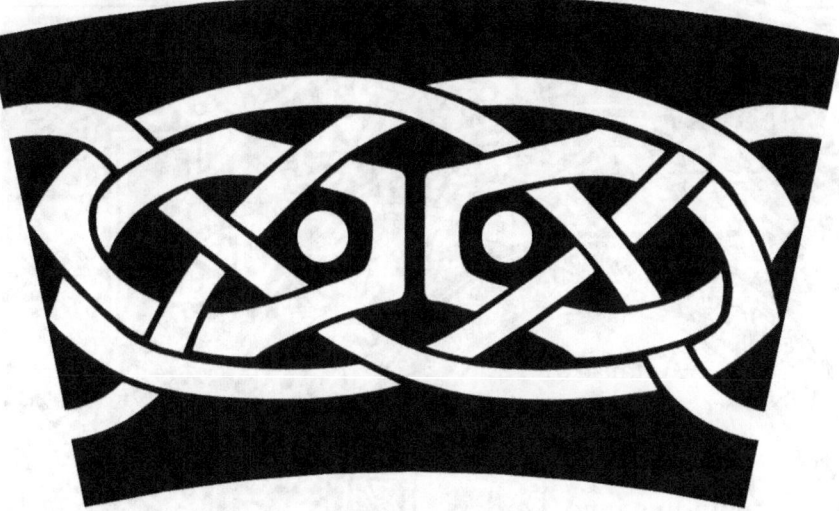

Repeats 15 times around
an 8" circle (o.d.)

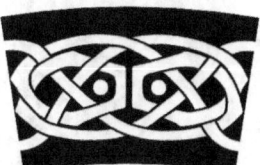

Repeats 15 times around a 22" circle (o.d.)

Repeats 20 times around
a 9" circle (o.d.)

Repeats 15 times around a 14" circle (o.d.)

Repeats 20 times around a 17" circle (o.d.)

Repeats 20 times around a 13" circle (o.d.)

Repeats 10 times around a 7" circle (o.d.)

Repeats 10 times around a 12" circle (o.d.)

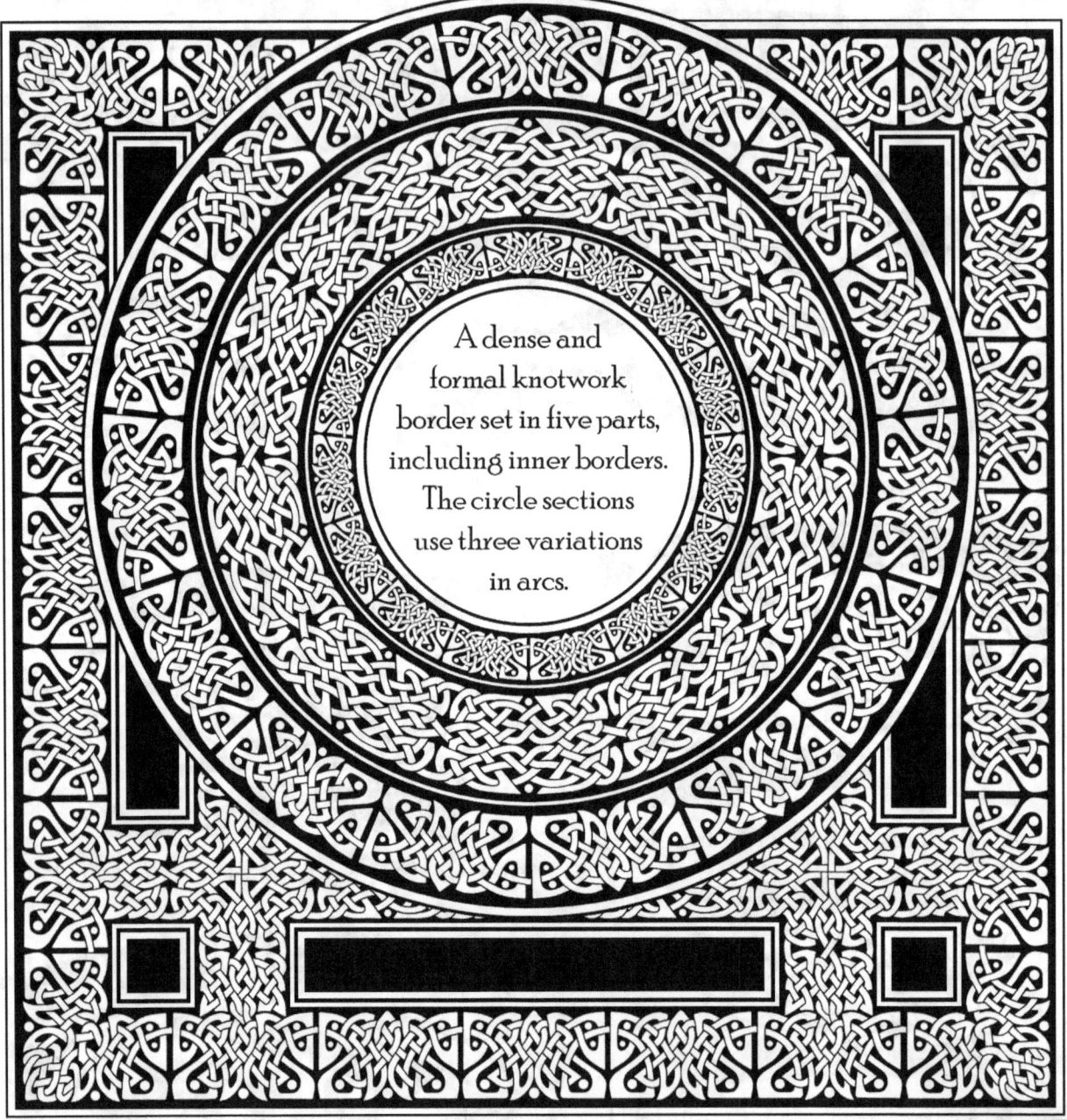

A dense and
formal knotwork
border set in five parts,
including inner borders.
The circle sections
use three variations
in arcs.

Structure:

Straight Sections, using only corners and outer border: one band.

Straight Sections, including Inner Border: multiple bands.

Circle Sections, Page One: design is a single band.

Circle Sections, Page Two: design is a multiple bands.

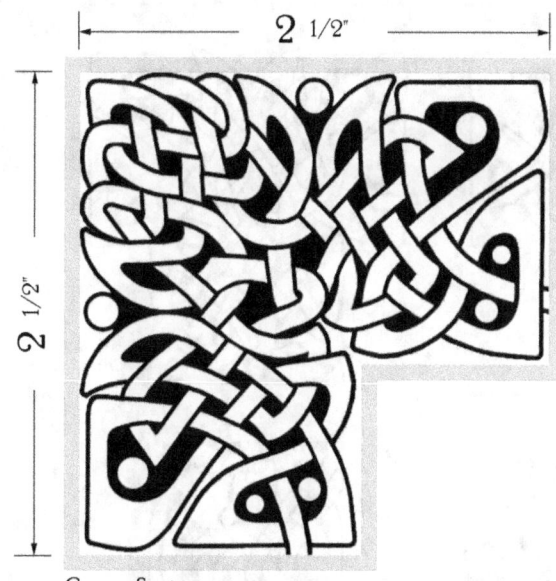

2 1/2"

2 1/2"

Corner Section

Unlike the preceding designs, this one can be laid out on a square grid. That's because the corner and the Outer Border/Inner Border T are perfectly square, making this one very simple to lay out accurately.

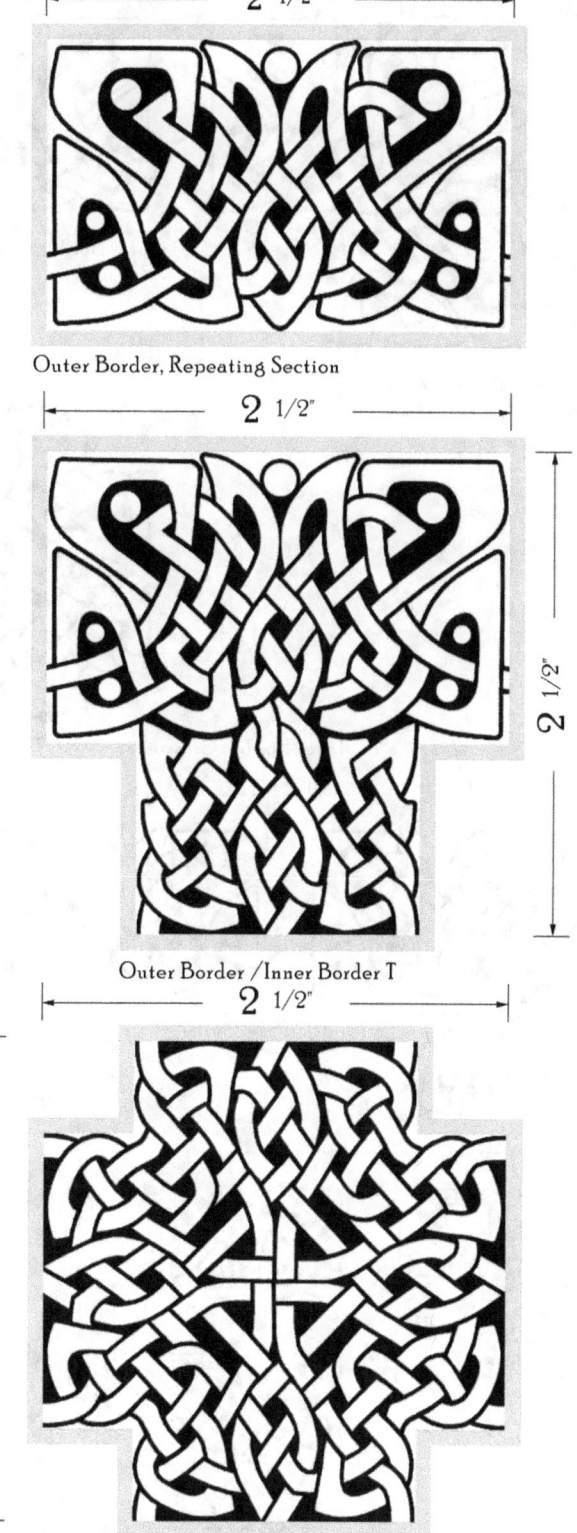

2 1/2"

Outer Border, Repeating Section

2 1/2"

2 1/2"

Outer Border /Inner Border T

2 1/2"

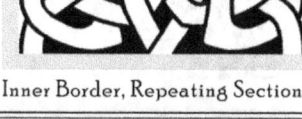

2 1/2"

Inner Border, Repeating Section

Inner Border, Crosspiece

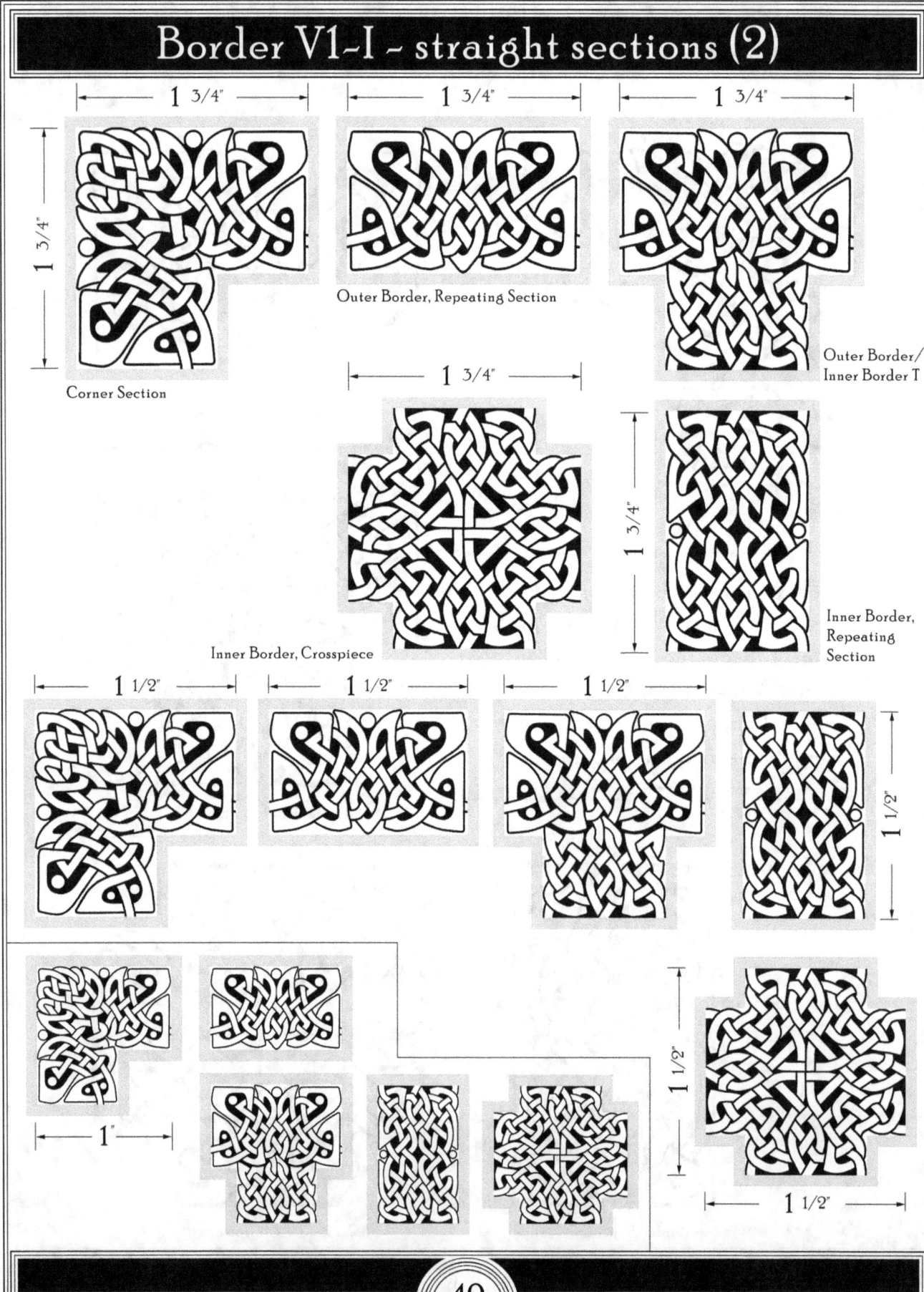

Corner Section

Outer Border, Repeating Section

Outer Border/ Inner Border T

Inner Border, Crosspiece

Inner Border, Repeating Section

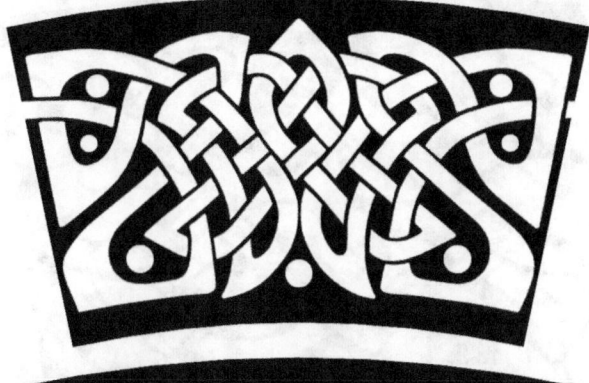

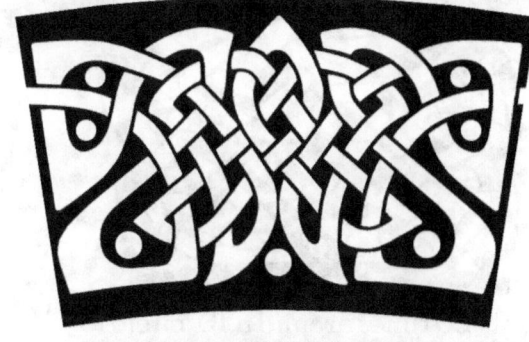

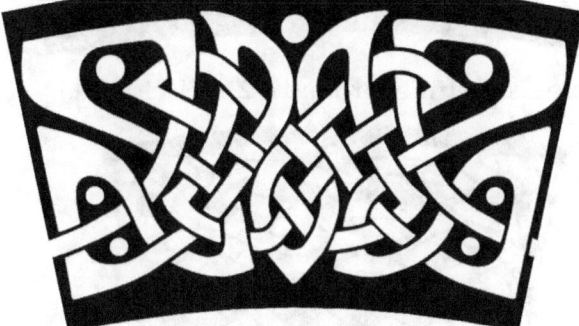

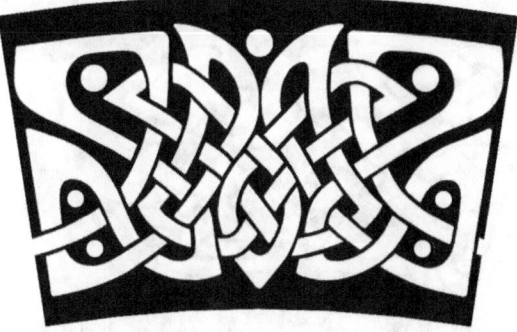

Each repeats 20 times around an 18" circle (o.d.)

Each repeats 15 times
around a 15" circle (o.d.)

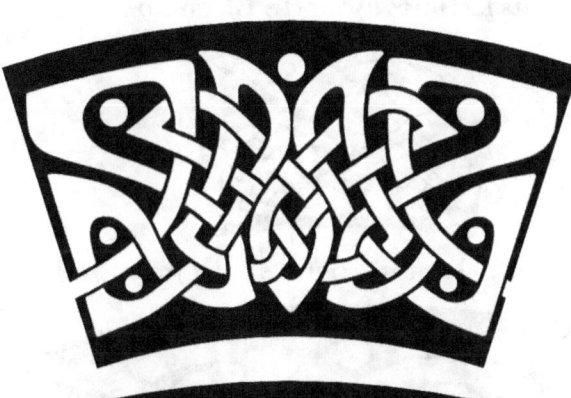

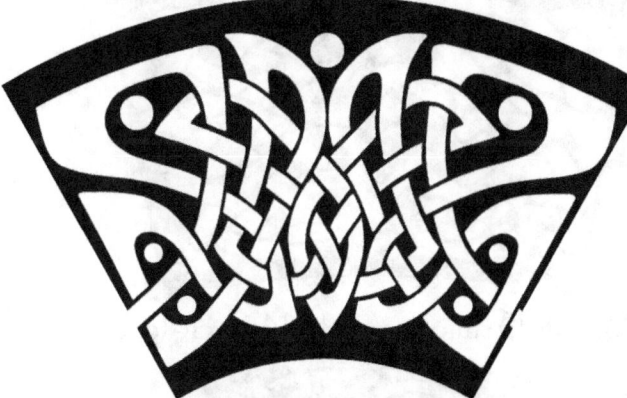

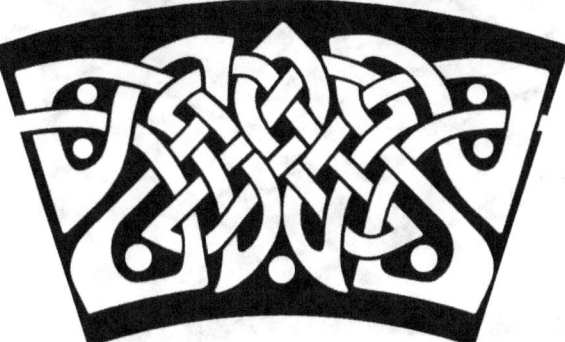

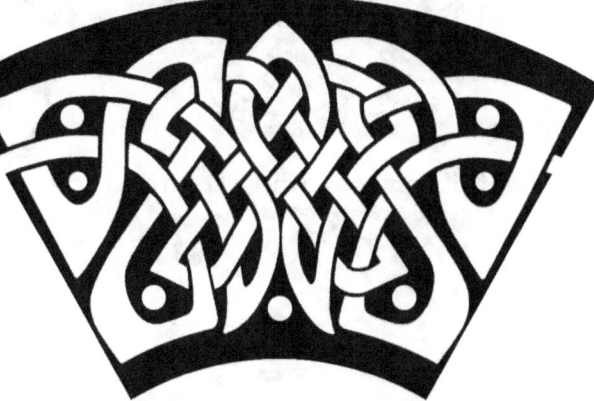

Each repeats 10 times around a 10" circle (o.d.)

Each repeats 6 times around a 7" circle (o.d.)

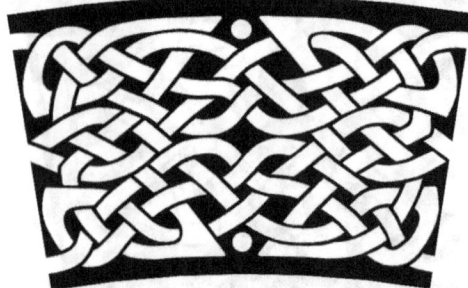

Repeats 20 times around a 16" circle (o.d.)

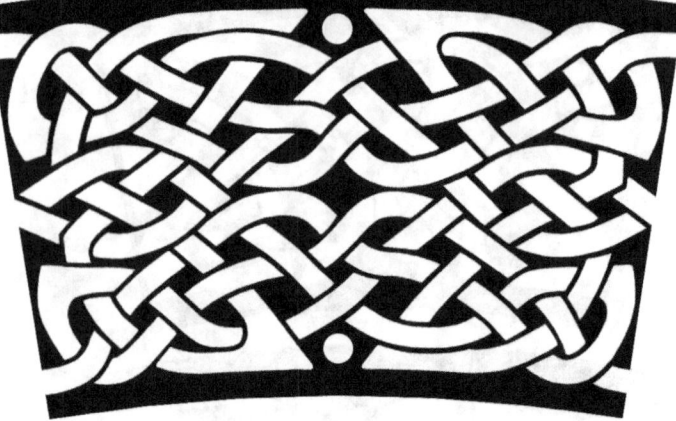

Repeats 20 times around a 24" circle (o.d.)

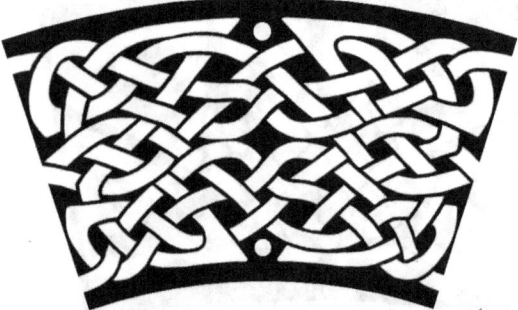

Repeats 10 times around a 9" circle (o.d.)

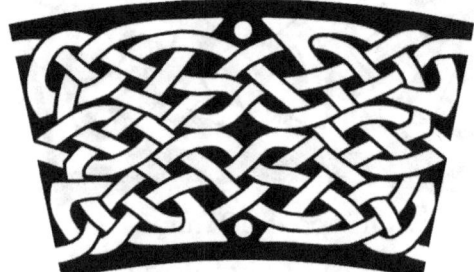

Repeats 15 times around a 12" circle (o.d.)

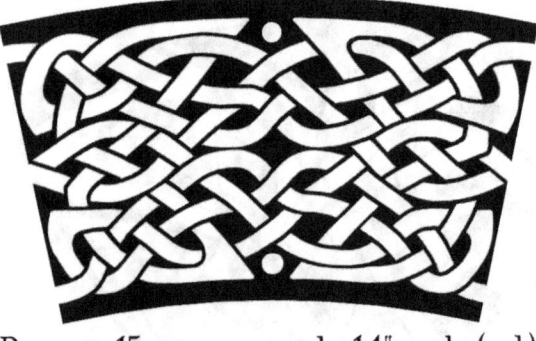

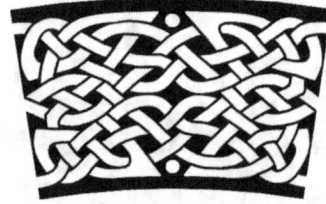

Repeats 20 times around an 11" circle (o.d.)

Repeats 15 times around a 14" circle (o.d.)

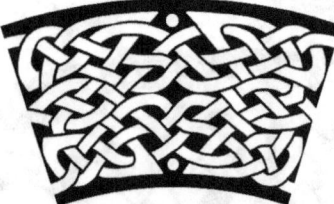

Repeats 10 times around a 6" circle (o.d.)

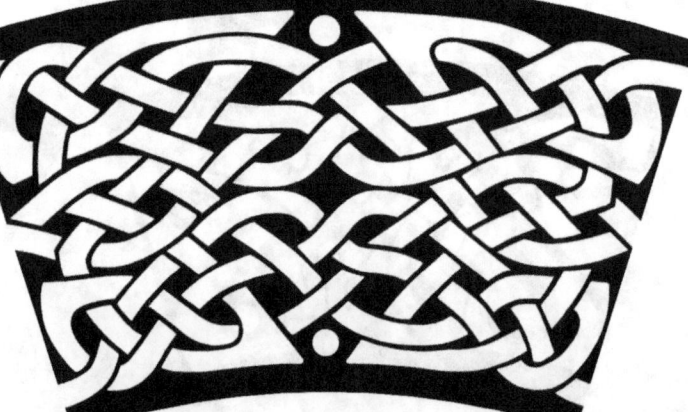

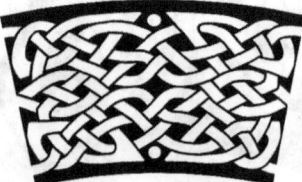

Repeats 15 times around an 8" circle (o.d.)

Repeats 10 times around a 13" circle (o.d.)

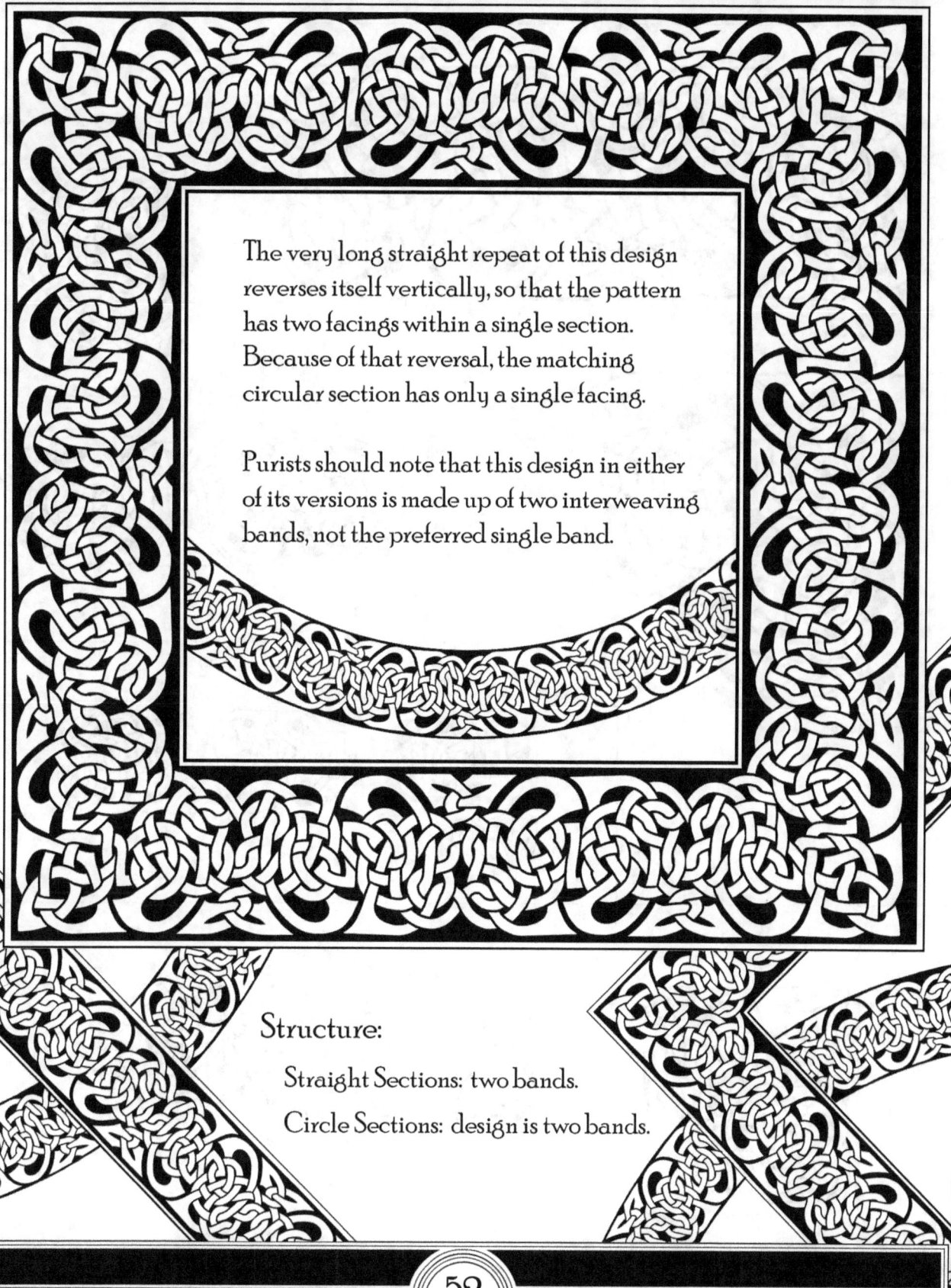

The very long straight repeat of this design reverses itself vertically, so that the pattern has two facings within a single section. Because of that reversal, the matching circular section has only a single facing.

Purists should note that this design in either of its versions is made up of two interweaving bands, not the preferred single band.

Structure:

Straight Sections: two bands.

Circle Sections: design is two bands.

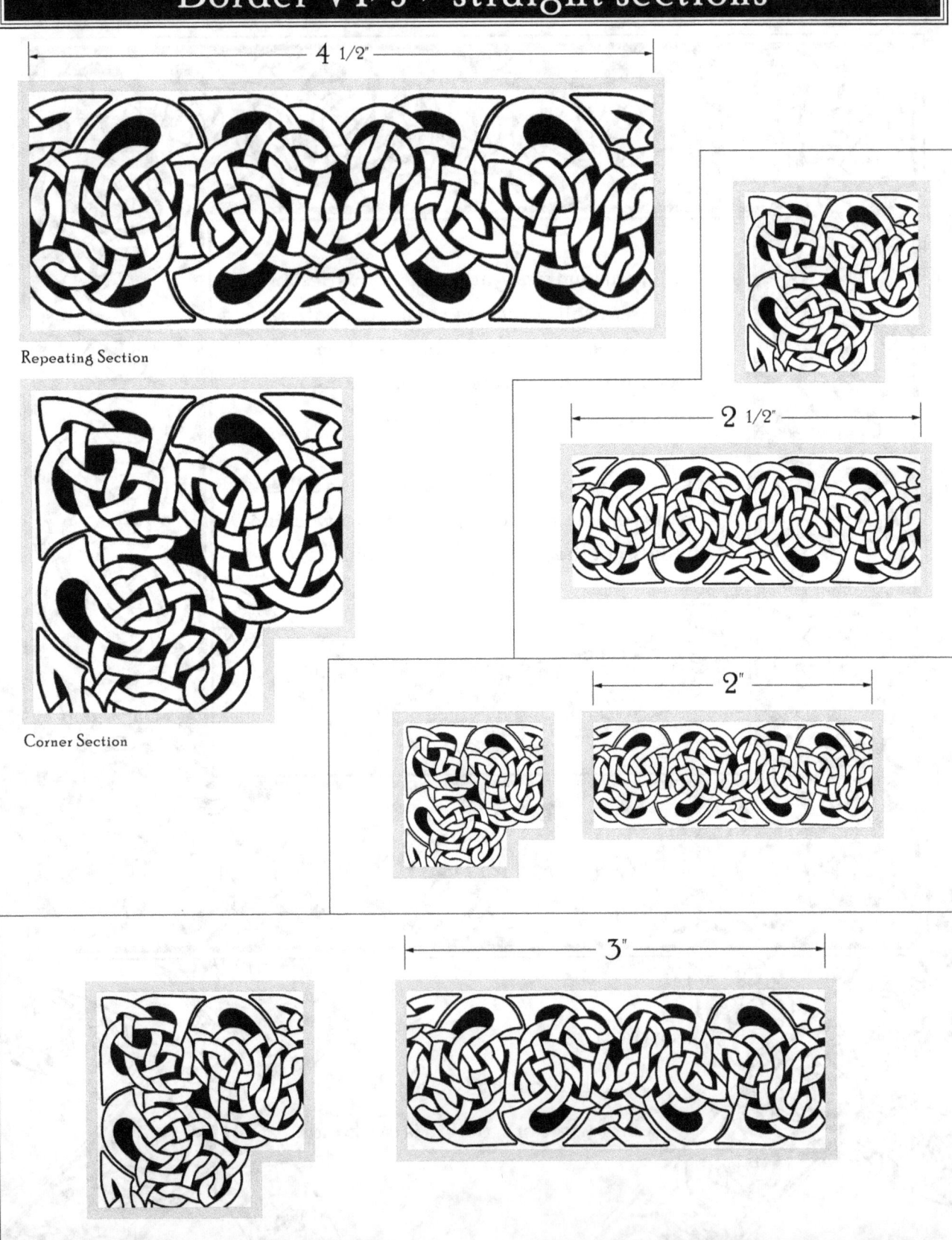

4 1/2"

Repeating Section

2 1/2"

Corner Section

2"

3"

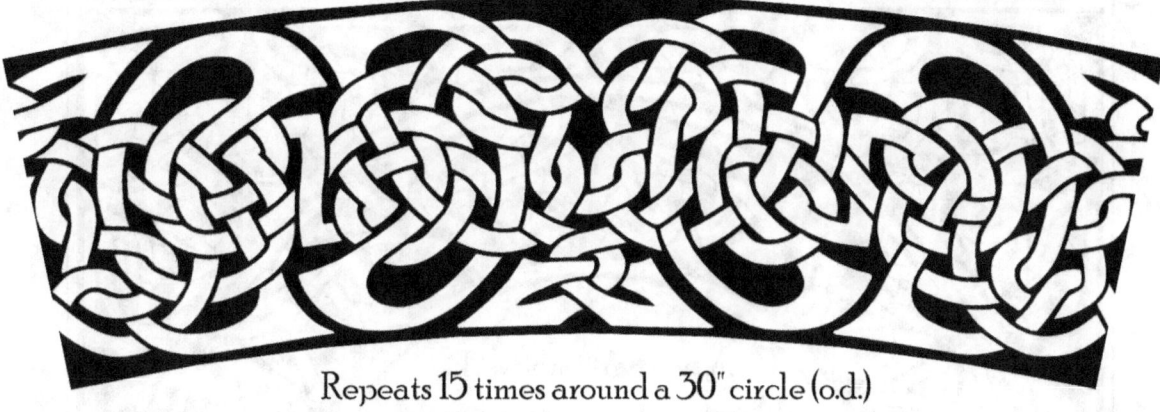

Repeats 15 times around a 30" circle (o.d.)

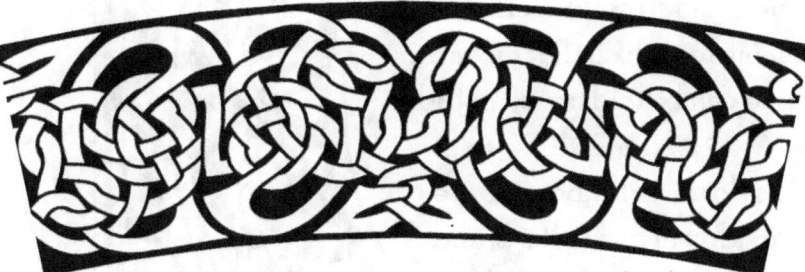

Repeats 15 times around a 21" circle (o.d.)

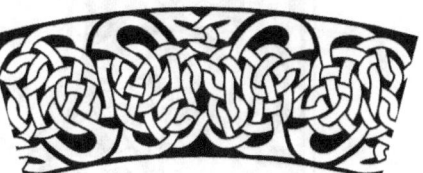

Repeats 12 times around
a 9" circle (o.d.)

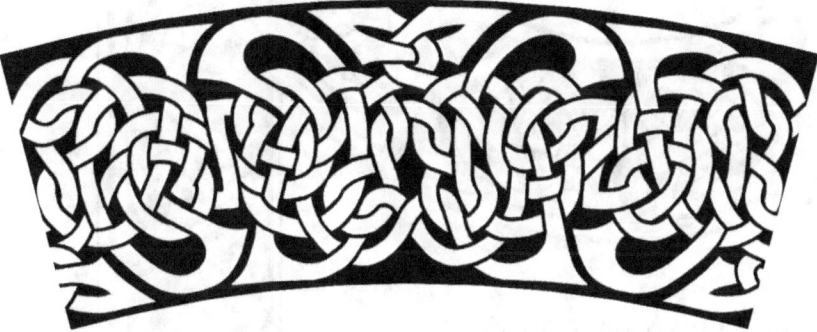

Repeats 12 times around a 17" circle (o.d.)

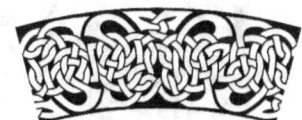

Repeats 12 times around
a 6" circle (o.d.)

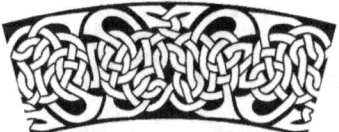

Repeats 12 times around
a 7" circle (o.d.)

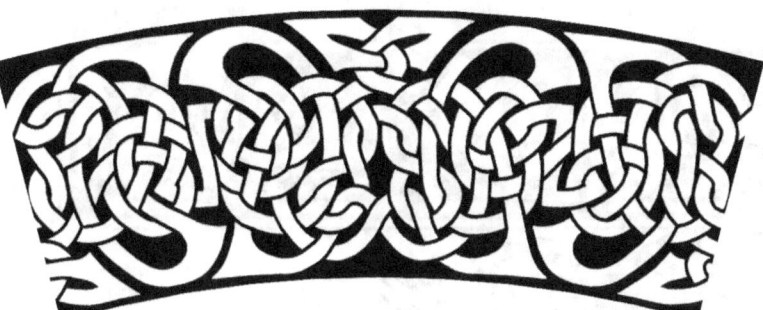

Repeats 12 times around a 16" circle (o.d.)

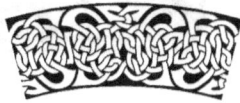

Repeats 12 times around
a 5" circle (o.d.)

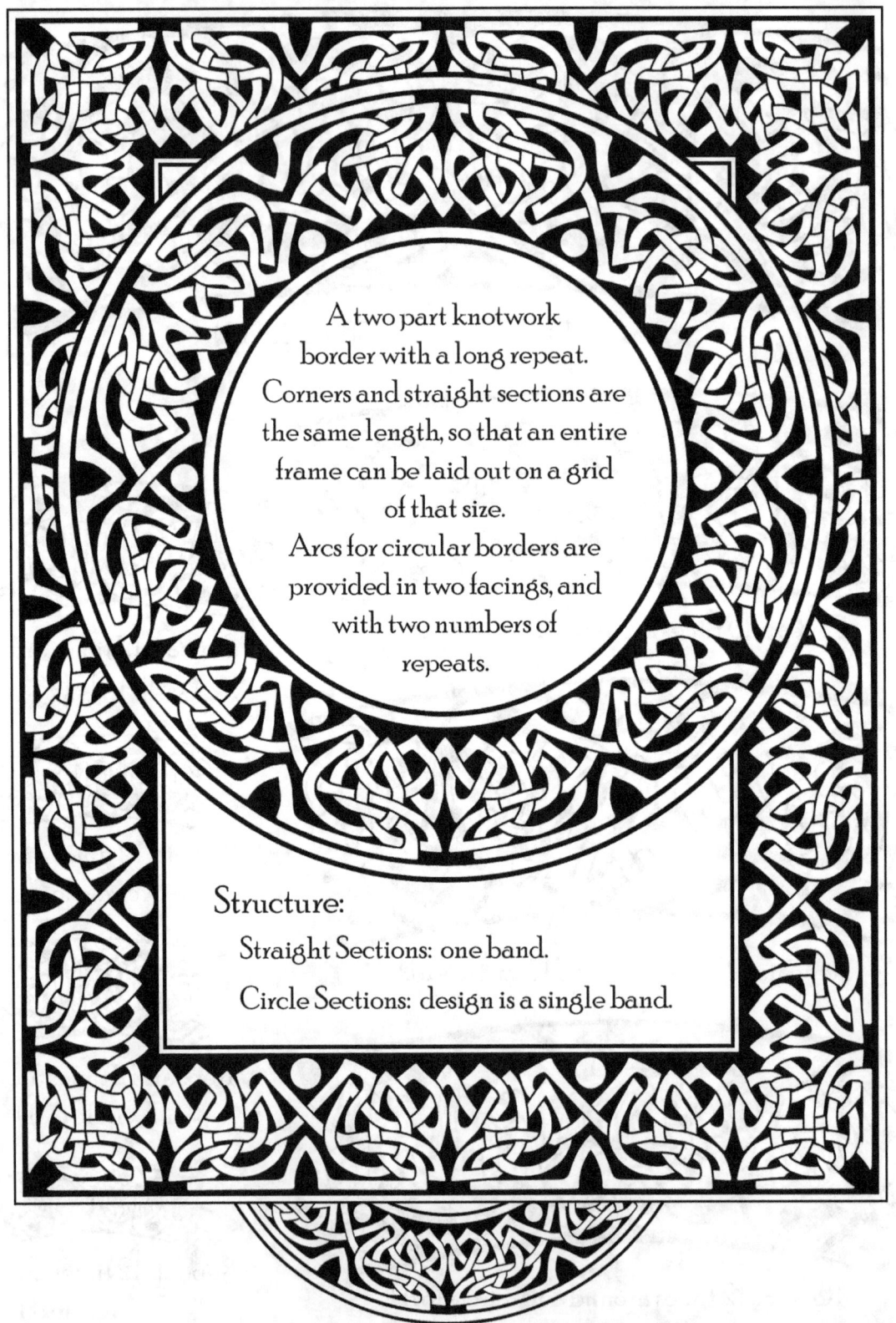

A two part knotwork
border with a long repeat.
Corners and straight sections are
the same length, so that an entire
frame can be laid out on a grid
of that size.
Arcs for circular borders are
provided in two facings, and
with two numbers of
repeats.

Structure:

Straight Sections: one band.

Circle Sections: design is a single band.

5"

5"

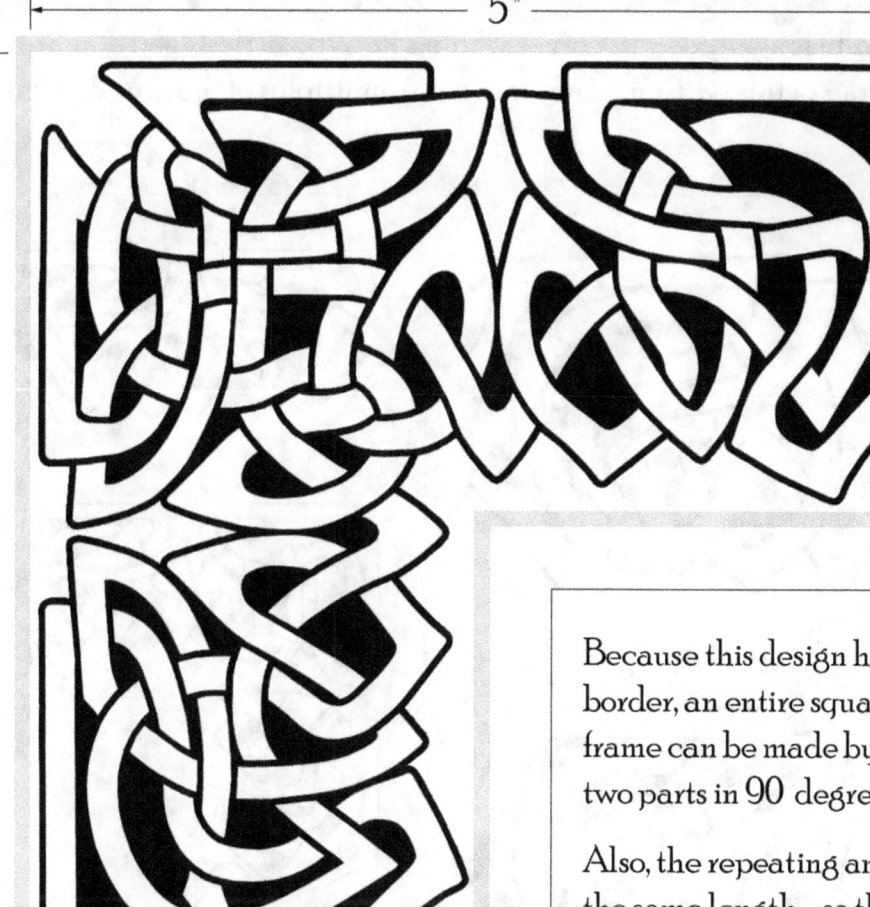

Corner Section

Because this design has no separate inner border, an entire square or rectangular frame can be made by rotating just these two parts in 90 degree increments.

Also, the repeating and corner sections are the same length ~ so this border can be very easily laid out in multiples of that length.

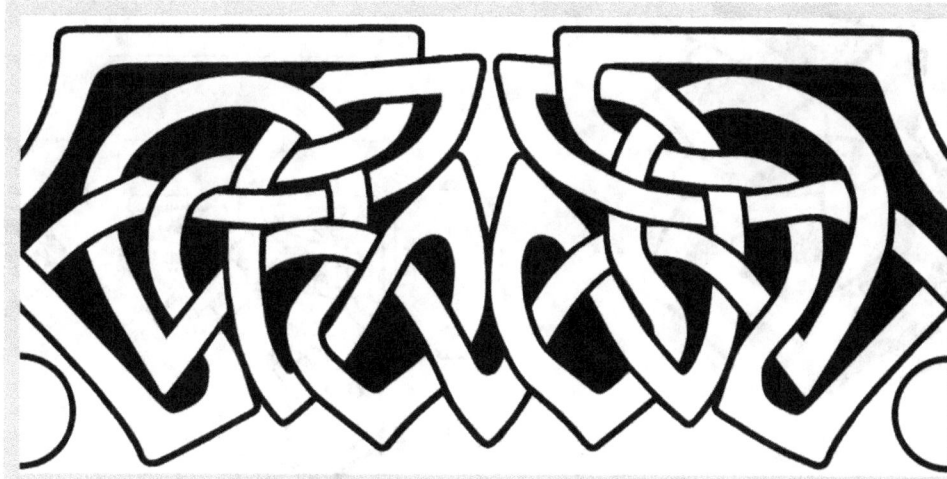

Repeating Section

5"

This pattern has an unusually long repeat. Its corner sections have been designed at that same full length ~ so a border of this pattern can be laid out in multiples of the sizes shown.

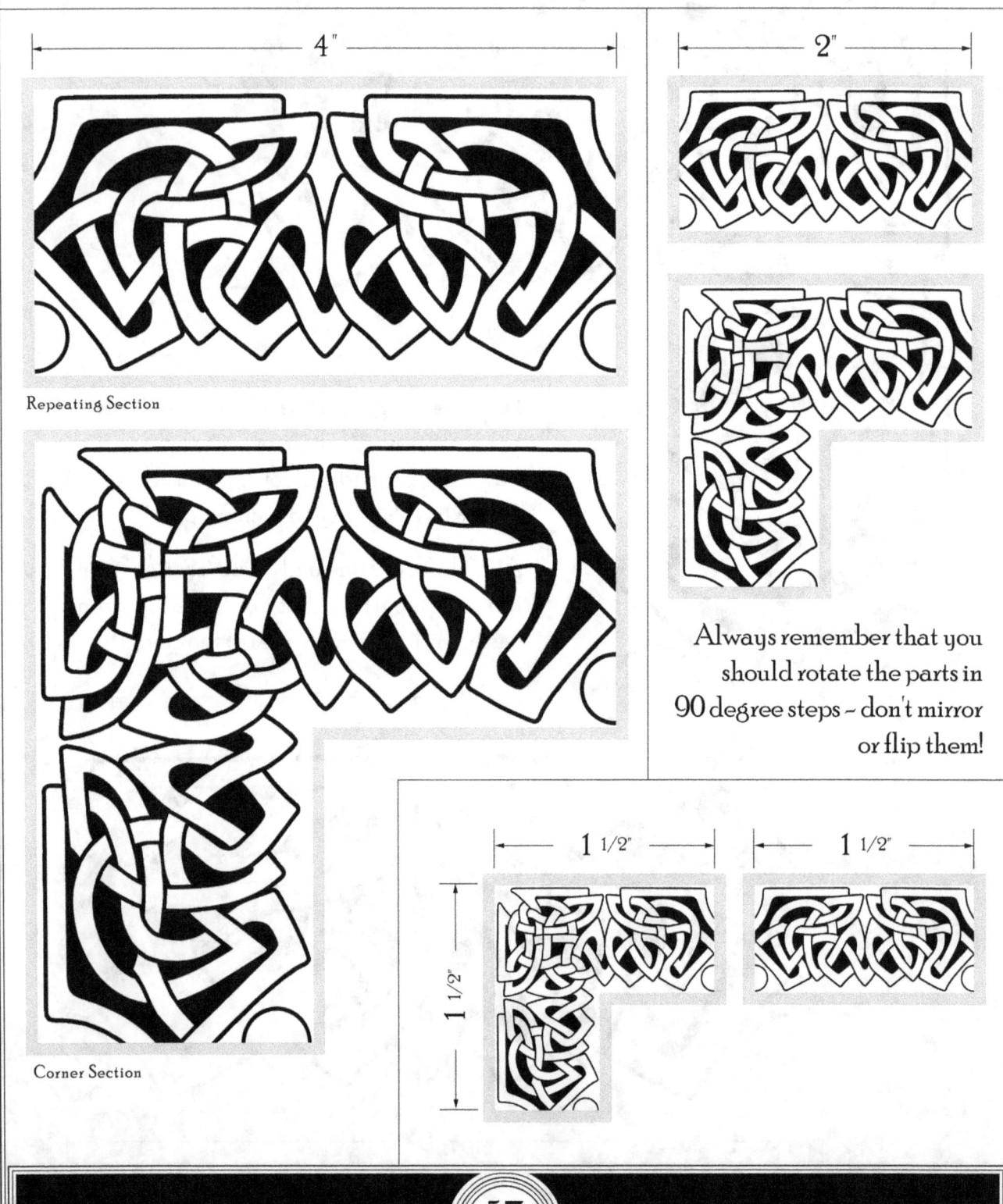

4"

Repeating Section

Corner Section

2"

Always remember that you should rotate the parts in 90 degree steps ~ don't mirror or flip them!

1 1/2"

1 1/2"

1 1/2"

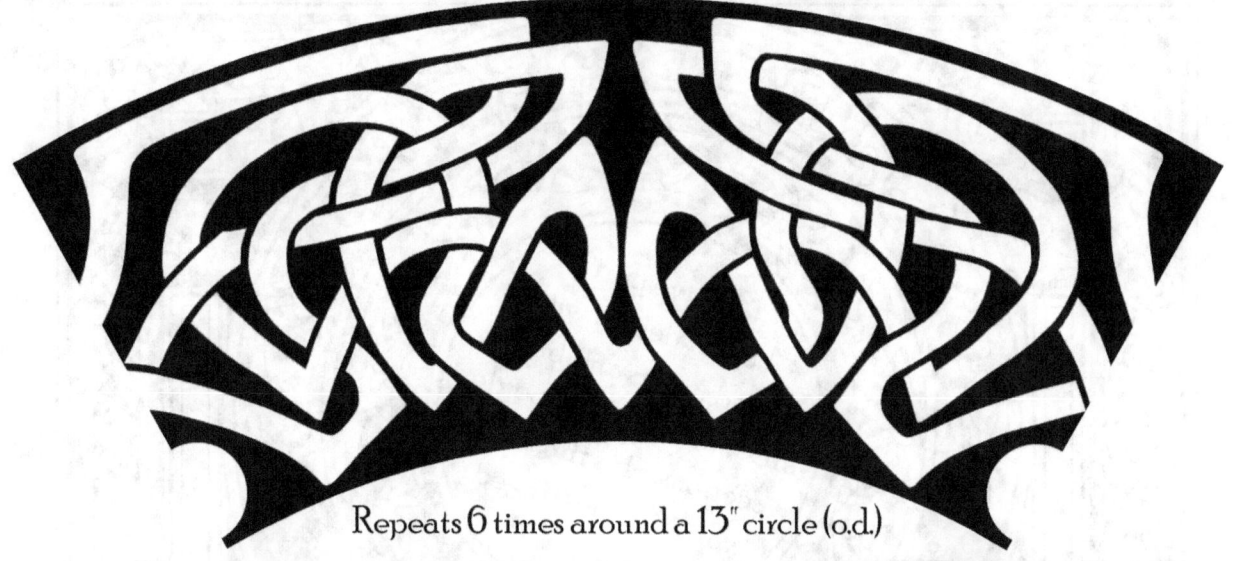

Repeats 6 times around a 13" circle (o.d.)

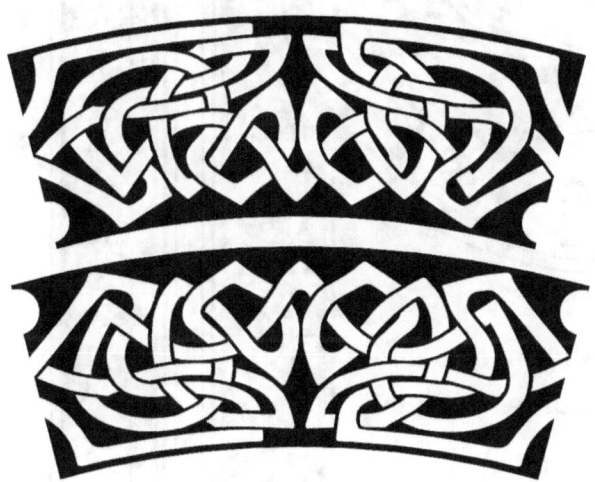

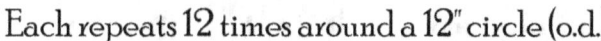

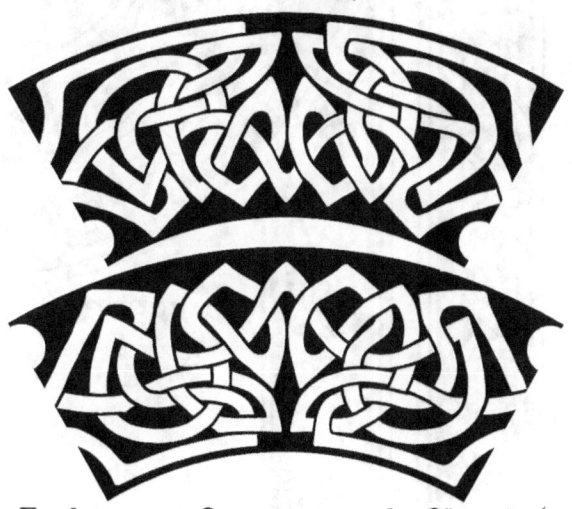

Each repeats 12 times around a 12" circle (o.d.)

Each repeats 6 times around a 6" circle (o.d.)

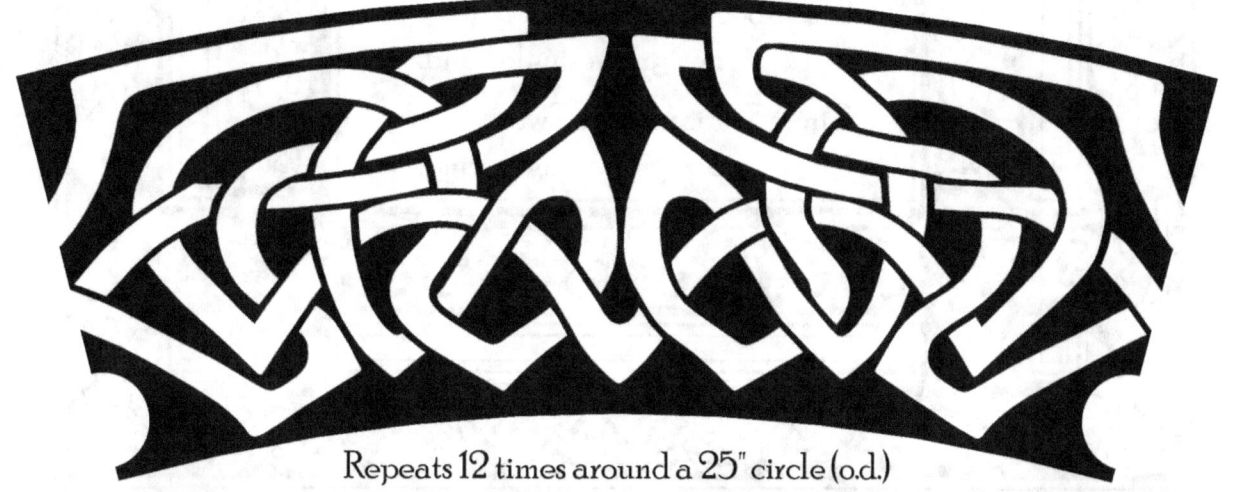

Repeats 12 times around a 25" circle (o.d.)

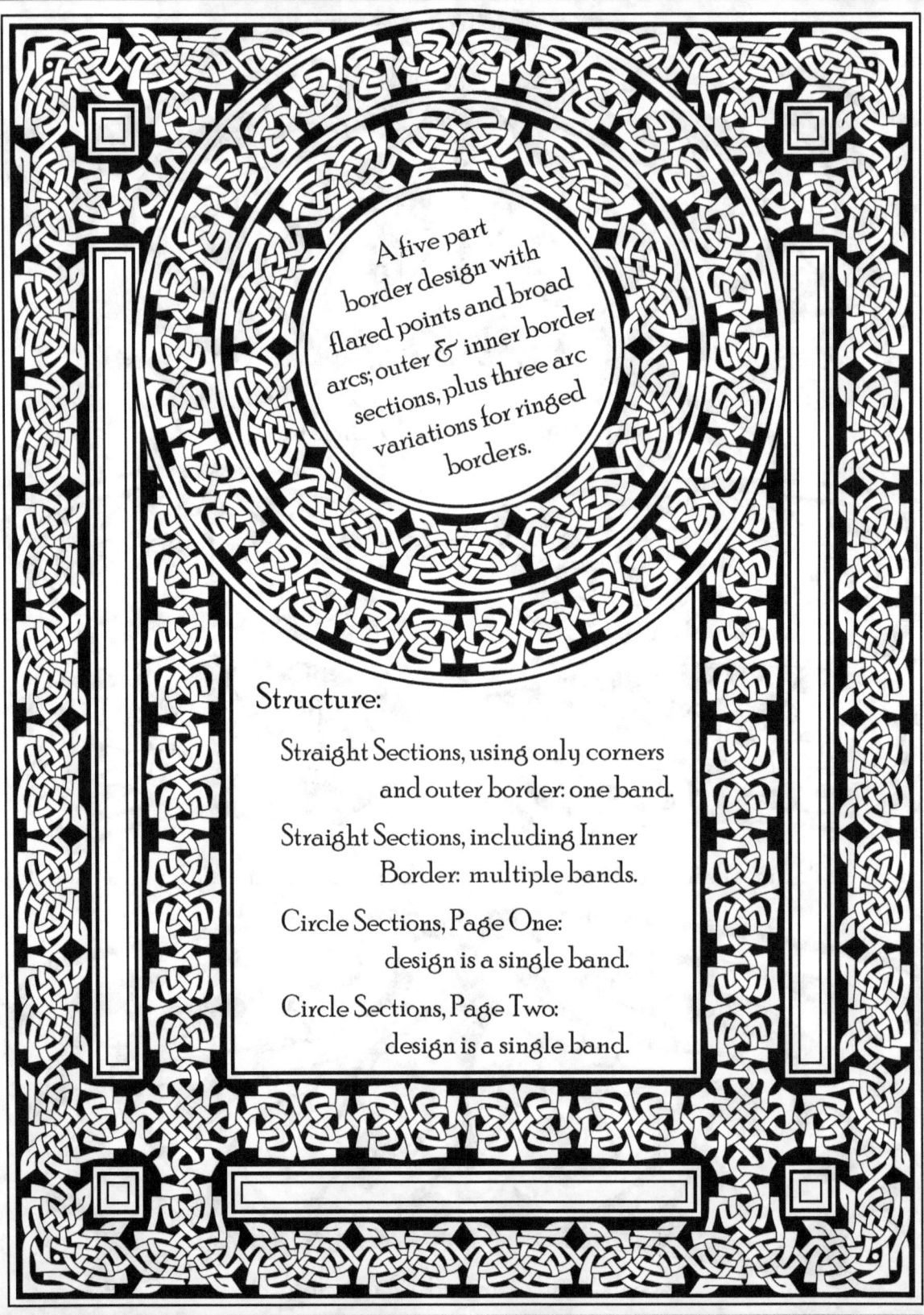

A five part border design with flared points and broad arcs; outer & inner border sections, plus three arc variations for ringed borders.

Structure:

Straight Sections, using only corners and outer border: one band.

Straight Sections, including Inner Border: multiple bands.

Circle Sections, Page One: design is a single band.

Circle Sections, Page Two: design is a single band.

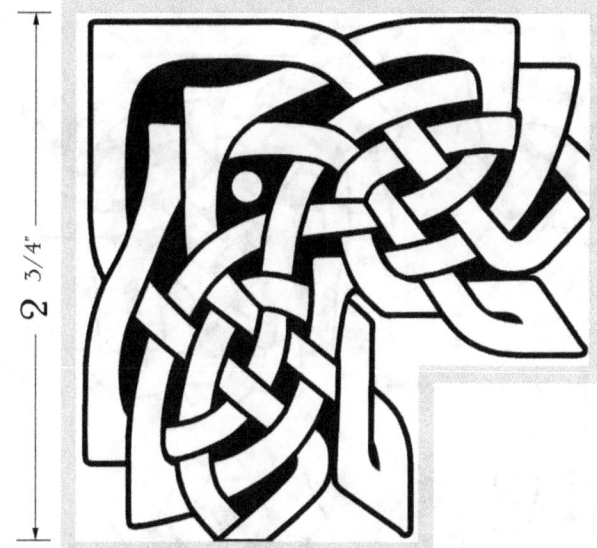

2 3/4"

Corner Section

2 3/4"

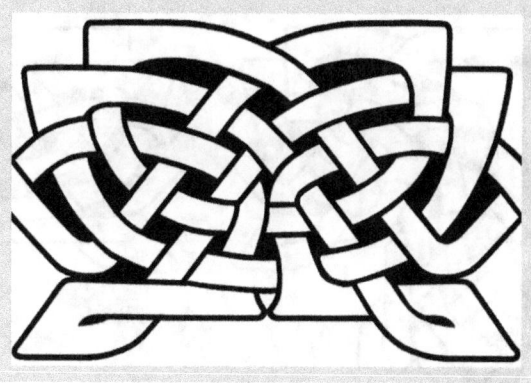

Outer Border, Repeating Section

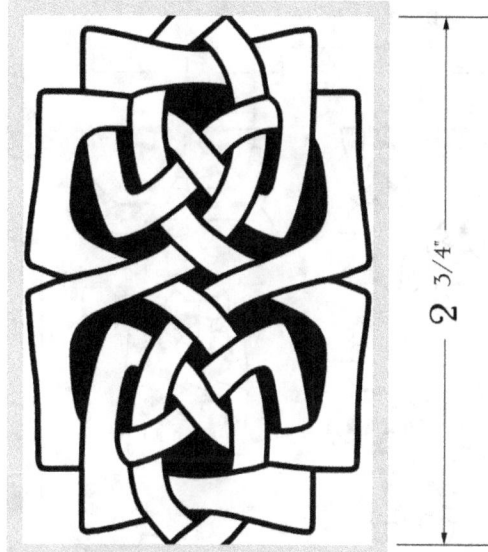

2 3/4"

Inner Border, Repeating Section

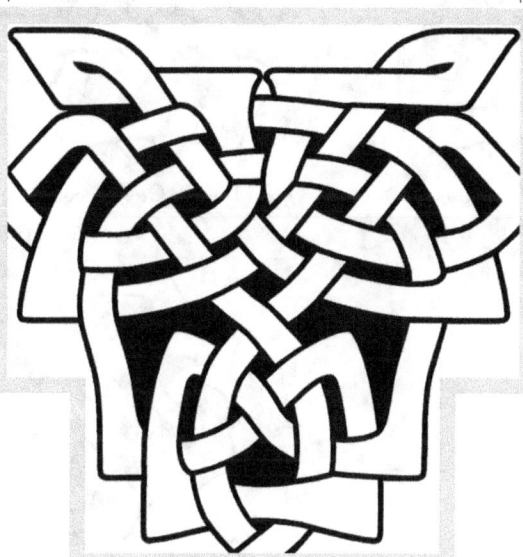

Outer Border / Inner Border T

The repeating, corner and "T" sections
are the same length ~ so this border
can be laid out on a square grid of that
same size.

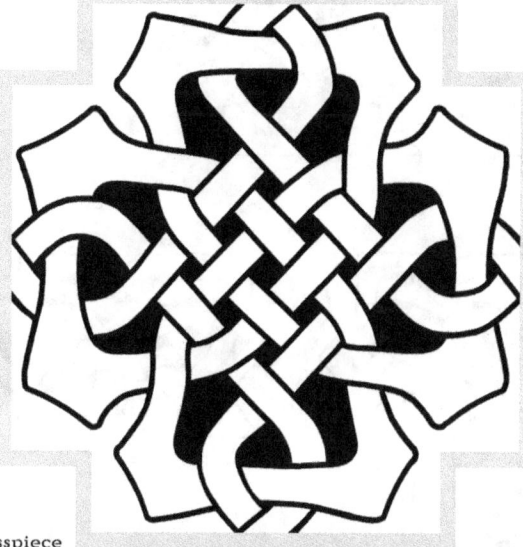

Inner Border, Crosspiece

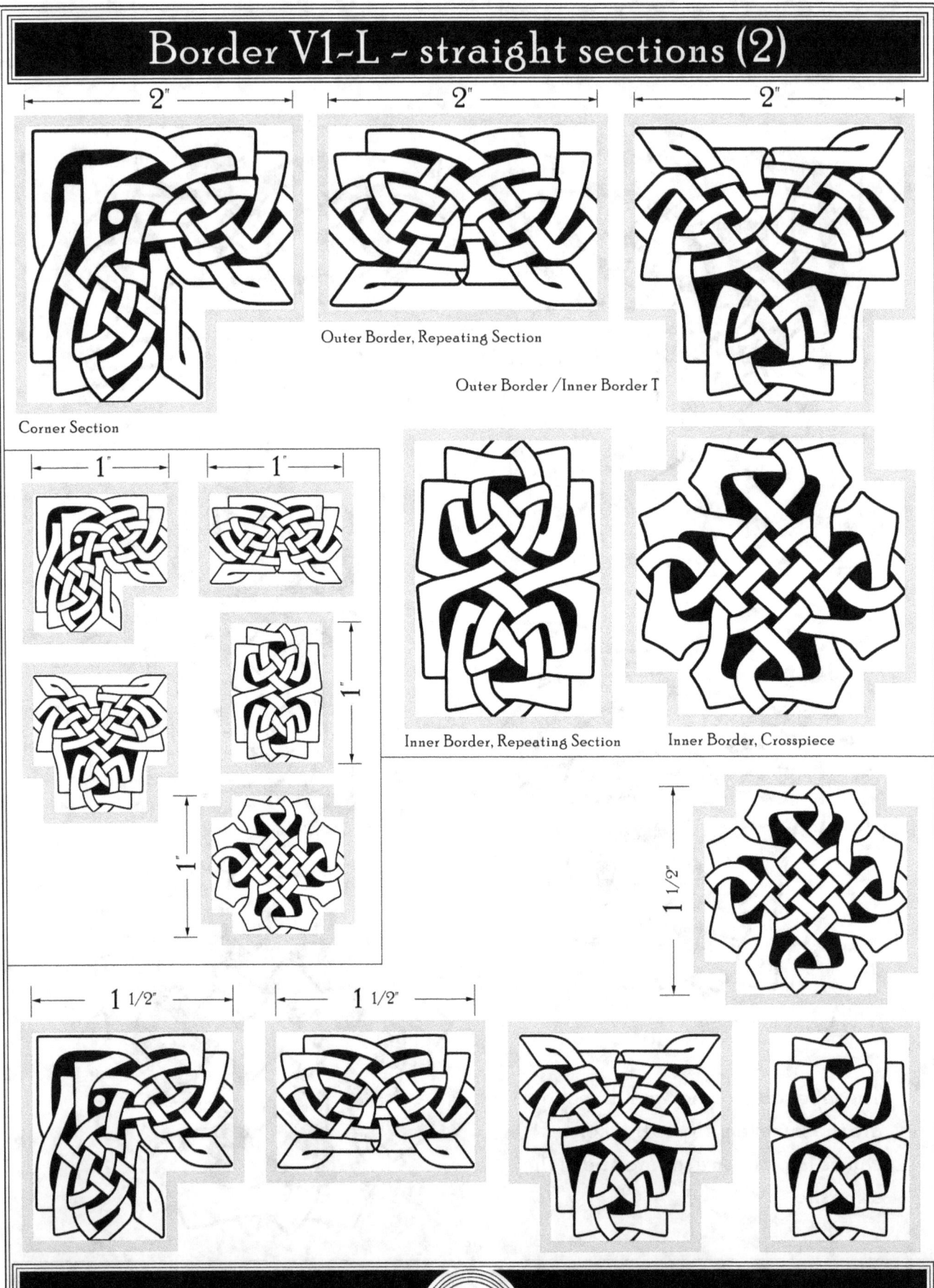

2"

2"

2"

Outer Border, Repeating Section

Outer Border / Inner Border T

Corner Section

1"

1"

1"

1"

Inner Border, Repeating Section

Inner Border, Crosspiece

1 1/2"

1 1/2"

1 1/2"

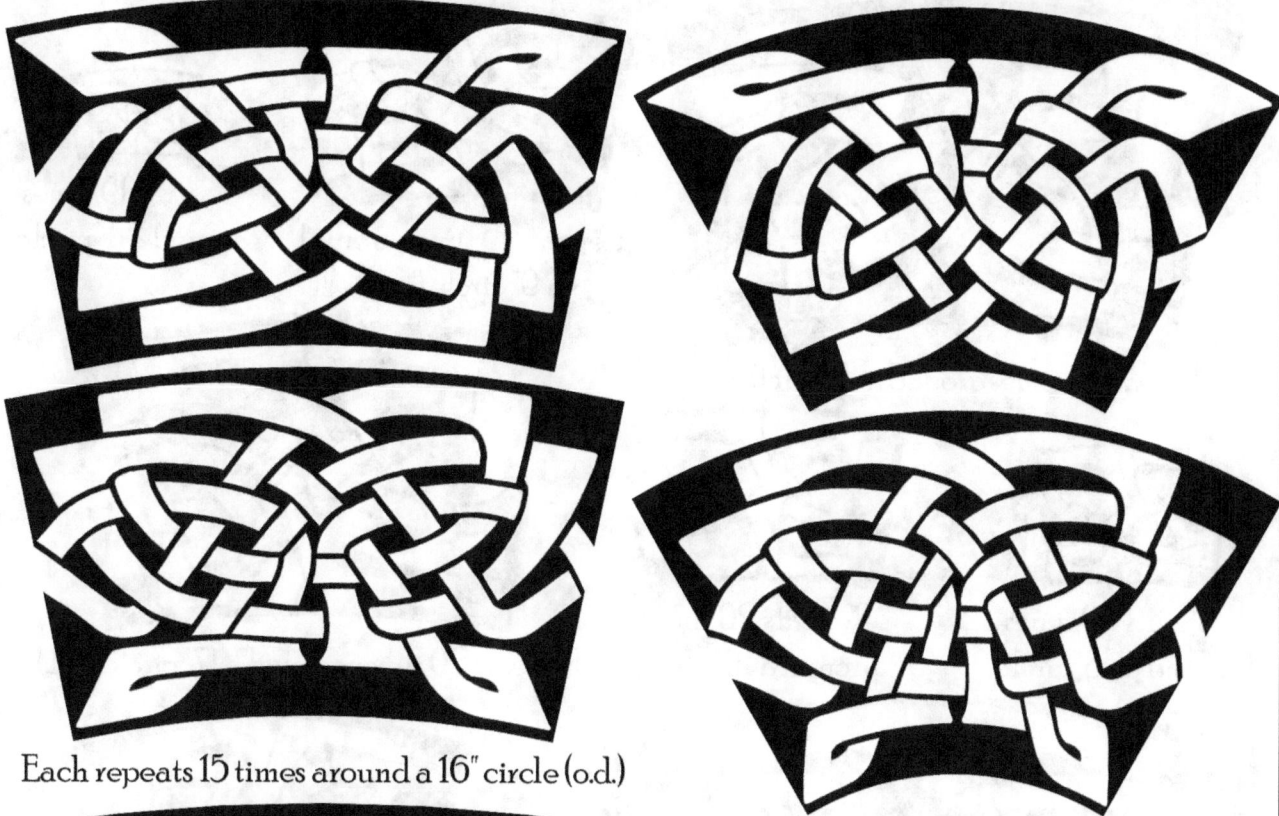

Each repeats 15 times around a 16" circle (o.d.)

Each repeats 6 times around a 7" circle (o.d.)

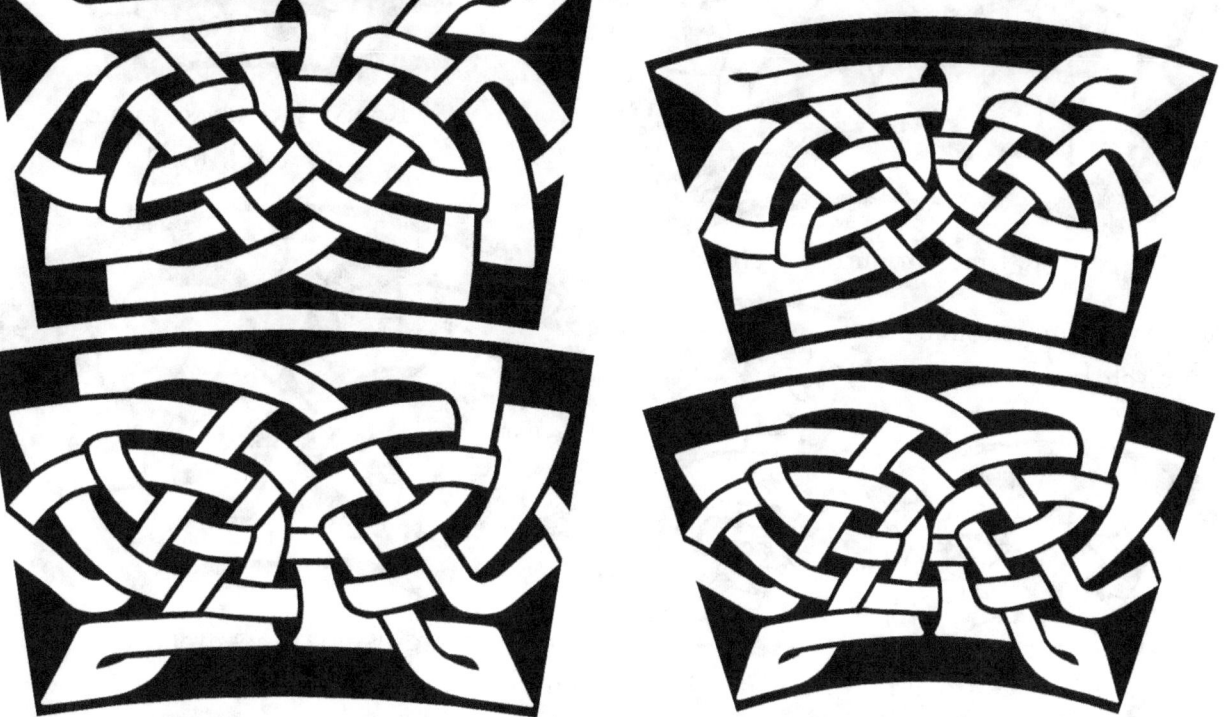

Each repeats 20 times around a 21" circle (o.d.)   Each repeats 10 times around a 10" circle (o.d.)

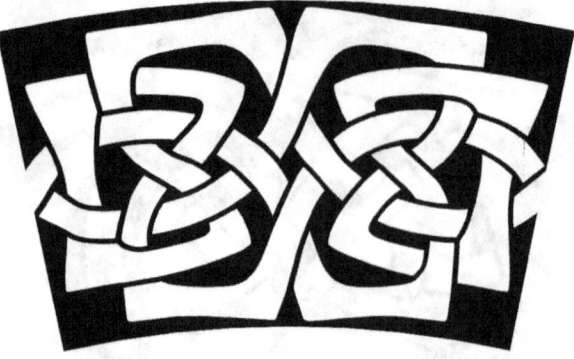

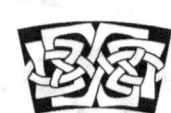

Repeats 15 times around a 9" circle (o.d.)

Repeats 15 times around a 4" circle

Repeats 15 times around a 15" circle (o.d.)

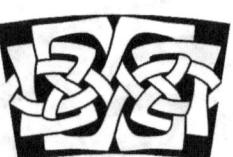

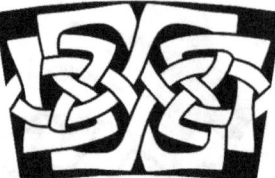

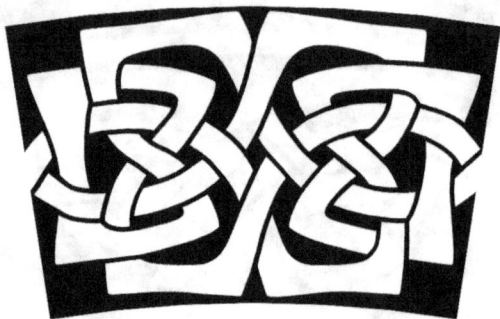

Repeats 20 times around an 8" circle

Repeats 20 times around a 10" circle

Repeats 20 times around a 17" circle (o.d.)

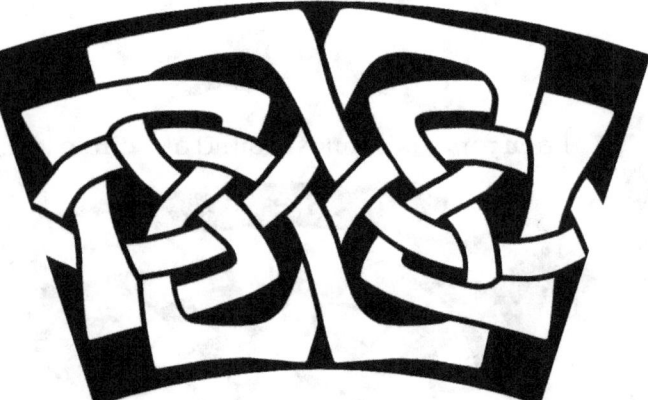

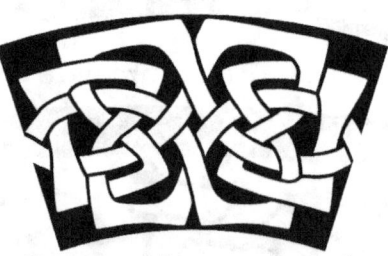

Repeats 10 times around a 7" circle (o.d.)

Repeats 10 times around a 12" circle (o.d.)

Repeats 6 times around a 3" circle (o.d.) →

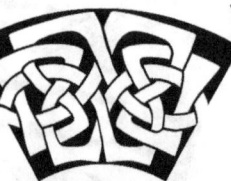

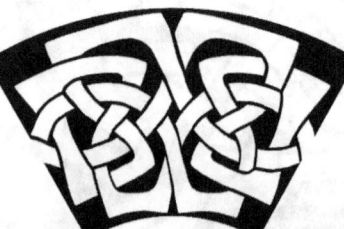

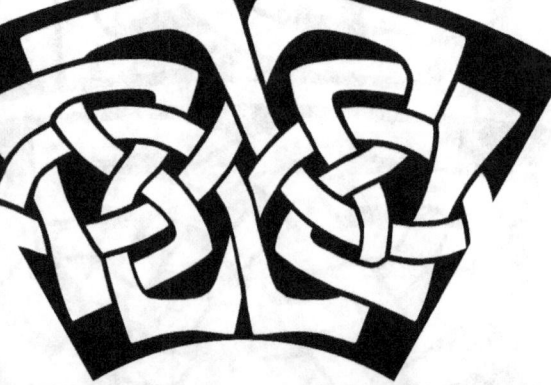

Repeats 6 times around a 4" circle (o.d.)

Repeats 10 times around a 5" circle (o.d.)

Repeats 6 times around a 7" circle (o.d.)

Border V1-M

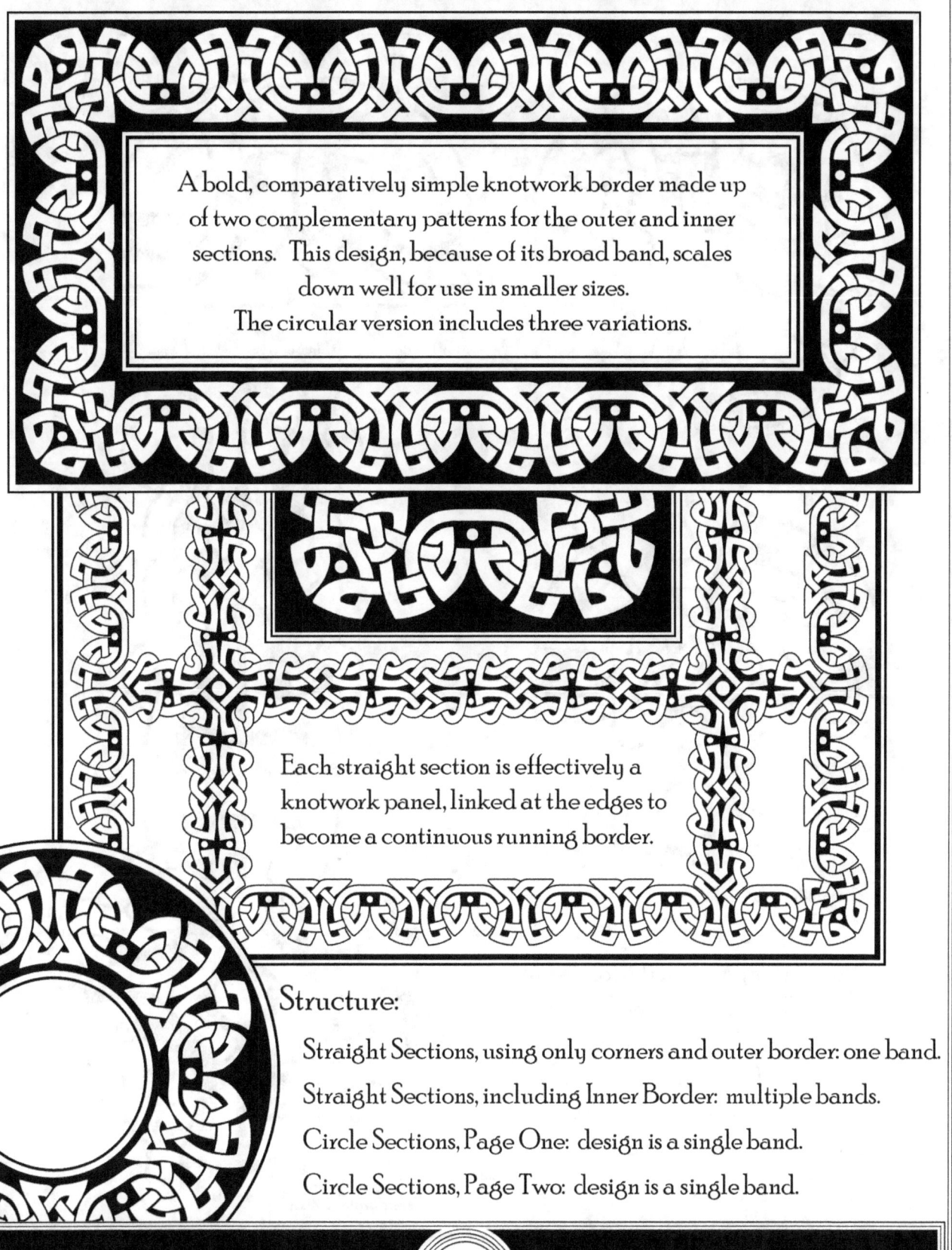

A bold, comparatively simple knotwork border made up of two complementary patterns for the outer and inner sections. This design, because of its broad band, scales down well for use in smaller sizes.
The circular version includes three variations.

Each straight section is effectively a knotwork panel, linked at the edges to become a continuous running border.

Structure:

Straight Sections, using only corners and outer border: one band.

Straight Sections, including Inner Border: multiple bands.

Circle Sections, Page One: design is a single band.

Circle Sections, Page Two: design is a single band.

2 1/2"

2 1/2"

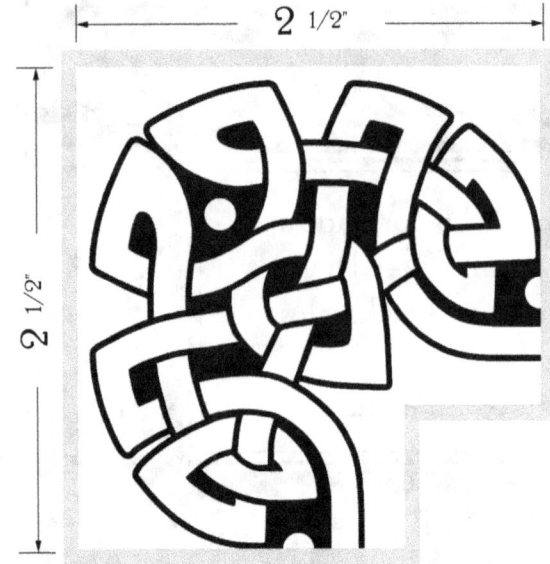

2 1/2"

Corner Section

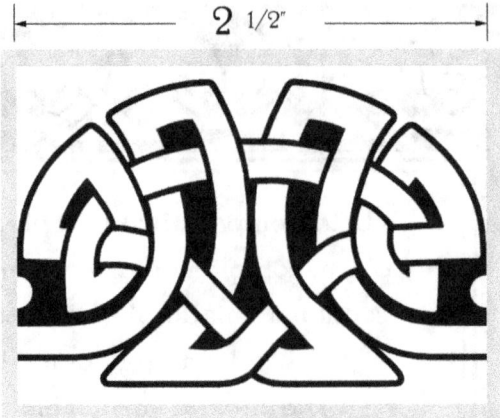

Outer Border, Repeating Section

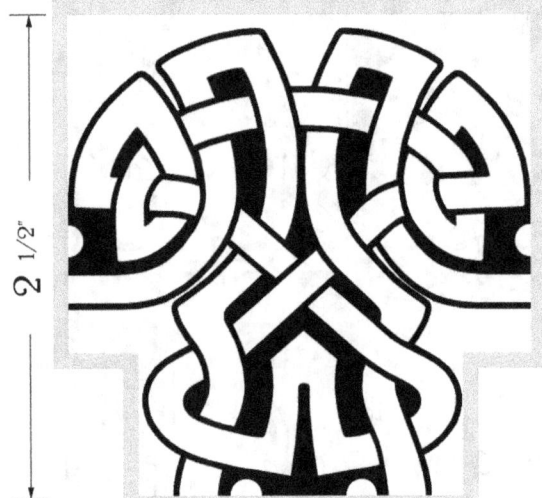

2 1/2"

Outer Border / Inner Border T

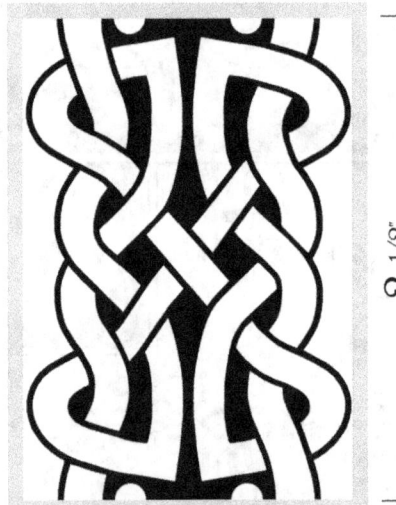

2 1/2"

Inner Border, Repeating Section

More sizes appear on the following page. The dimensions of this pattern are square (that is, all the repeats and sizes of the corners and T sections are the same) so the border may be laid out on a square grid.

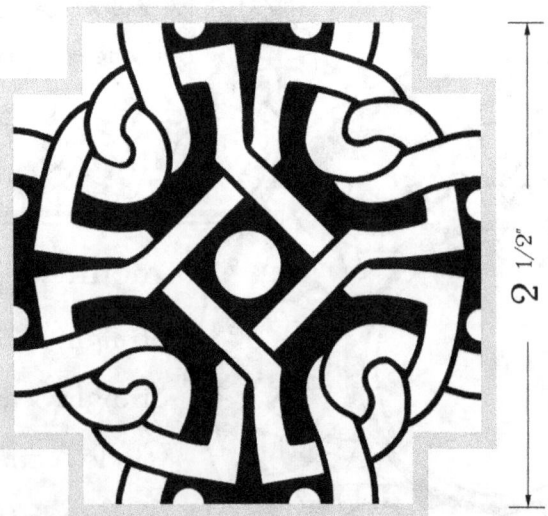

2 1/2"

Inner Border, Crosspiece

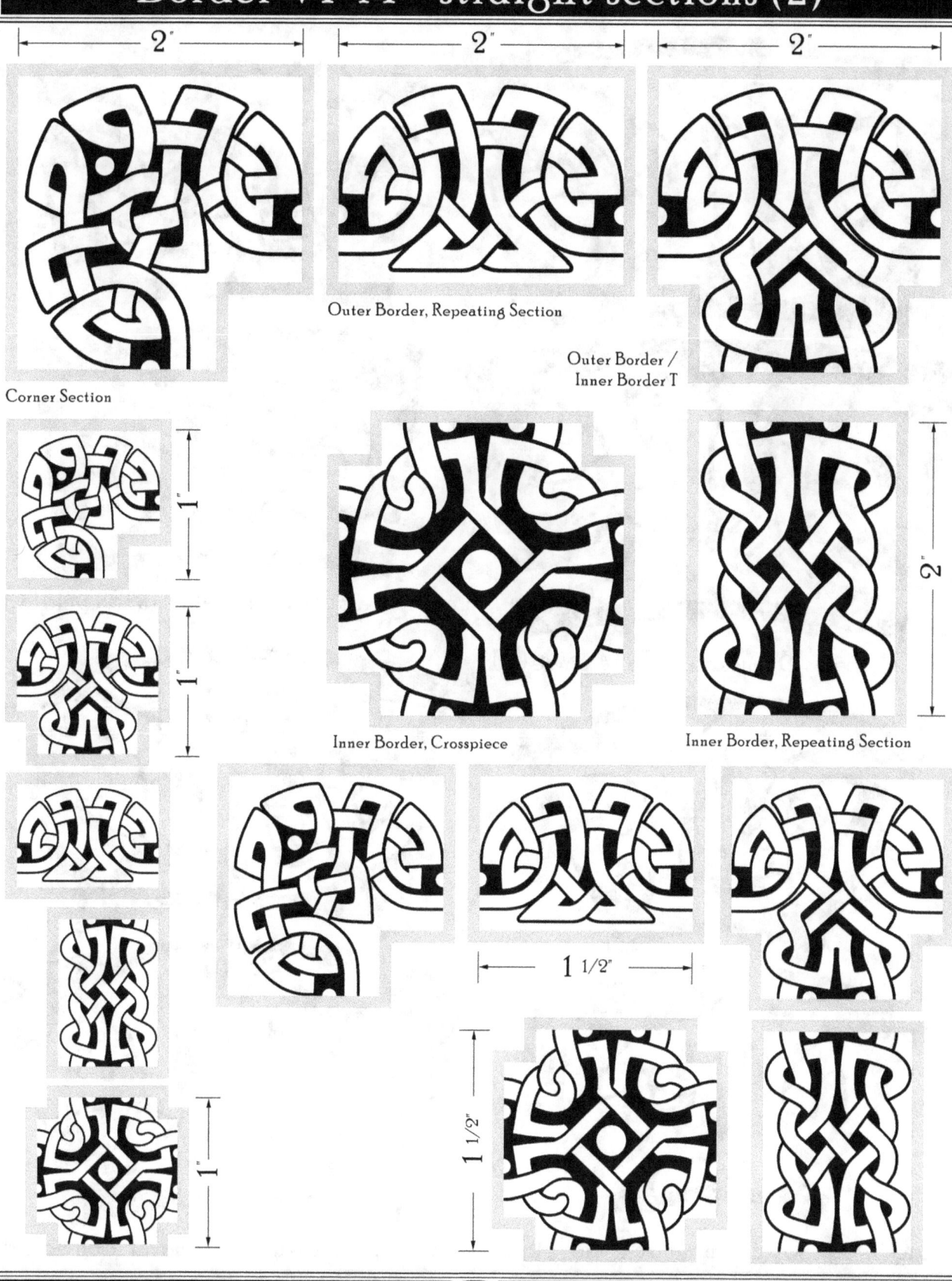

2" 2" 2"

Corner Section

Outer Border, Repeating Section

Outer Border /
Inner Border T

1"

1"

Inner Border, Crosspiece

2"

Inner Border, Repeating Section

1 1/2"

1"

1 1/2"

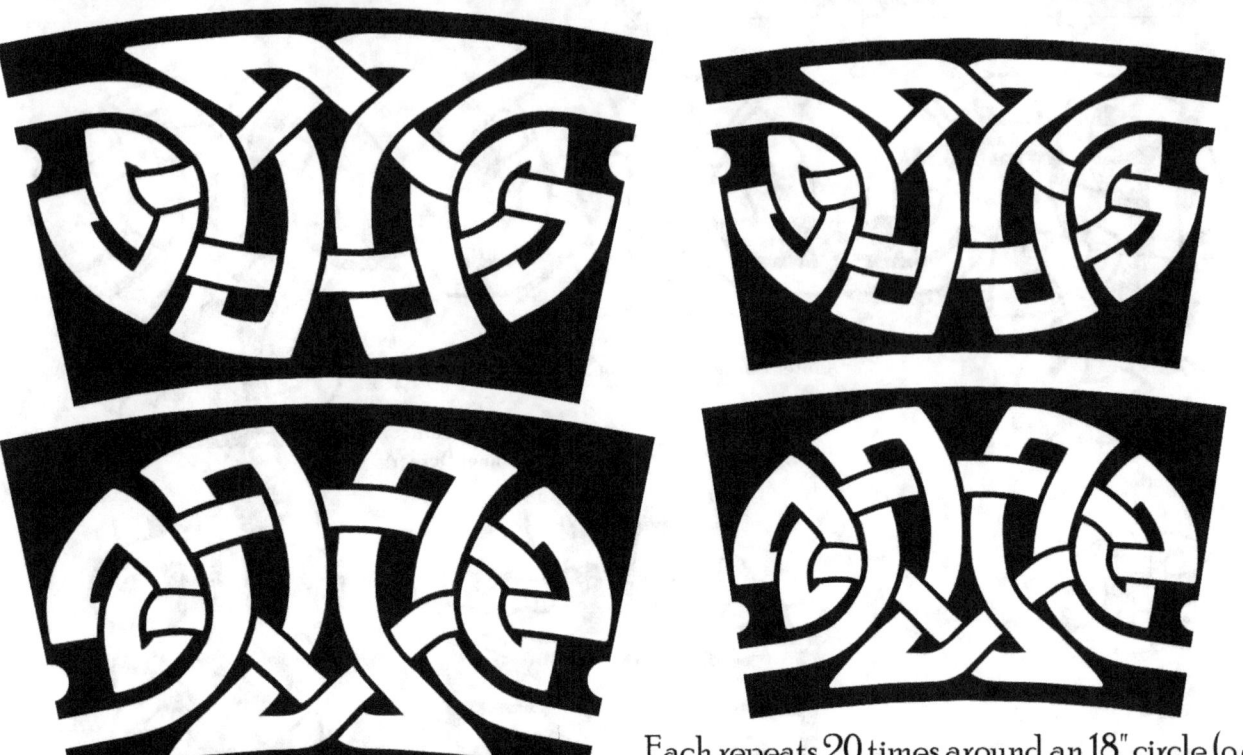

Each repeats 20 times around an 18" circle (o.d.)

Each repeats 15 times around a 17" circle (o.d.)

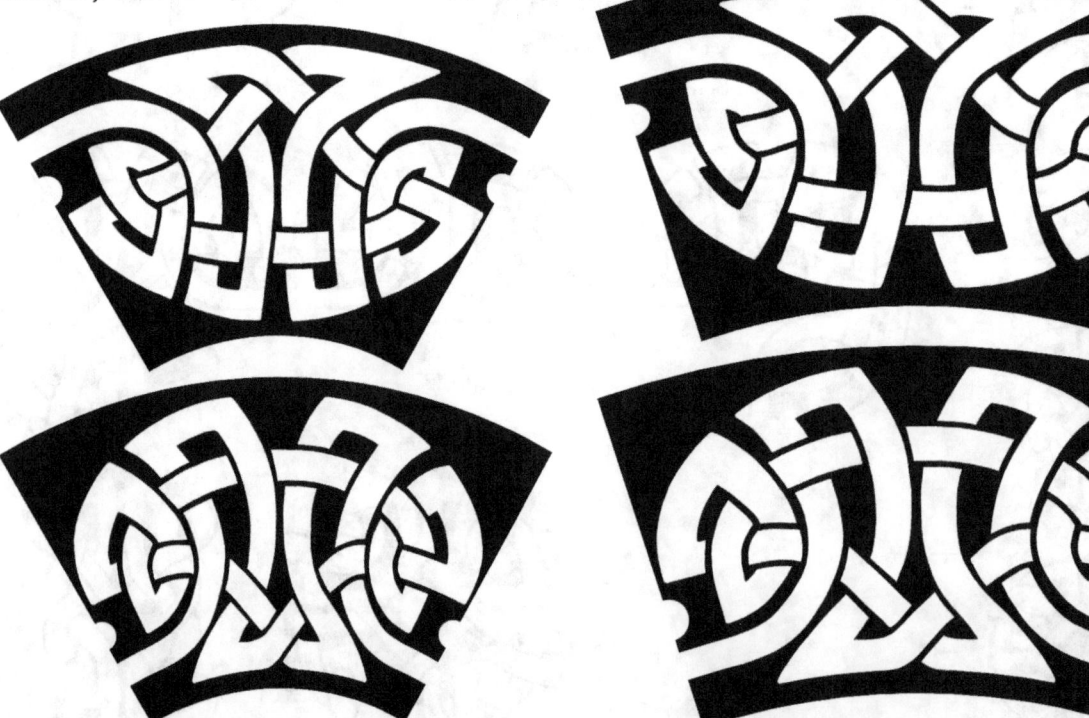

Each repeats 6 times around a 6" circle (o.d.)

Each repeats 10 times around an 11" circle (o.d.)

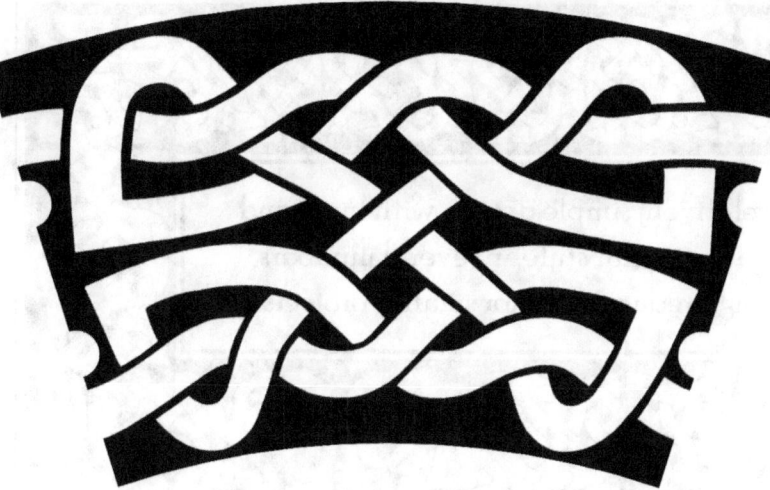

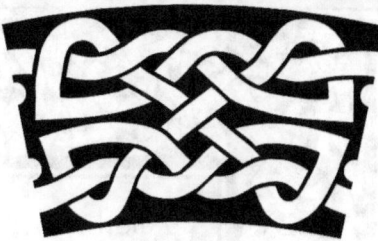

Repeats 15 times around
a 10" circle (o.d.)

Repeats 10 times around a 14" circle (o.d.)

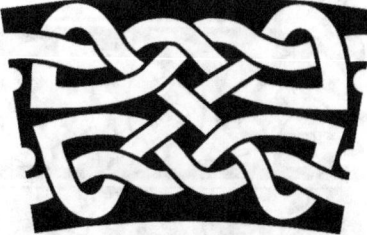

Repeats 20 times around a 13" circle (o.d.)

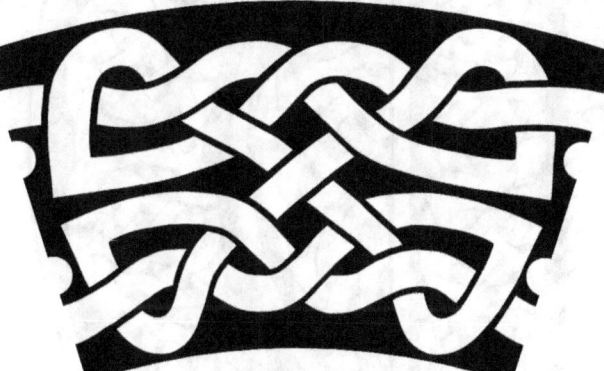

Repeats 10 times around
an 11" circle (o.d.)

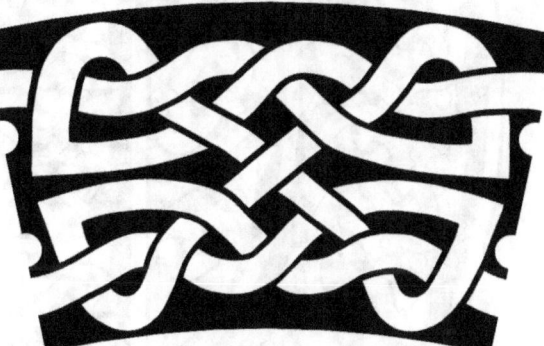

Repeats 15 times around a 15" circle (o.d.)

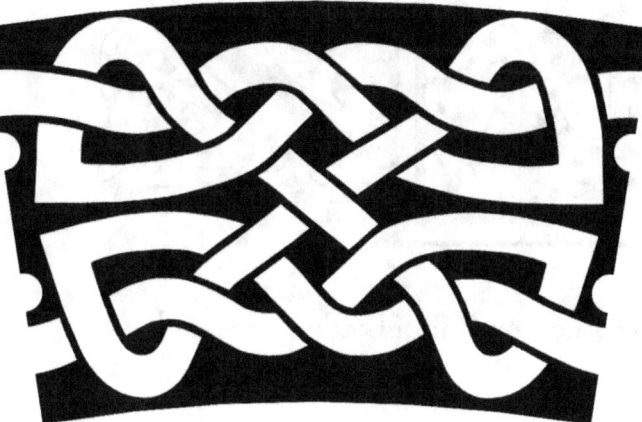

Repeats 20 times around a 23" circle (o.d.)

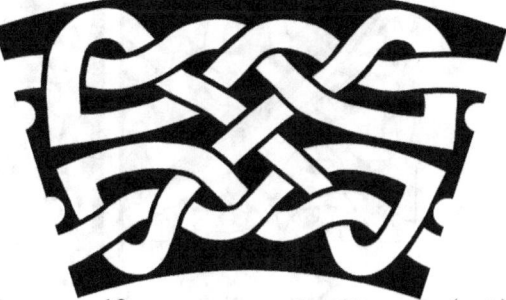

Repeats 10 times around a 9" circle (o.d.)

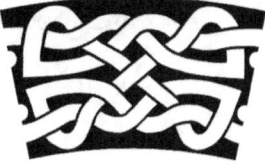

Repeats 15 times around a 7" circle (o.d.)

Border V1-N

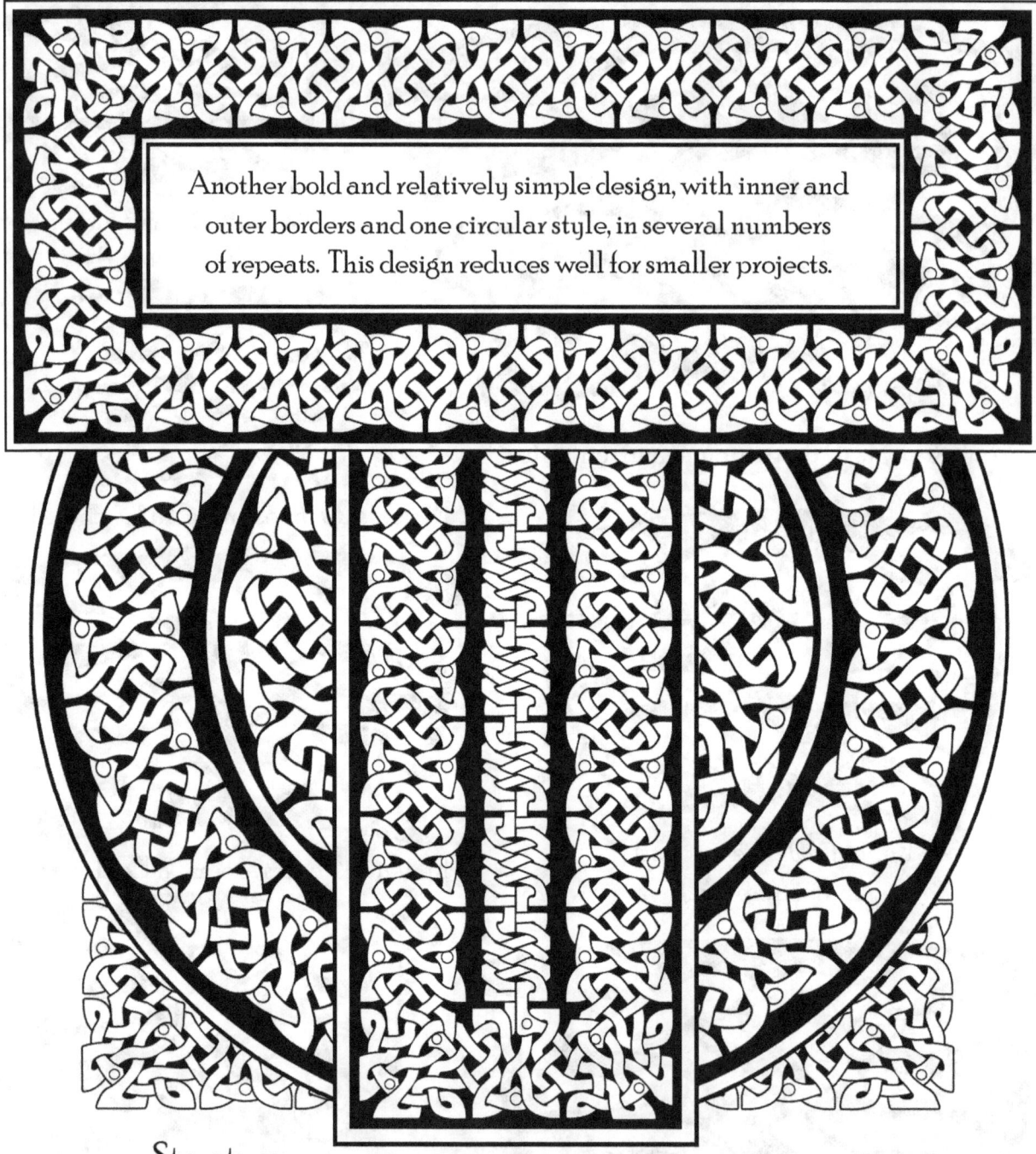

Another bold and relatively simple design, with inner and outer borders and one circular style, in several numbers of repeats. This design reduces well for smaller projects.

Structure:

Straight Sections, using only corners and outer border: one band.

Straight Sections, including Inner Border: multiple bands.

Circle Sections: design is a single band.

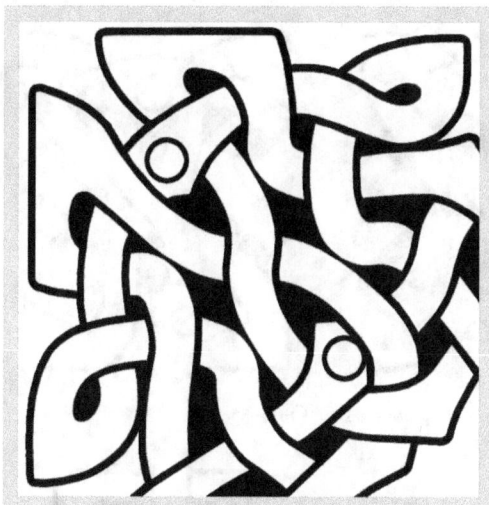

Corner Section

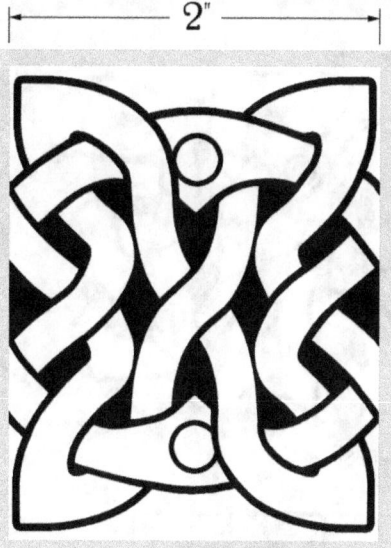

2"

Outer Border, Repeating Section

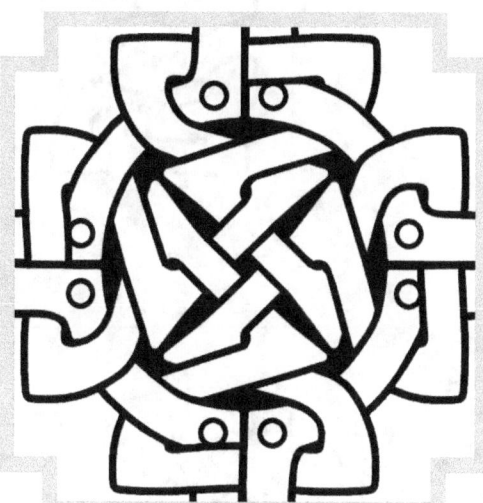

Inner Border, Crosspiece

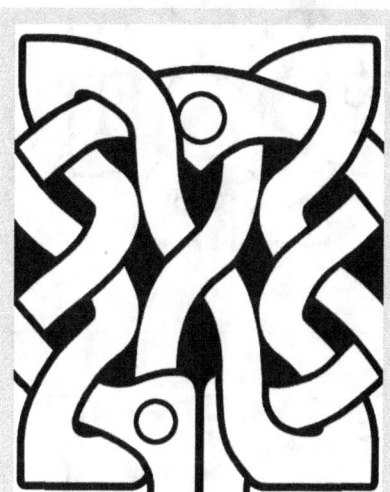

Outer Border /Inner Border T

See the following page for additional sizes. Refer to the text for layout tips on how to build a complete square or rectangular border by using just the corner and outer border sections, or a divided border by using all five.

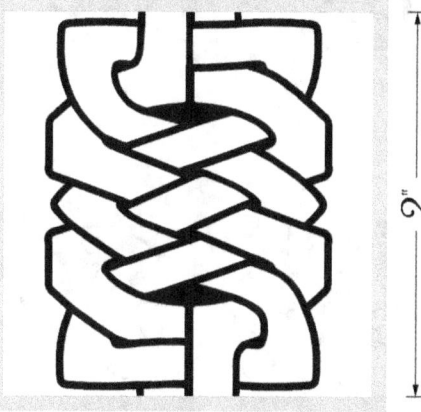

2"

Inner Border, Repeating Section

1 1/2"   1 1/2"

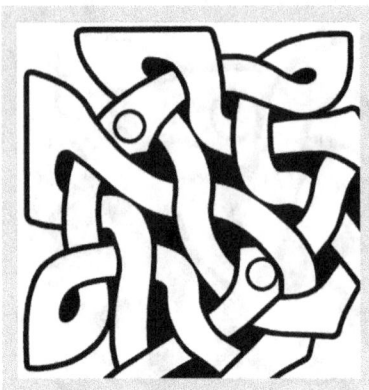

Corner Section

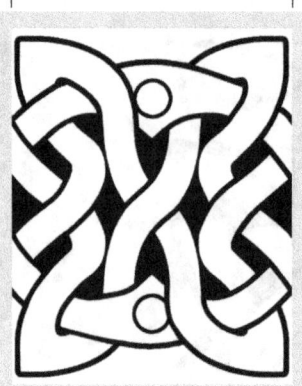

Outer Border, Repeating Section

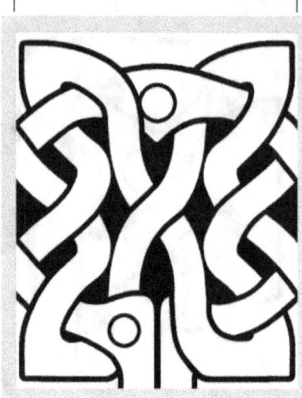

Outer Border / Inner Border T

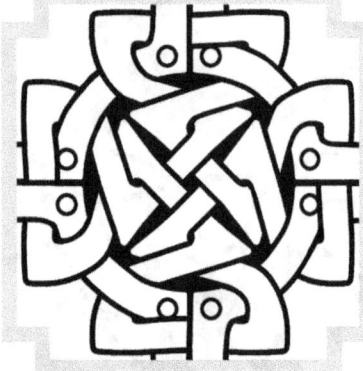

Inner Border, Repeating Section

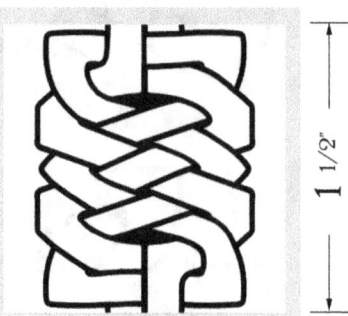

1 1/2"

Inner Border, Crosspiece

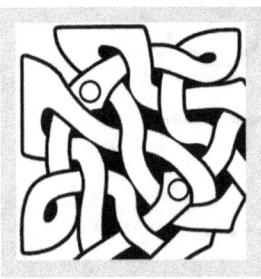

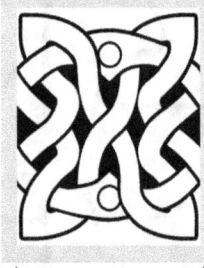

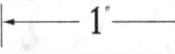
1"

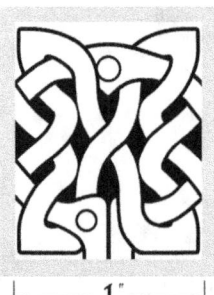
1"

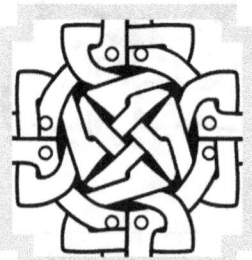

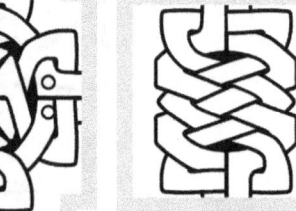

3/4"   3/4"

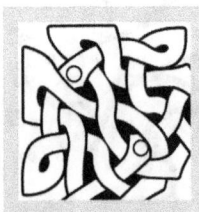

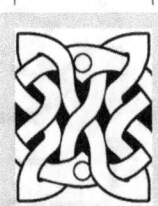

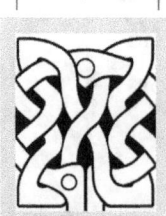

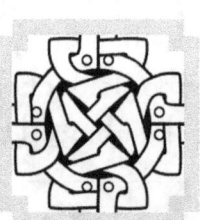

3/4"

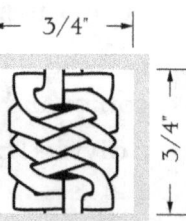
3/4"

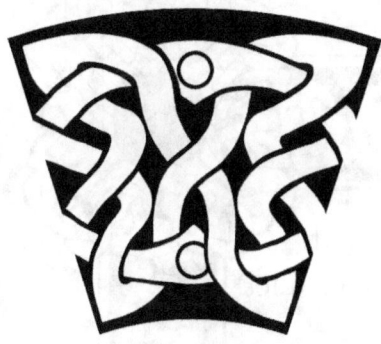

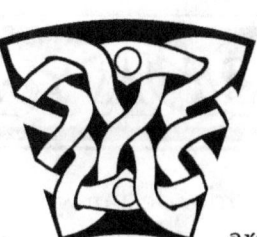

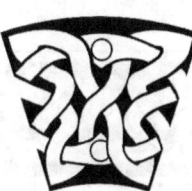

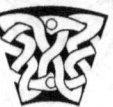

Repeats 10 times around a 2" circle (o.d.)

Repeats 10 times around a 3 1/2" circle (o.d.)

Repeats 10 times around a 4 1/2" circle (o.d.)

Repeats 10 times around a 6 1/2" circle (o.d.)

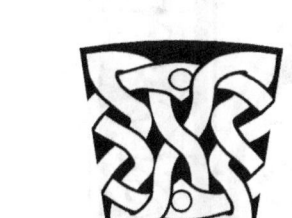

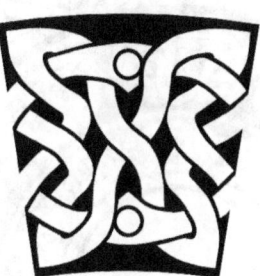

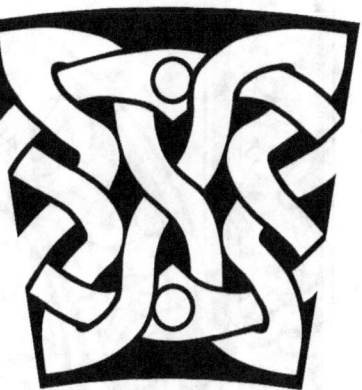

Repeats 20 times around a 7" circle (o.d.)

Repeats 20 times around a 9" circle (o.d.)

Repeats 20 times around a 13" circle (o.d.)

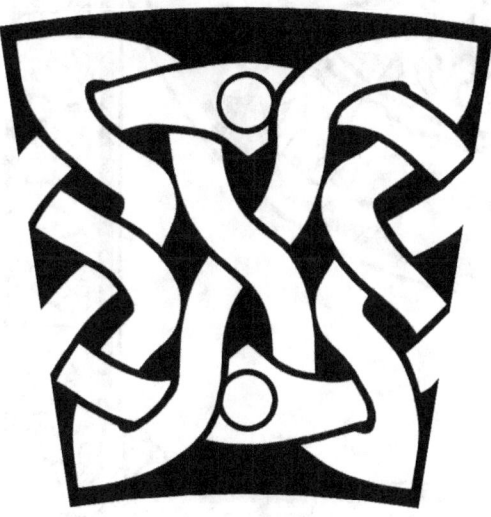

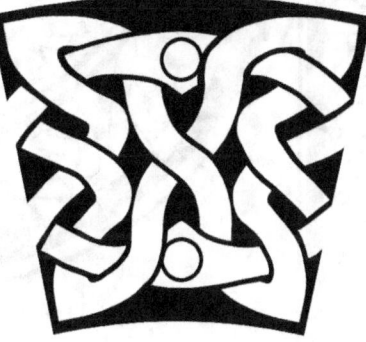

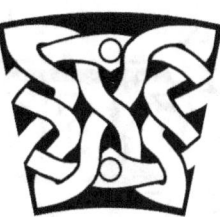

Repeats 15 times around a 10" circle (o.d.)

Repeats 20 times around a 17" circle (o.d.)

Repeats 15 times around a 6" circle (o.d.)

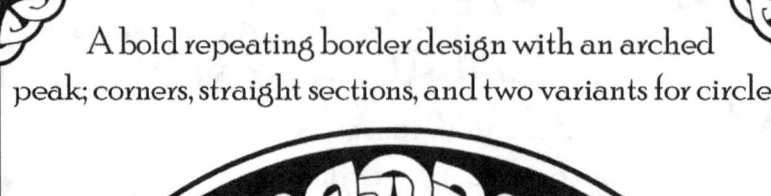

A bold repeating border design with an arched peak; corners, straight sections, and two variants for circles.

Structure:

Straight Sections: one band.

Circle Sections: design is a single band.

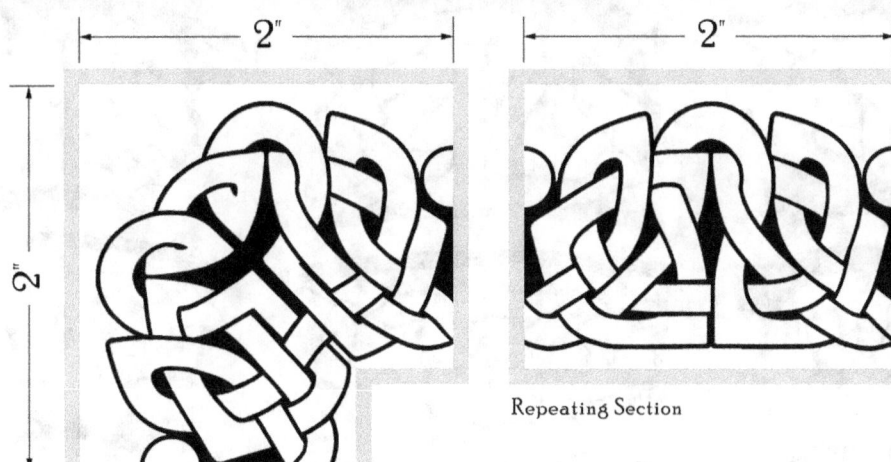

2"

2"

2"

Repeating Section

Corner Section

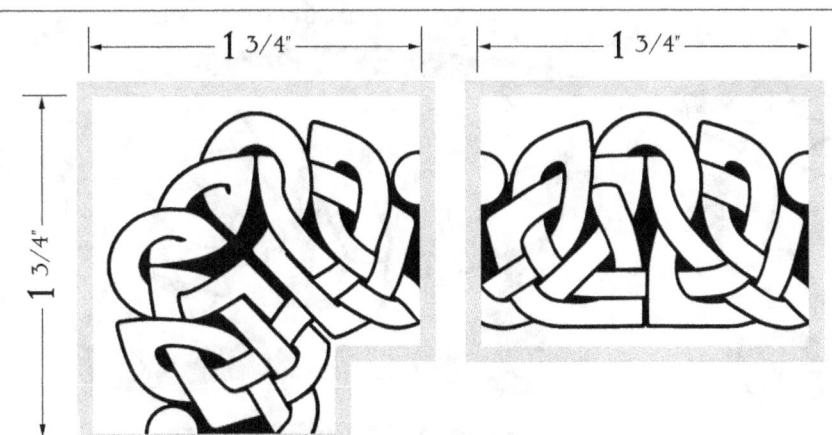

1 3/4"

1 3/4"

1 3/4"

Because this design has no separate inner border, a square or rectangular frame can be made by rotating just these two parts in **90** degree increments.

We can also see here that all the sections have the same dimen~sions: so it can be plotted on a square grid.

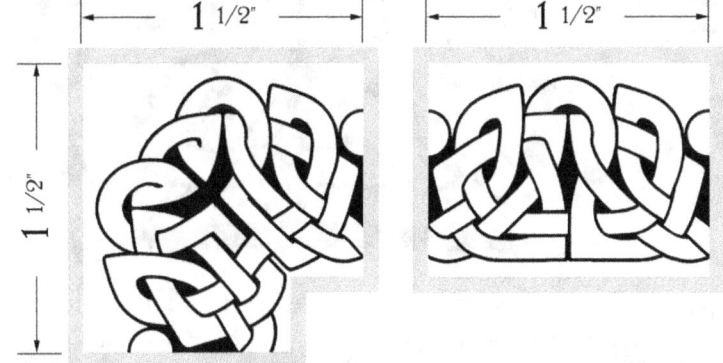

1 1/2"

1 1/2"

1 1/2"

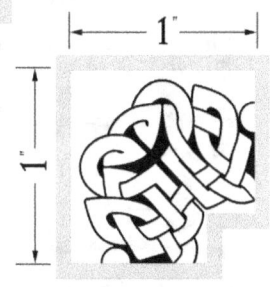

1"

1"

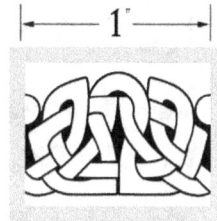

1"

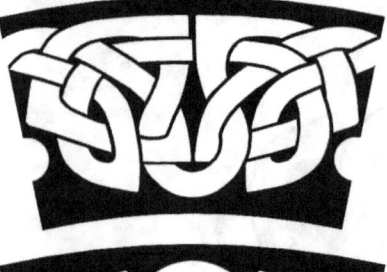

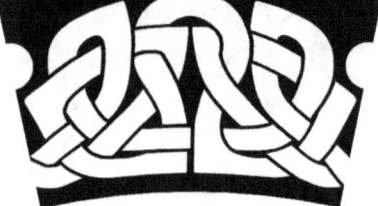

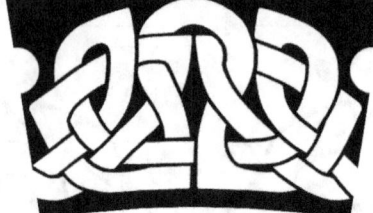

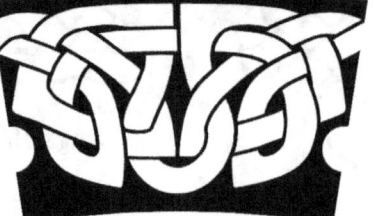

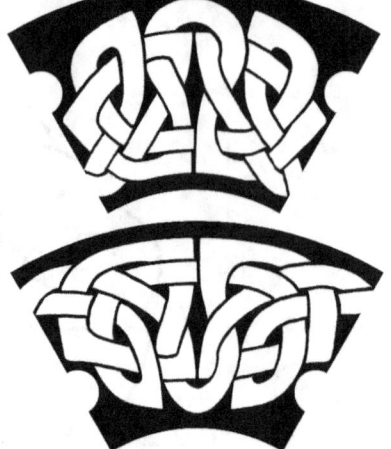

Each repeats 15 times around a 10" circle (o.d.)

Each repeats 20 times around a 13" circle (o.d.)

Each repeats 6 times around a 4" circle (o.d.)

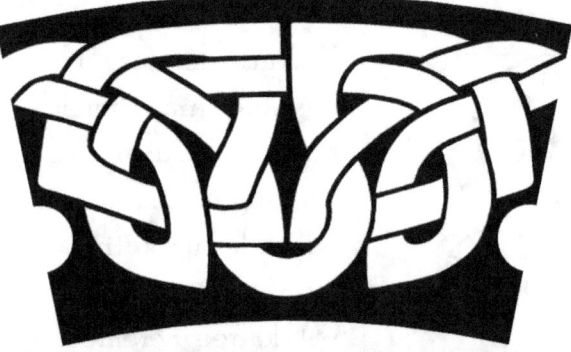

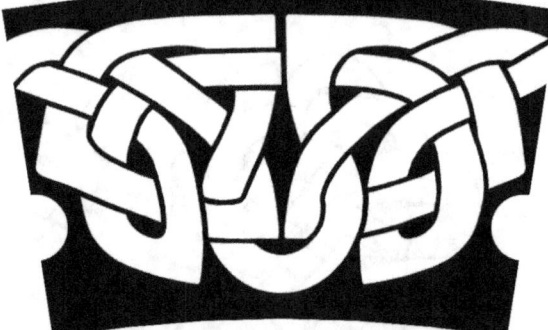

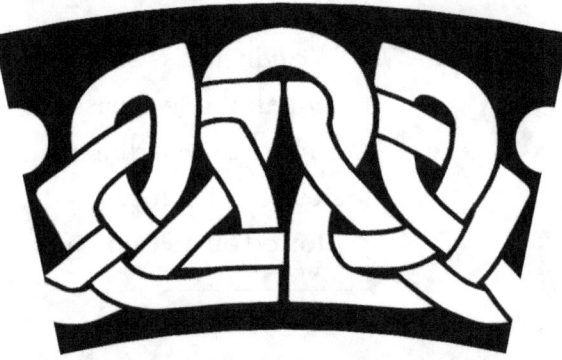

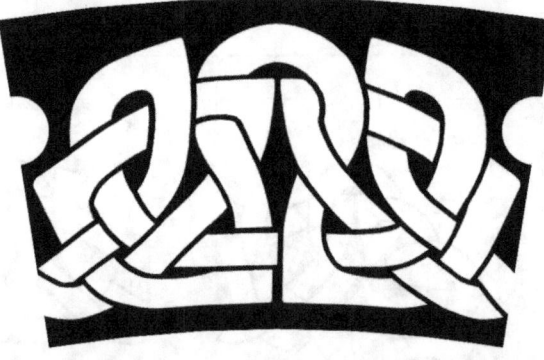

Each repeats 15 times around a 15" circle (o.d.)

Each repeats 20 times around a 19" circle (o.d.)

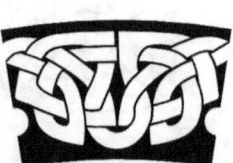
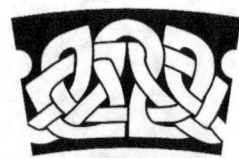
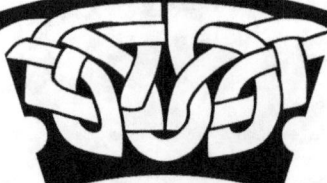
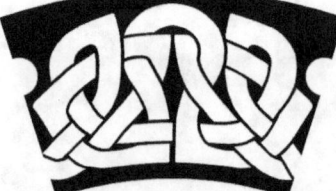

Each repeats 20 times around an 8" circle (o.d.)

Each repeats 10 times around a 6" circle (o.d.)

Border V1–P

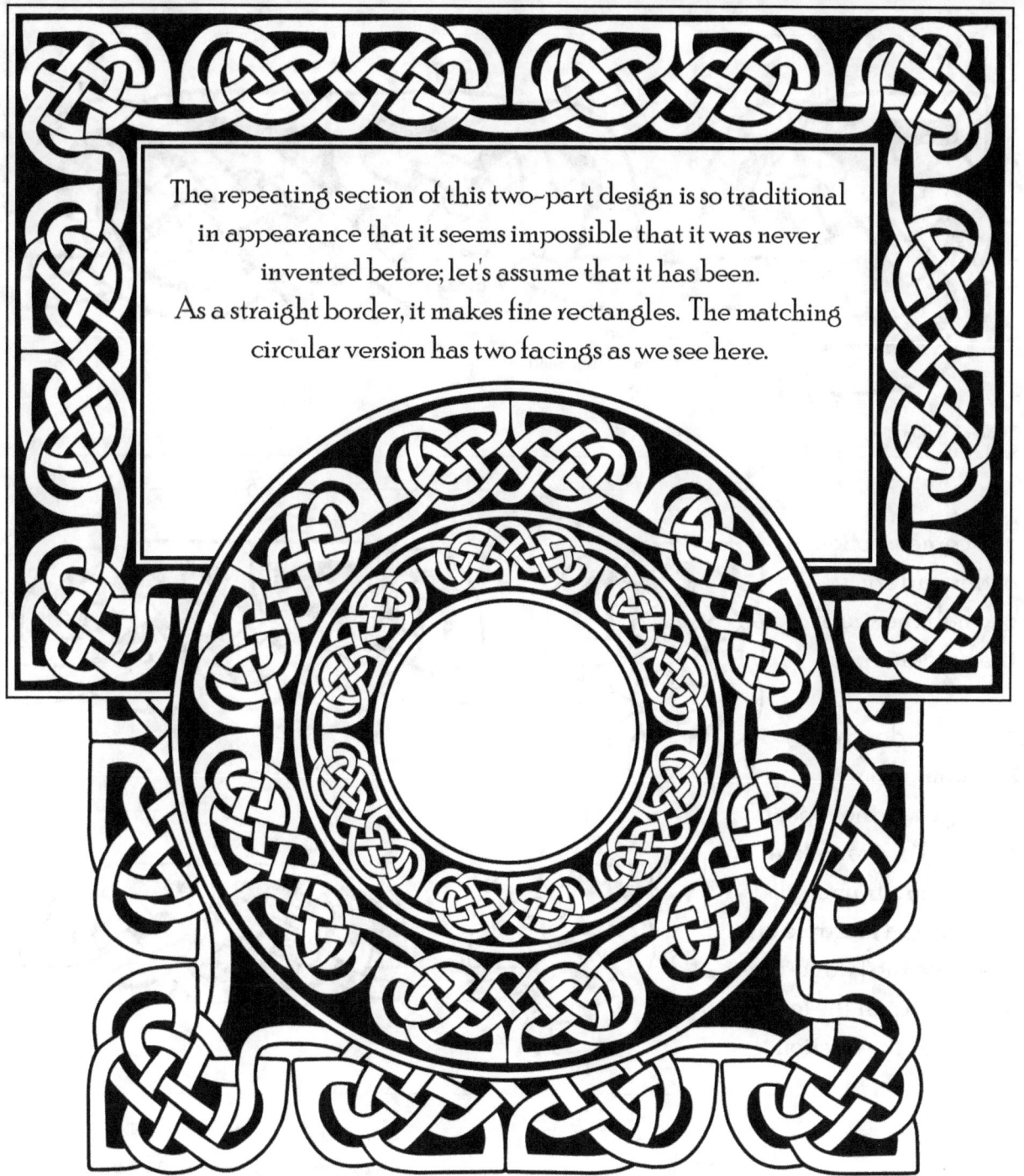

The repeating section of this two–part design is so traditional in appearance that it seems impossible that it was never invented before; let's assume that it has been.
As a straight border, it makes fine rectangles. The matching circular version has two facings as we see here.

Structure:

Straight Sections: one band.

Circle Sections: design is a single band.

2"   4"

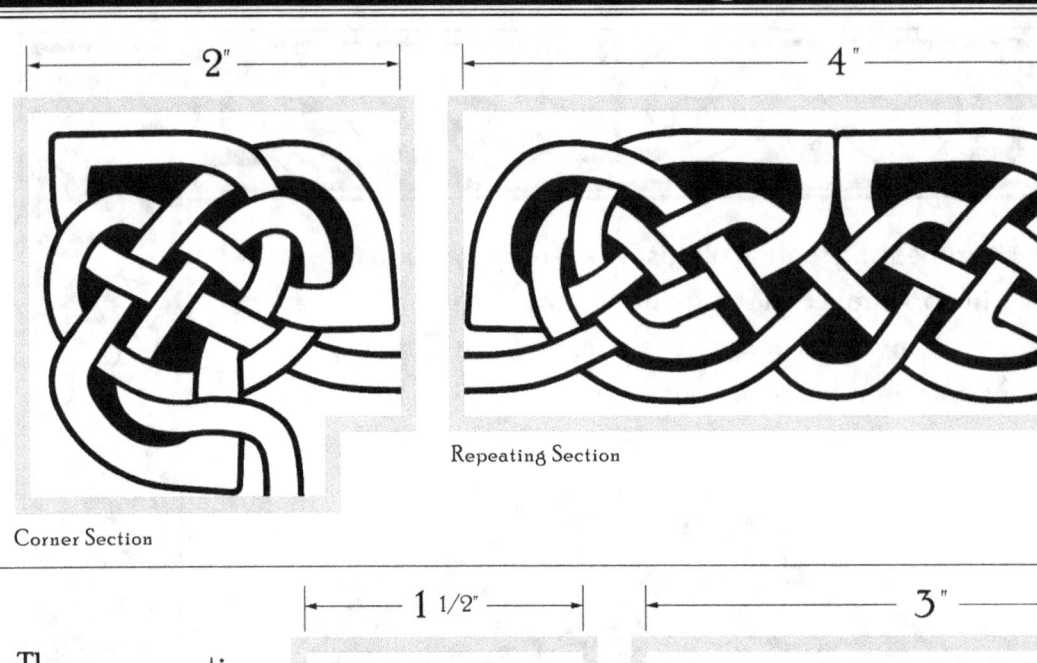

Corner Section

Repeating Section

The corner section of this pattern is one half the size of the border repeat.

So the border can be planned out in multiples of the repeat's length. For example, at the 4" size a frame will always be a multiple of 4" ~ since the two corner sections equal the length of a repeating section.

1 1/2"   3"

1 1/4"   1 1/4"   2 1/2"

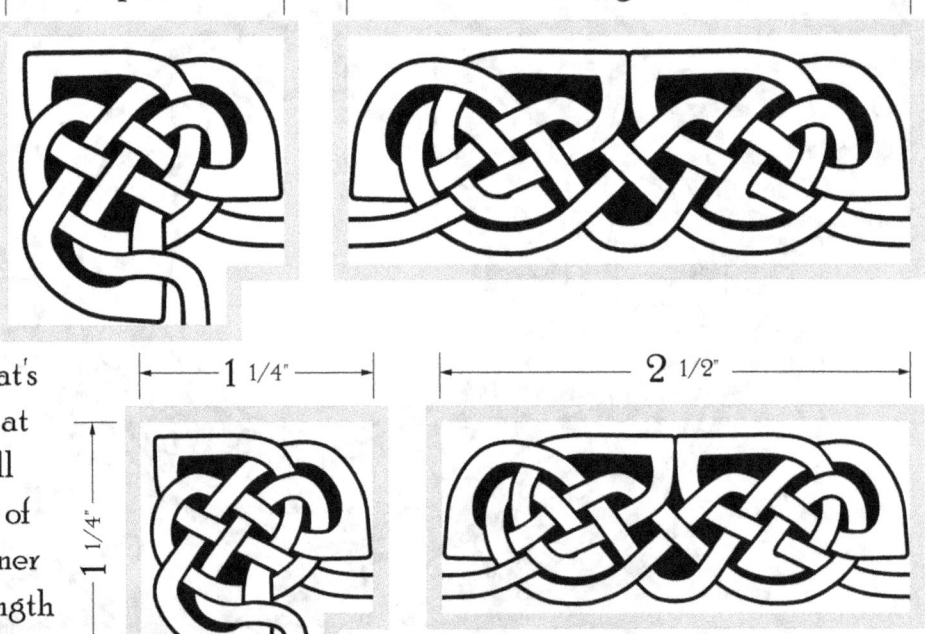

2"   1 1/2"

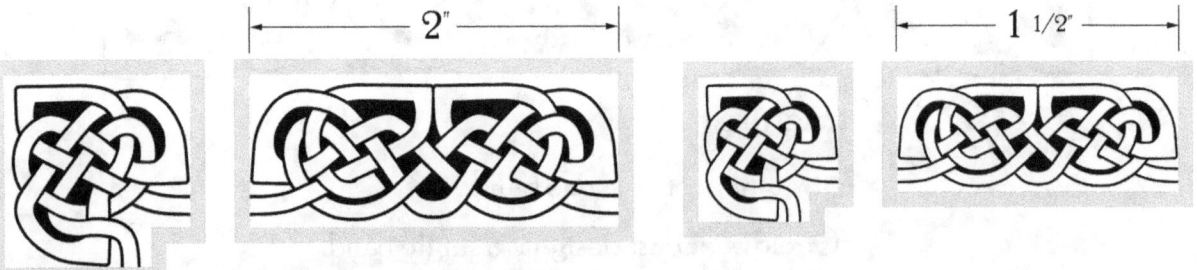

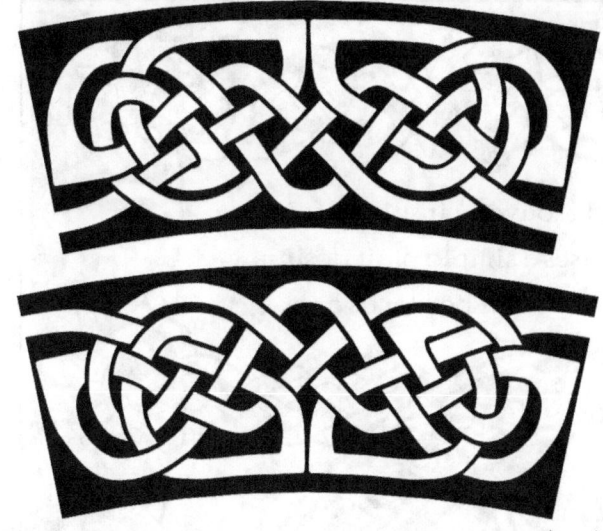

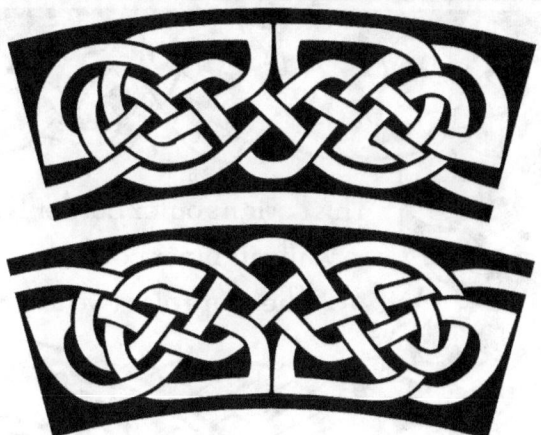

Each repeats 12 times
around an 11" circle (o.d.)

Each repeats 15 times around a 15" circle (o.d.)

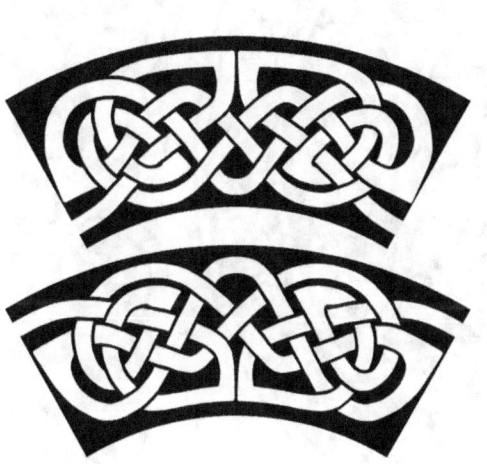

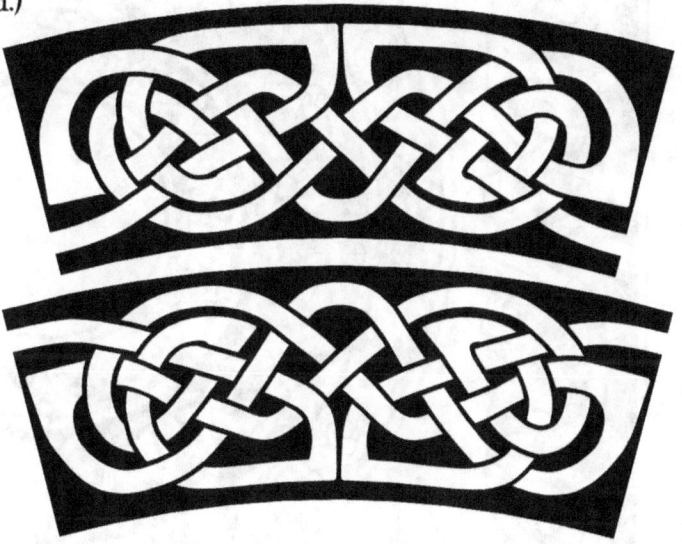

Each repeats 6 times around
a 5" circle (o.d.)

Each repeats 12 times around a 14" circle (o.d.)

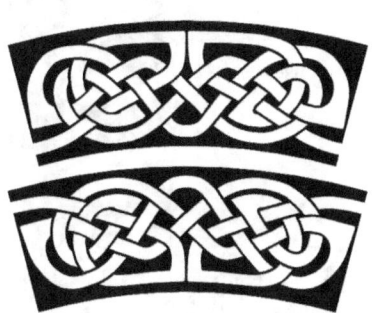

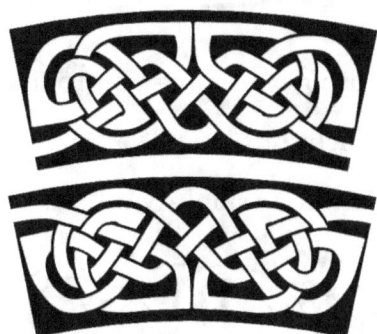

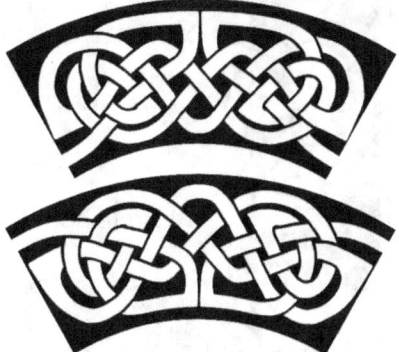

Each repeats 12 times around
a 7 1/2" circle (o.d.)

Each repeats 15 times
around a 9 1/2" circle (o.d.)

Each repeats 6 times around
a 4 1/4" circle (o.d.)

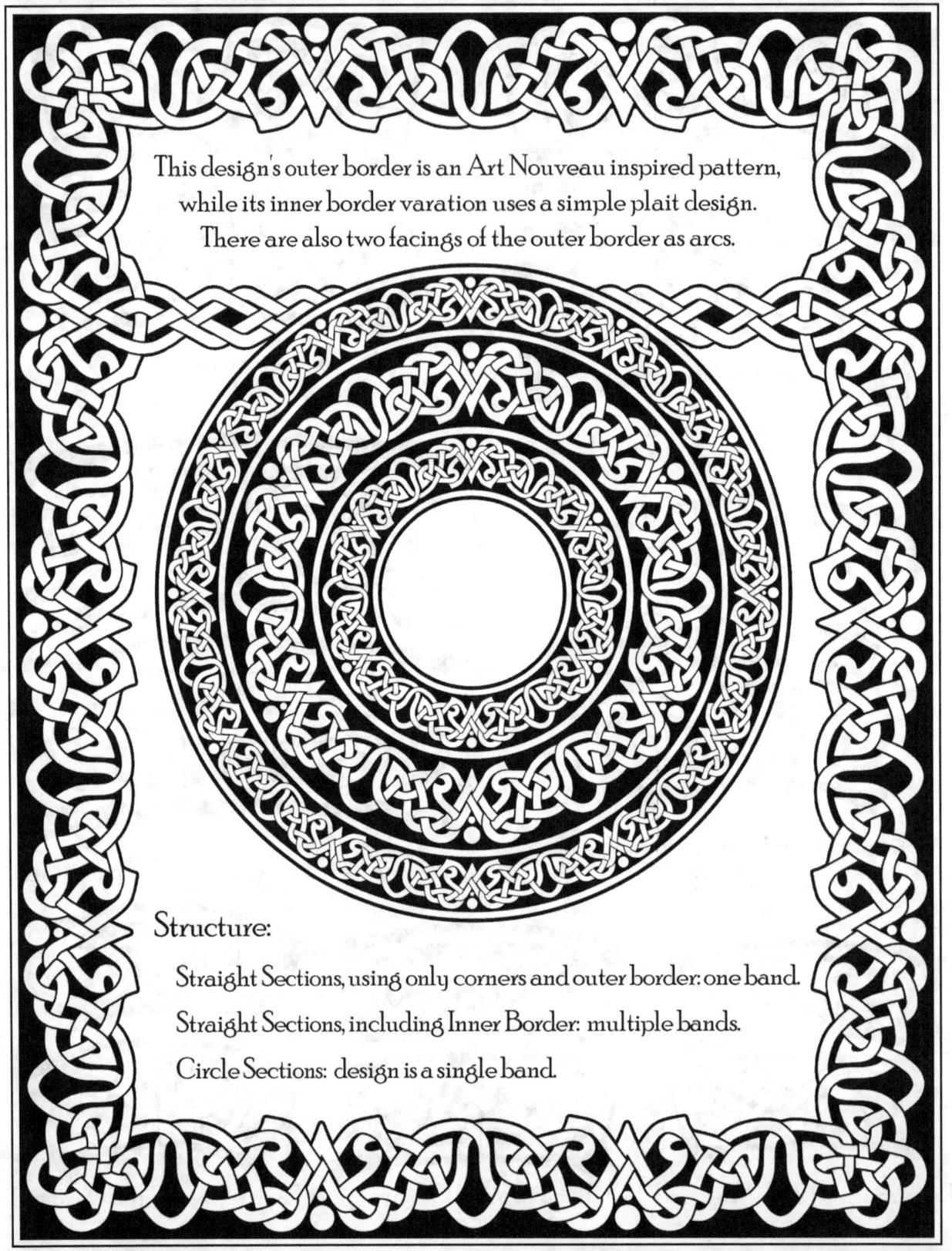

This design's outer border is an Art Nouveau inspired pattern, while its inner border varation uses a simple plait design. There are also two facings of the outer border as arcs.

Structure:

Straight Sections, using only corners and outer border: one band.

Straight Sections, including Inner Border: multiple bands.

Circle Sections: design is a single band.

The corner section of this pattern is one half the size of the border repeat.

So the border can be planned out in multiples of the repeat's length. For example, at the 3" size a frame will always be a multiple of 3" ~ since the length of the two corner sections (one on each side) equal the length of a single repeating section.

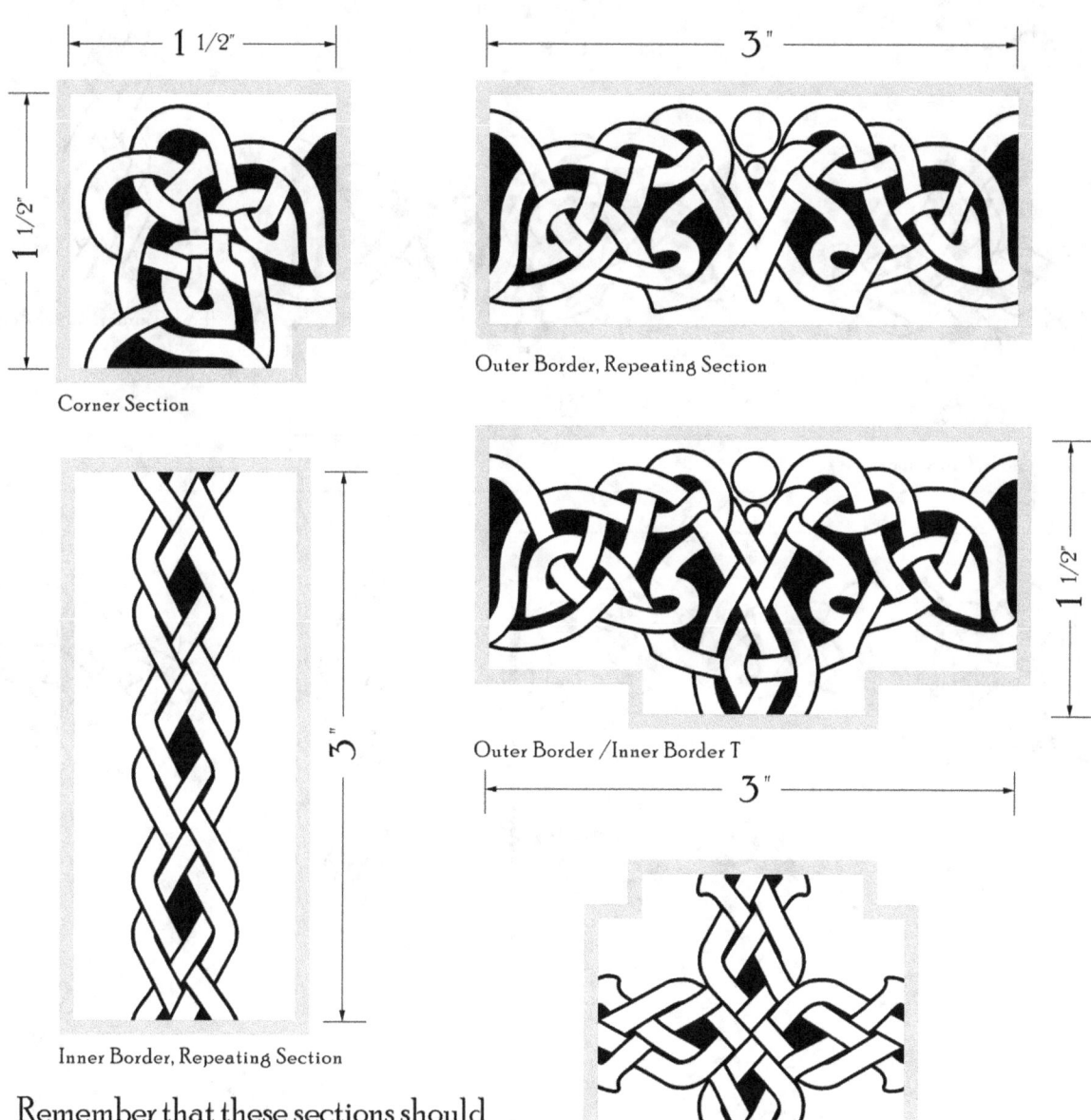

1 1/2"

1 1/2"

Corner Section

3"

Outer Border, Repeating Section

3"

Inner Border, Repeating Section

Outer Border / Inner Border T

1 1/2"

3"

Inner Border, Crosspiece

Remember that these sections should always be rotated, not mirrored ~ if you flip them, the pattern will not line up properly!

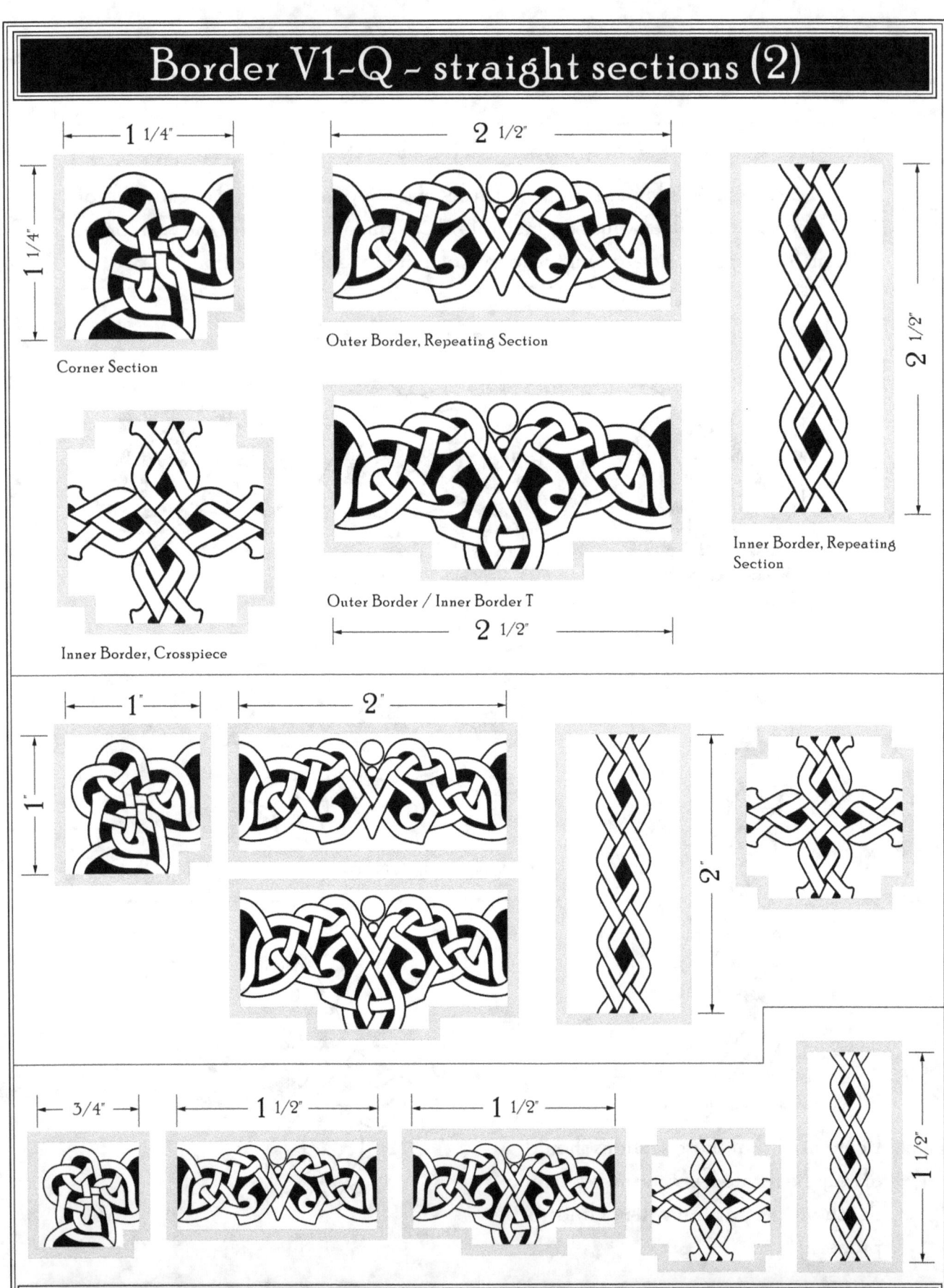

1 1/4"

1 1/4"

Corner Section

2 1/2"

Outer Border, Repeating Section

2 1/2"

Inner Border, Repeating Section

Inner Border, Crosspiece

Outer Border / Inner Border T

2 1/2"

1"

1"

2"

2"

3/4"

1 1/2"

1 1/2"

1 1/2"

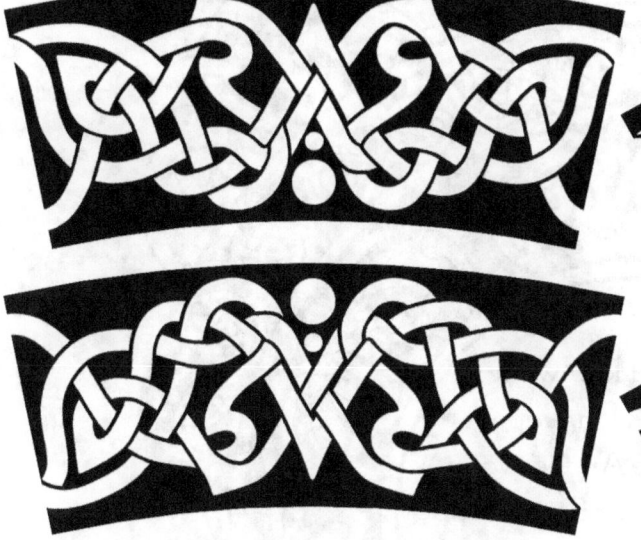

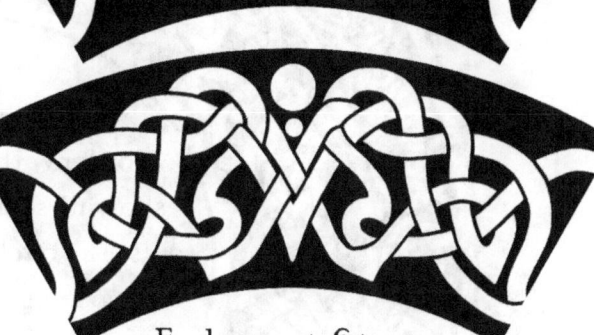

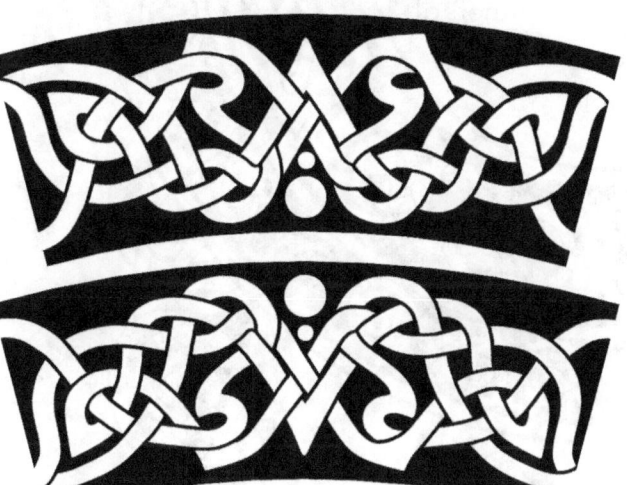

Each repeats 15 times around a 14" circle (o.d.)

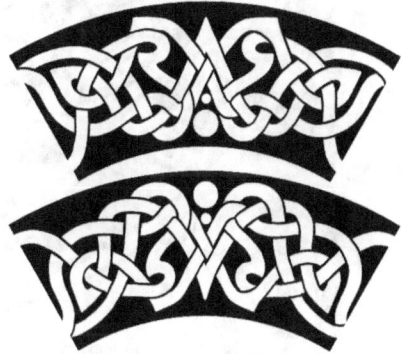

Each repeats 6 times
around a 7" circle (o.d.)

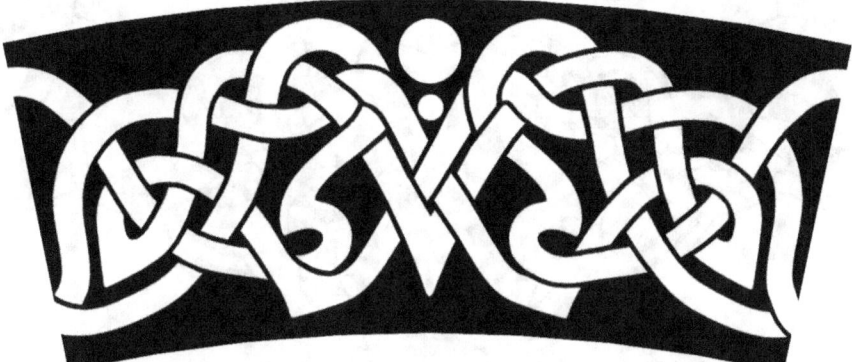

Each repeats 12 times around a 13" circle (o.d.)

Each repeats 6 times
around a 4 1/4" circle (o.d.)

Repeats 15 times around a 22" circle (o.d.)

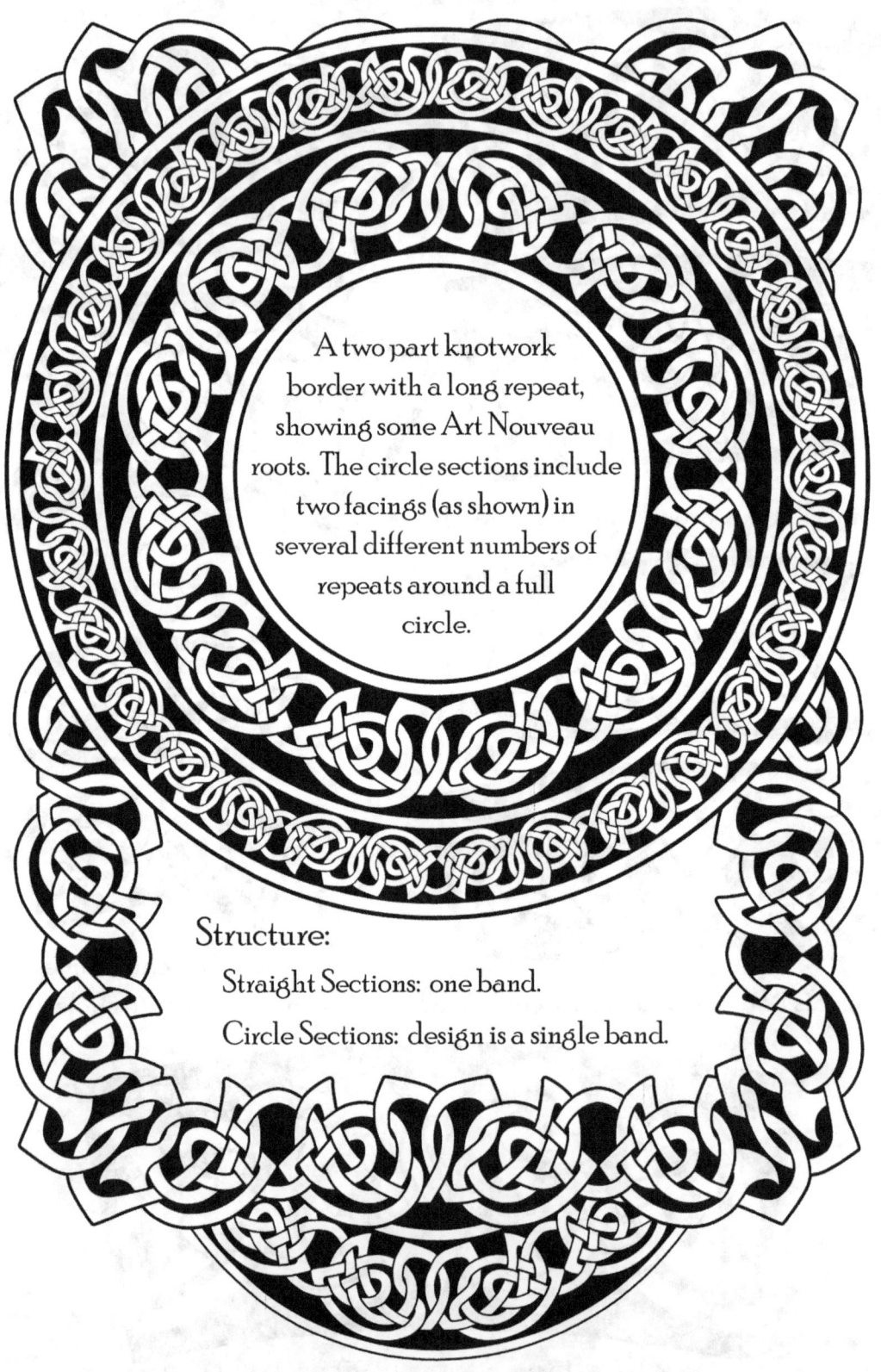

A two part knotwork border with a long repeat, showing some Art Nouveau roots. The circle sections include two facings (as shown) in several different numbers of repeats around a full circle.

Structure:

Straight Sections: one band.

Circle Sections: design is a single band.

5"

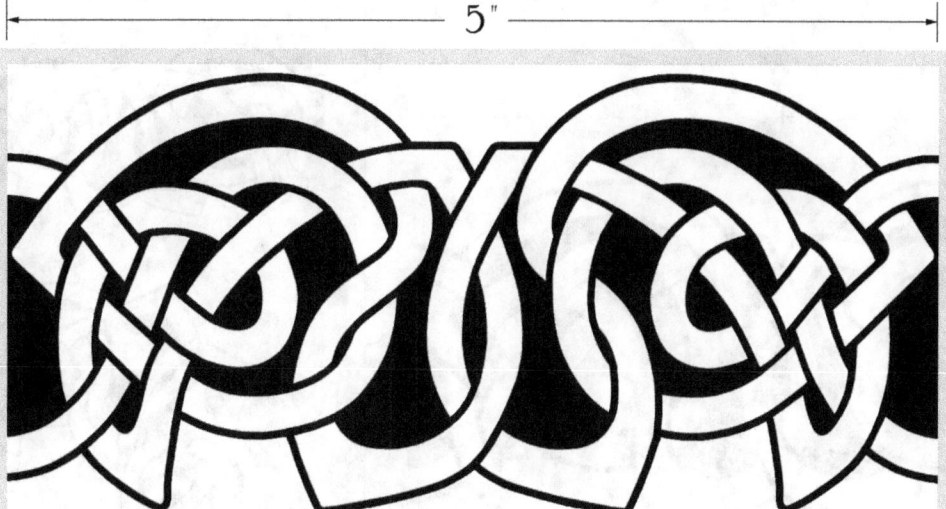

Repeating Section

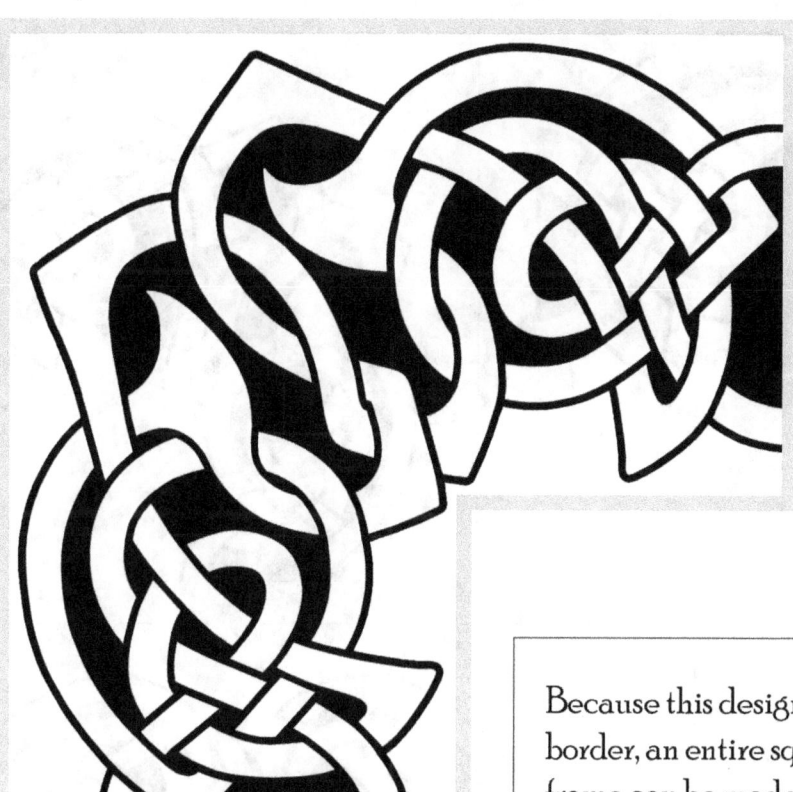

Corner Section

Because this design has no separate inner border, an entire square or rectangular frame can be made by rotating just these two parts in 90 degree increments.

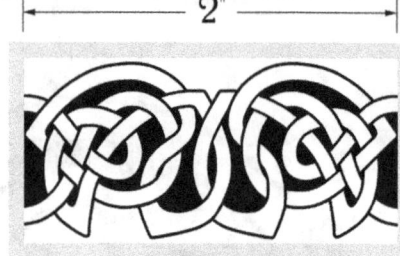

2"

4"

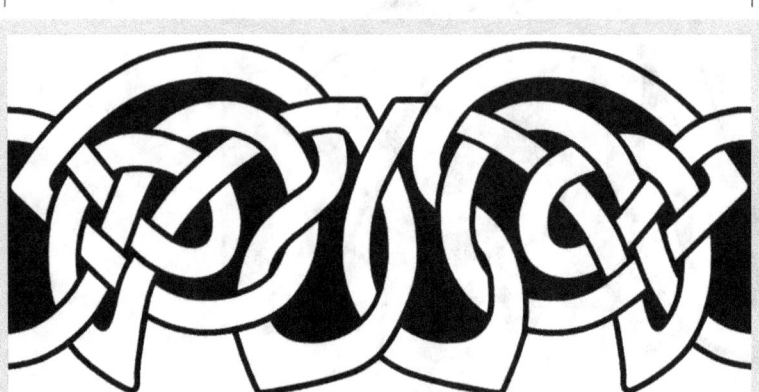

Repeating Section

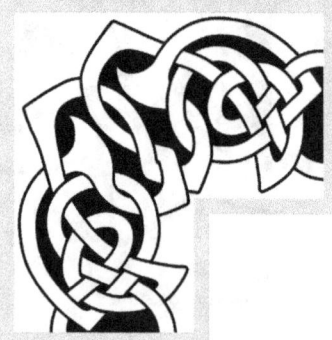

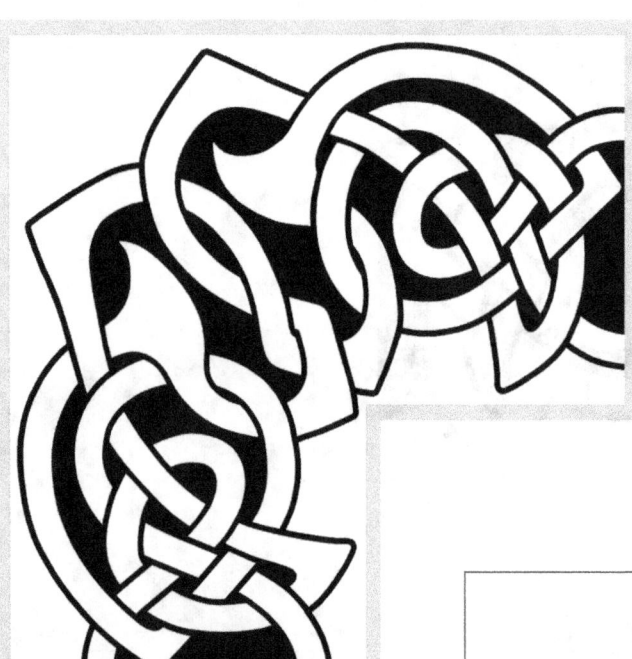

Corner Section

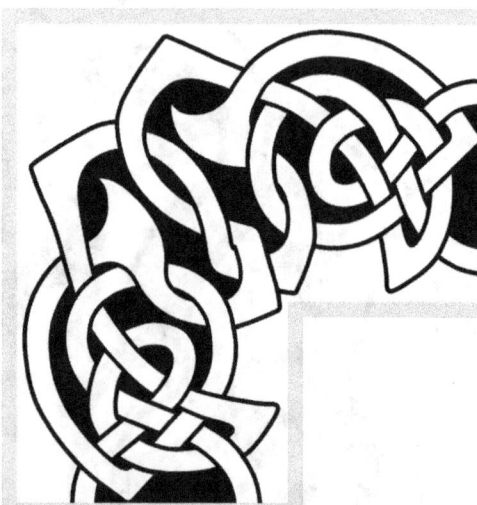

Remember that these sections should always be rotated, not mirrored ~ if you flip them, the pattern will not line up properly!

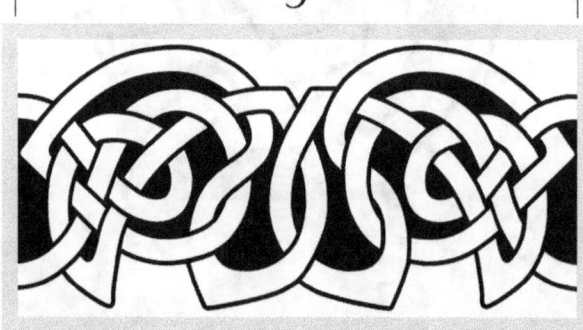

3"

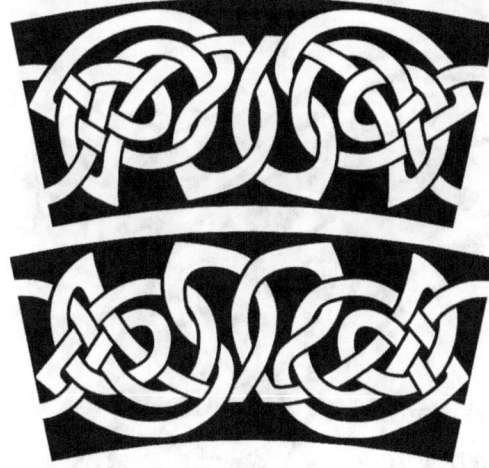

Each repeats 15 times around
a 12 1/2" circle (o.d.)

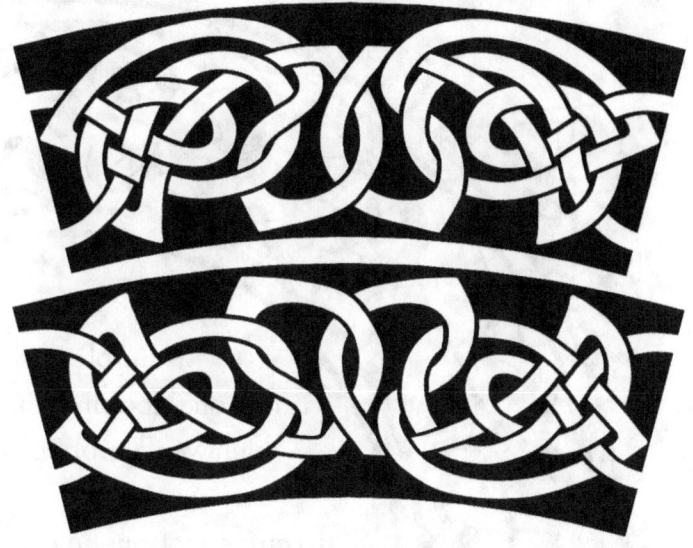

Each repeats 12 times around a 14" circle (o.d.)

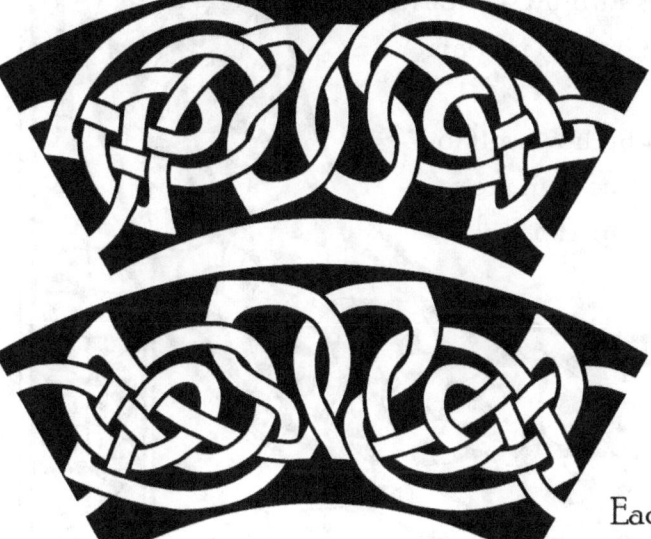

Each repeats 6 times around a 7" circle (o.d.)

Each repeats 6 times around a 5 1/2" circle (o.d.)

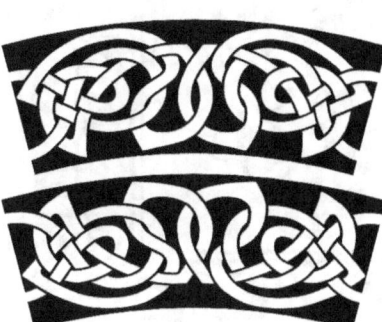

Each repeats 12 times
around an 8" circle (o.d.)

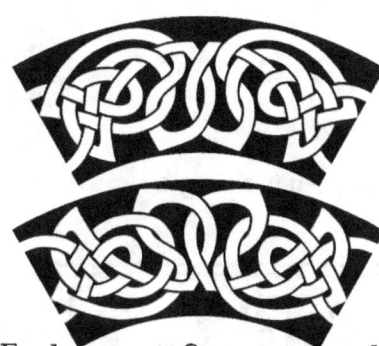

Each repeats 6 times around
a 4" circle (o.d.)

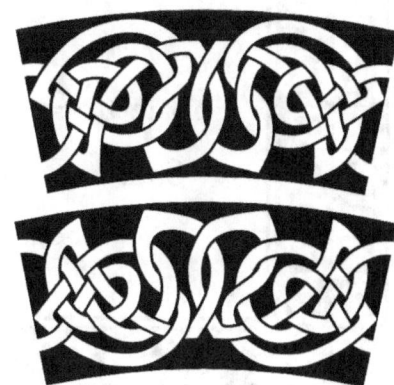

Each repeats 15 times around
a 10" circle (o.d.)

A simple and very
traditional looking knotwork border
which we've probably seen before.

Its circle sections have several numbers
of repeats, while its straight sections are
limited to corners and repeats.

Note (below right) how well four
corners combine to make a
diamond shaped panel.

Structure:

Straight Sections: one band.

Circle Sections: design is a single band.

2"

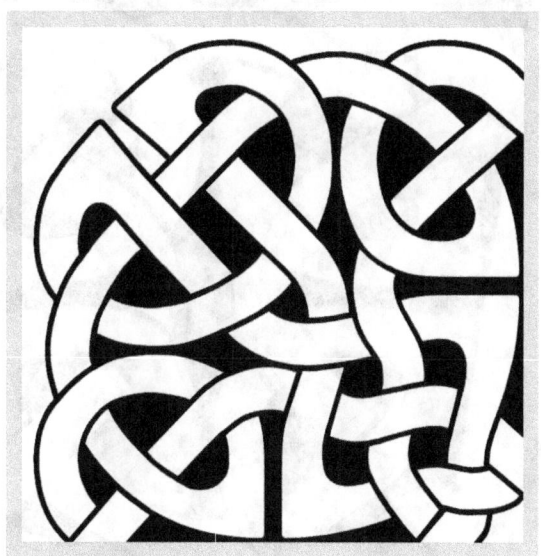
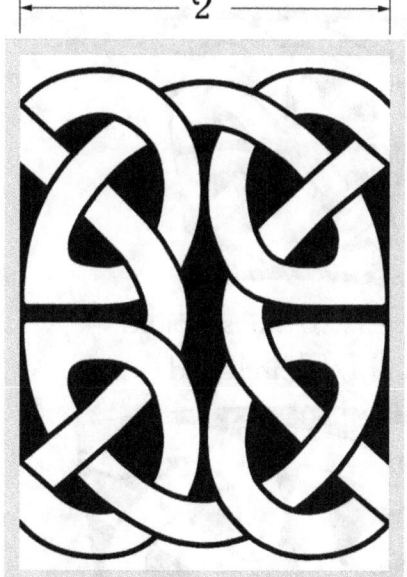

Corner Section

Repeating Section

1 1/2"

1"

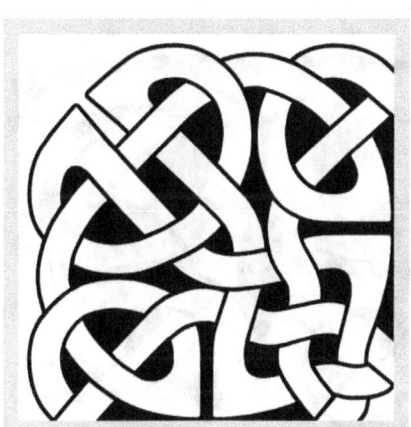
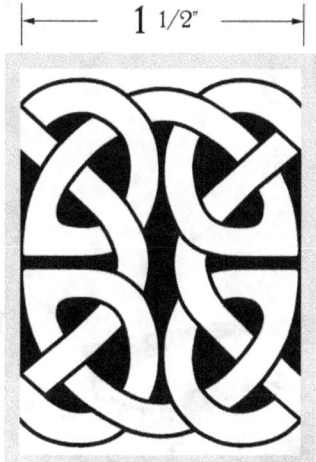
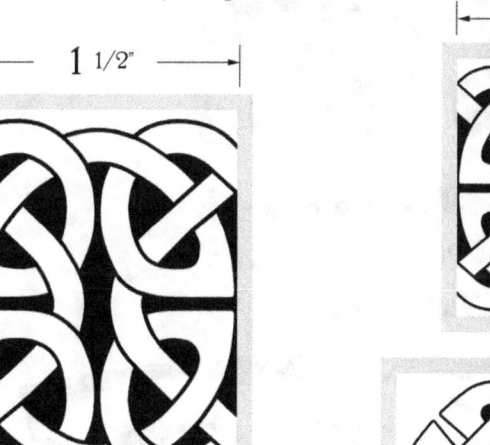
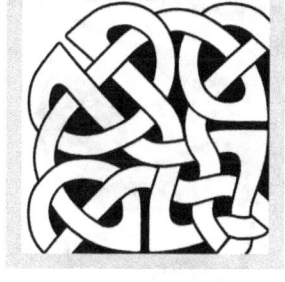

1 1/4"

3/4"

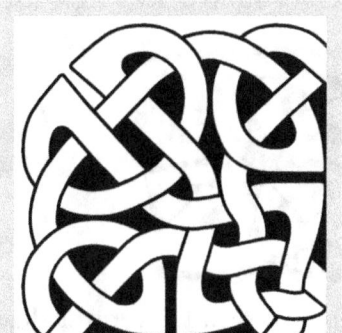
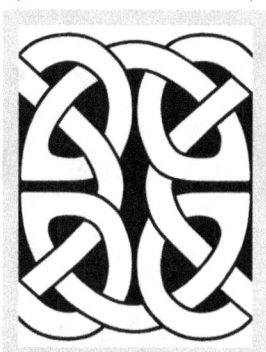
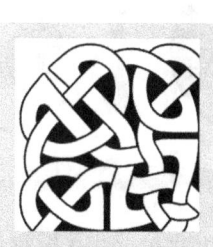
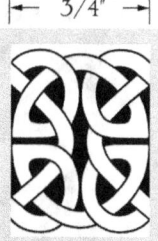

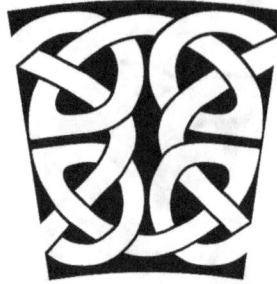

Repeats 20 times around
a 9 1/2" circle (o.d.)

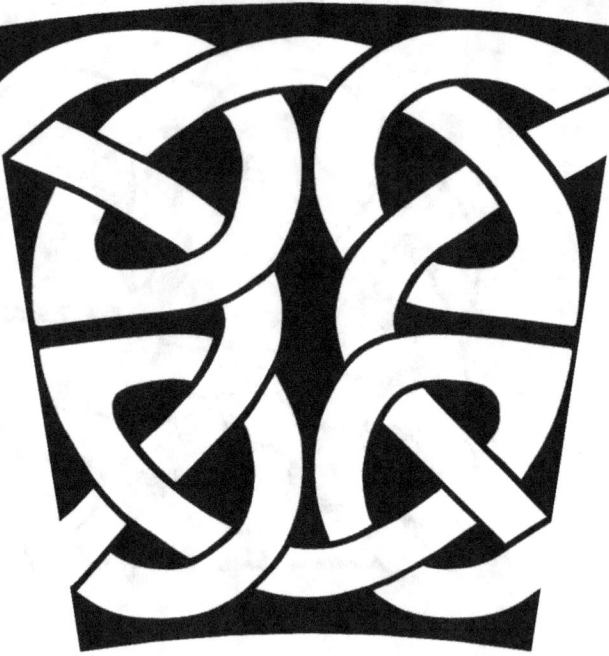

Repeats 20 times around a 22" circle (o.d.)

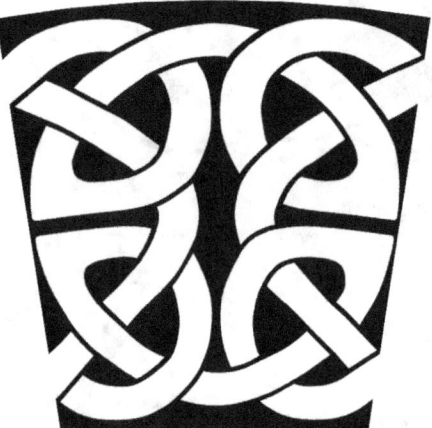

Repeats 20 times around
a 15" circle (o.d.)

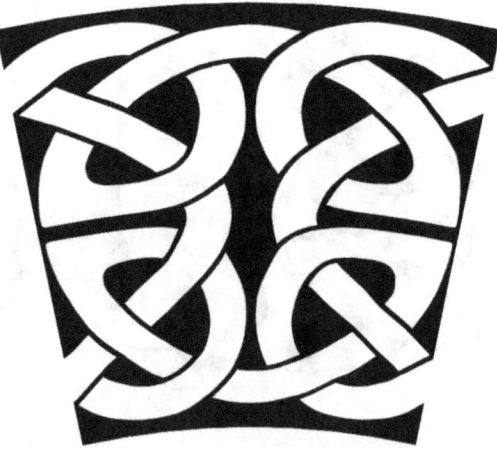

Repeats 15 times around a 13" circle (o.d.)

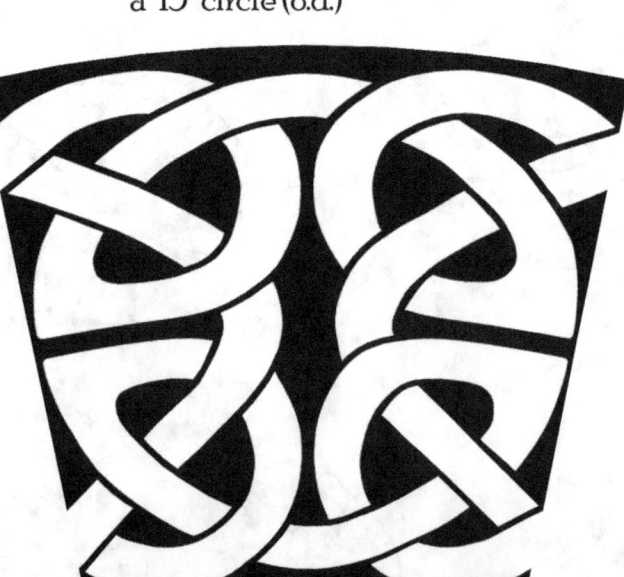

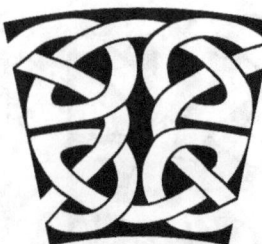

Repeats 15 times around a 7" circle (o.d.)

Repeats 15 times around a 17" circle (o.d.)

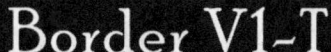

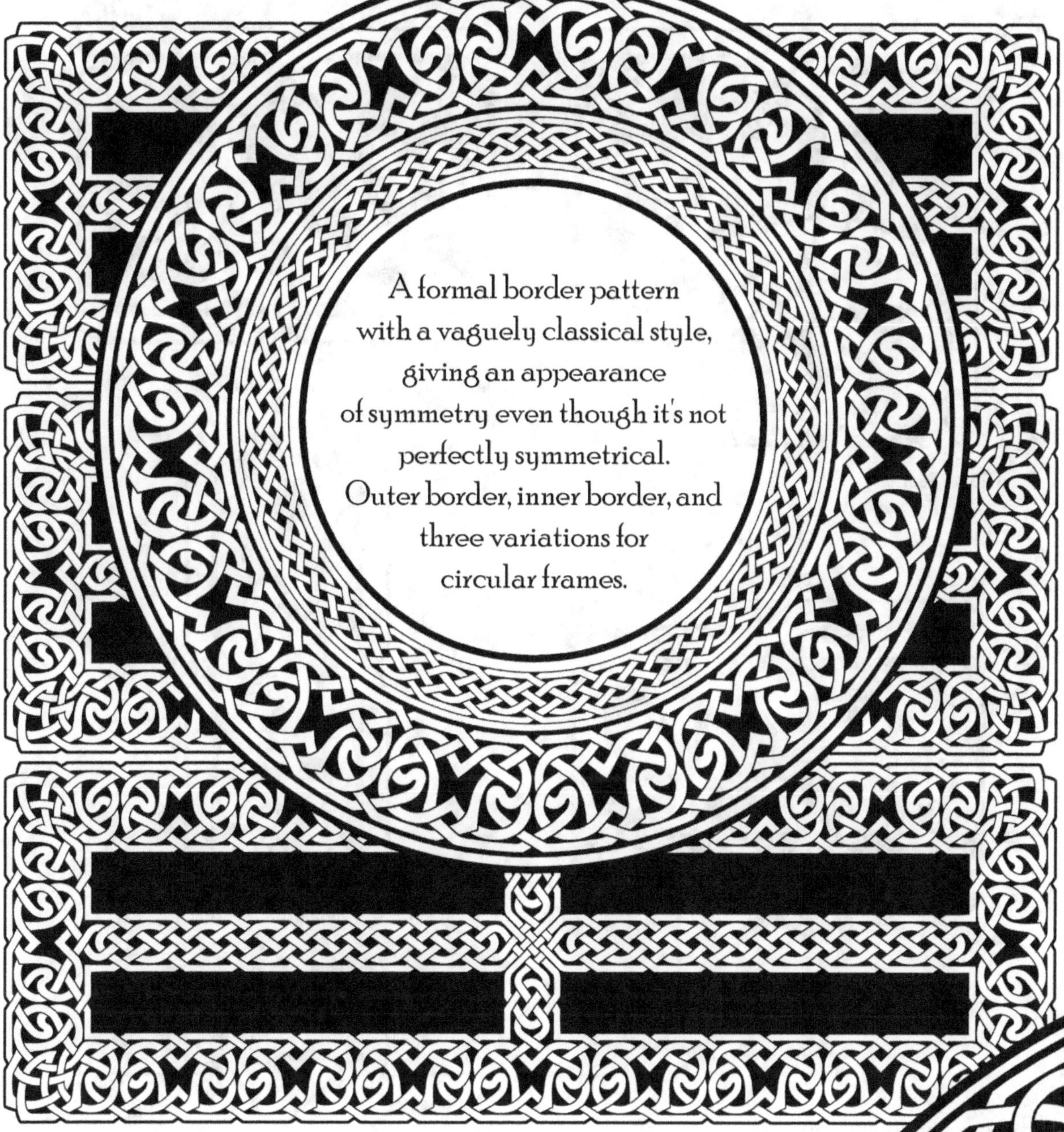

A formal border pattern
with a vaguely classical style,
giving an appearance
of symmetry even though it's not
perfectly symmetrical.
Outer border, inner border, and
three variations for
circular frames.

Structure:

Straight Sections, using only corners and outer border: one band.

Straight Sections, including Inner Border: multiple bands.

Circle Sections, Page One: design is a single band.

Circle Sections, Page Two: design is multiple bands.

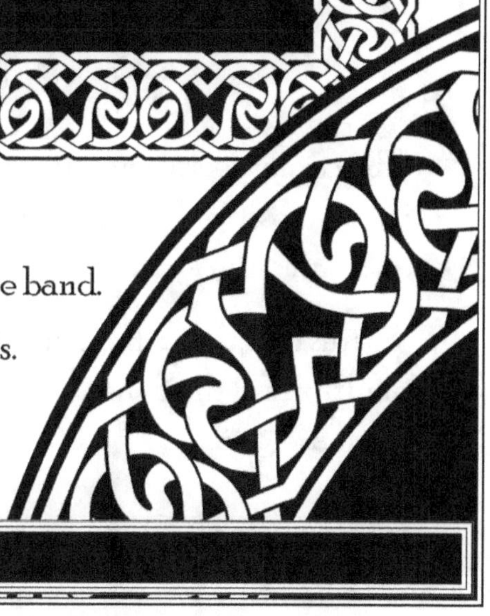

2 1/2"   2 1/2"

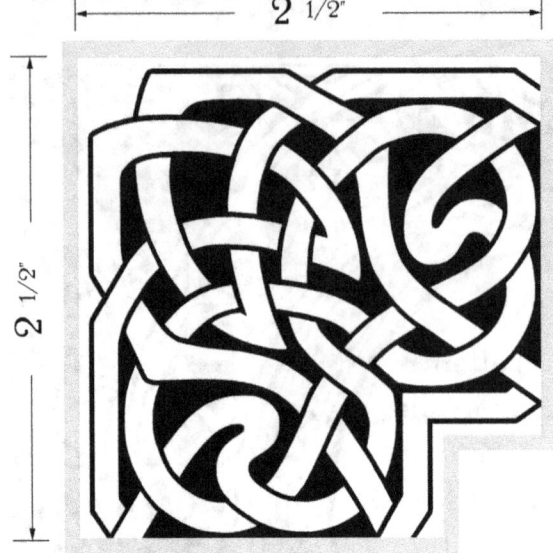

2 1/2"

Corner Section

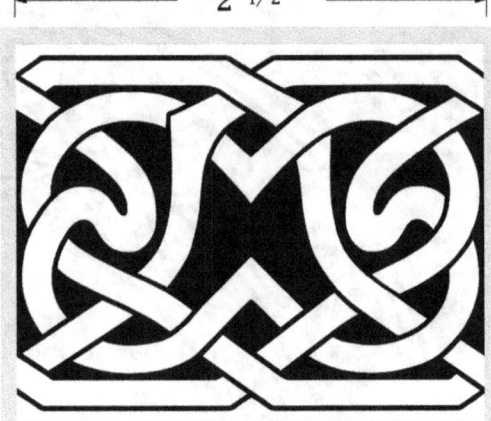

Outer Border, Repeating Section

2 1/2"

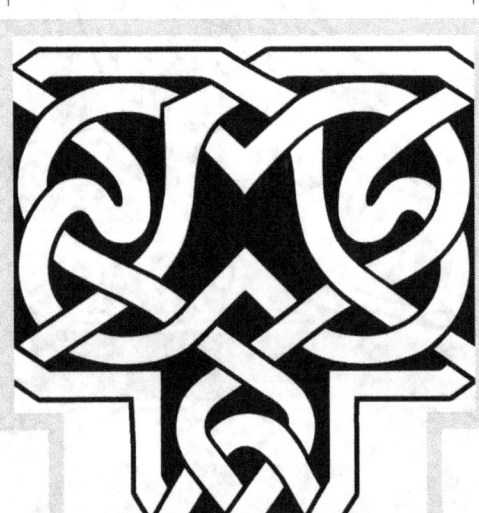

Outer Border / Inner Border T

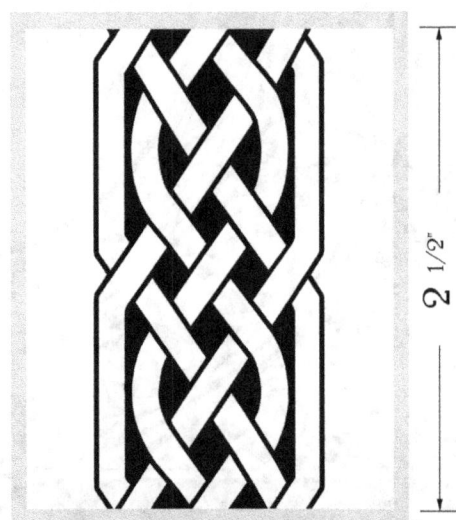

2 1/2"

Inner Border, Repeating Section

The corner section and the inner border T and crosspiece have square dimensions, matching the length of the repeats.

So this design can be laid out in multiples of the dimension shown„ on a square grid.

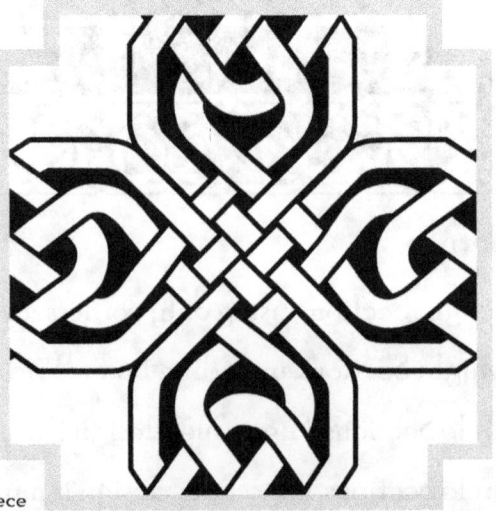

2 1/2"

Inner Border, Crosspiece

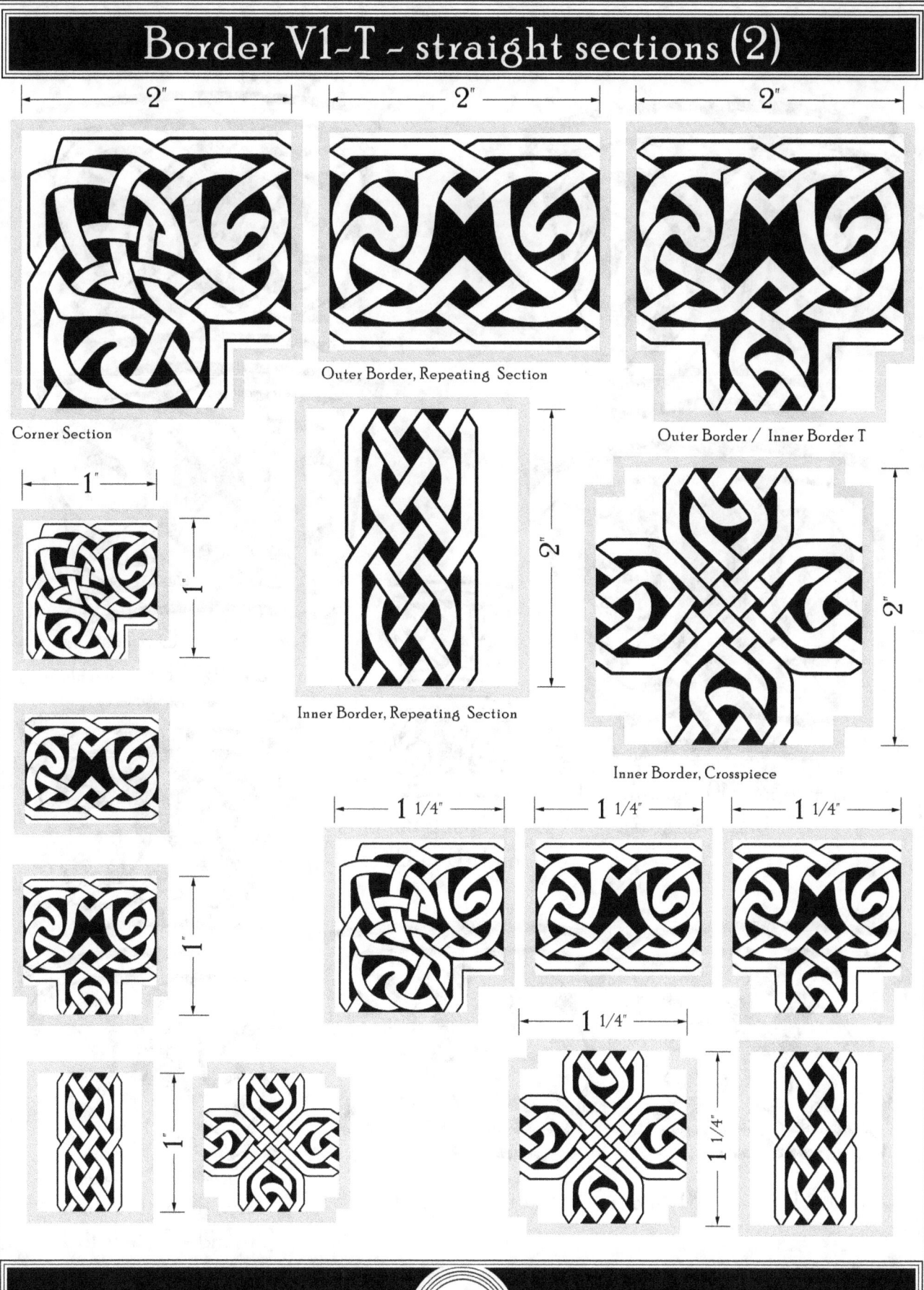

2"

2"

2"

Corner Section

Outer Border, Repeating Section

Outer Border / Inner Border T

1"

1"

1"

2"

Inner Border, Repeating Section

2"

Inner Border, Crosspiece

1"

1 1/4"

1 1/4"

1 1/4"

1"

1 1/4"

1 1/4"

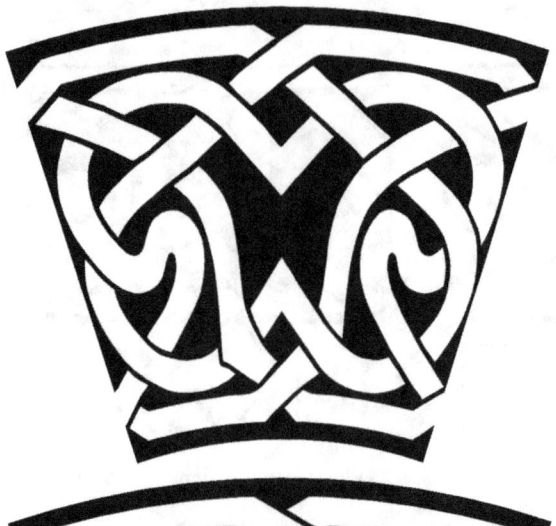

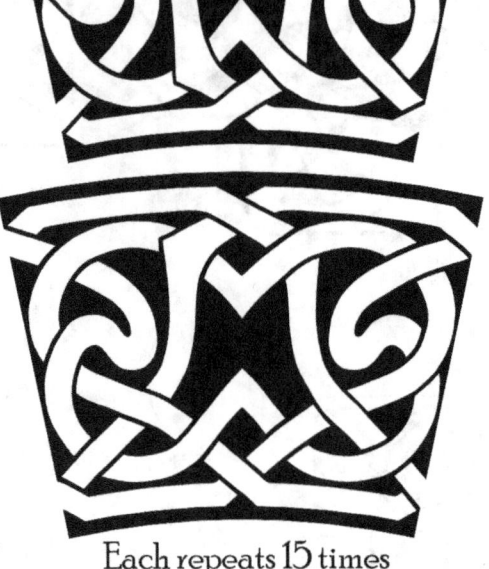

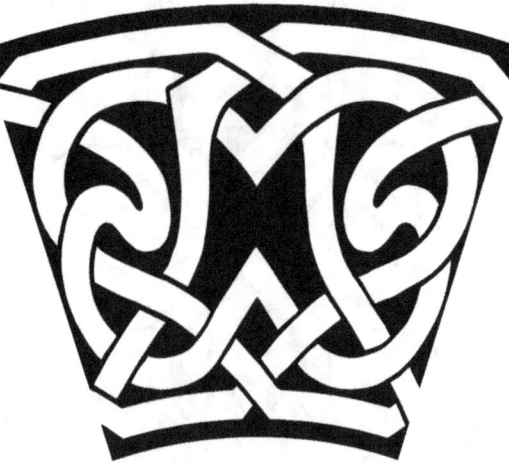

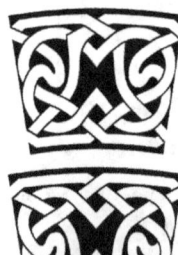

Each repeats 15 times
around a 12 1/2" circle (o.d.)

Each repeats 10 times around
a 9 1/2" circle (o.d.)

Each repeats 20 times
around a 6" circle (o.d.)

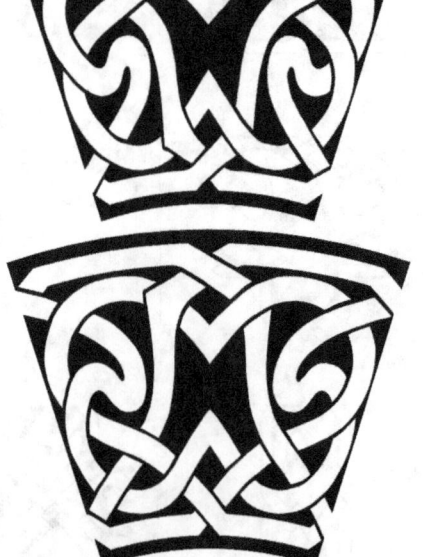

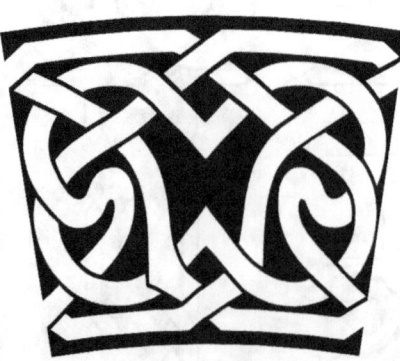

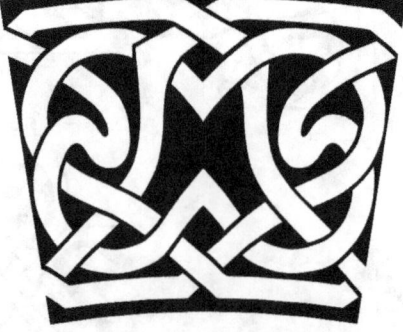

Each repeats 20 times around a 14" circle (o.d.)

Each repeats 10 times
around a 7" circle (o.d.)

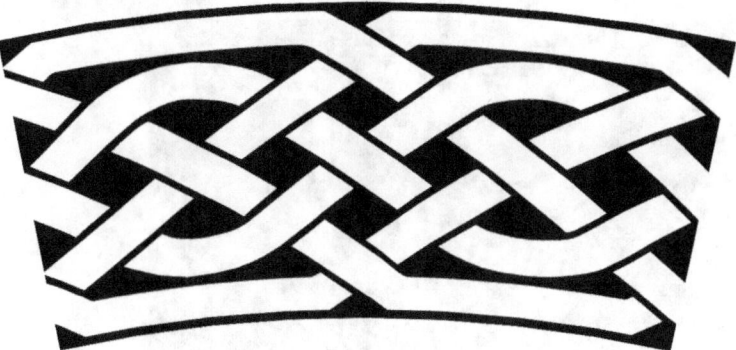

Repeats 15 times around a 19" circle (o.d.)

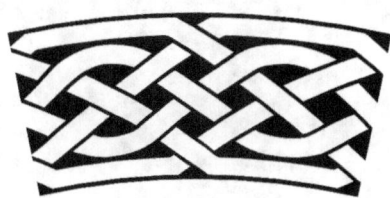

Repeats 15 times
around a 10" circle (o.d.)

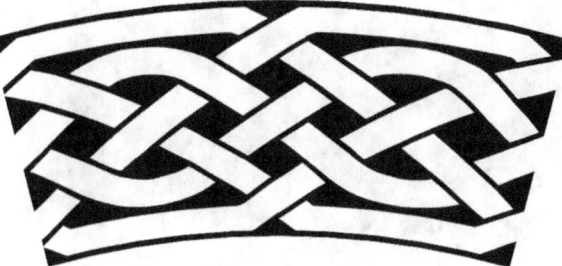

Repeats 12 times around a 12" circle (o.d.)

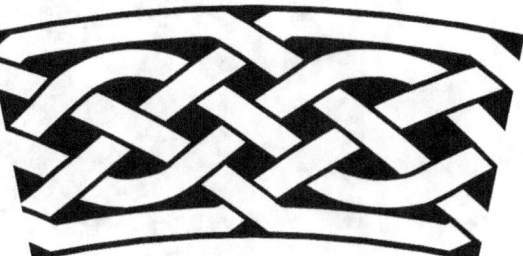

Repeats 15 times
around a 14" circle (o.d.)

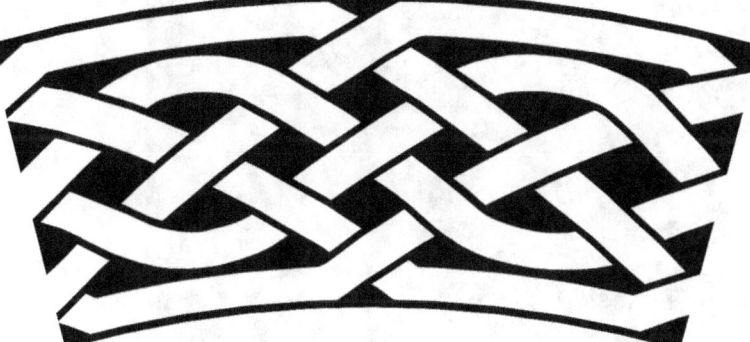

Repeats 12 times around a 16" circle (o.d.)

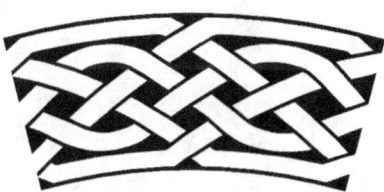

Repeats 12 times around
an 8" circle (o.d.)

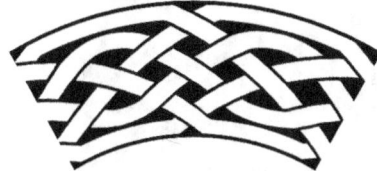

Repeats 6 times around a 4" circle (o.d.)

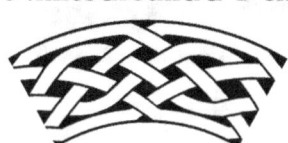

Repeats 6 times around a 3" circle (o.d.)

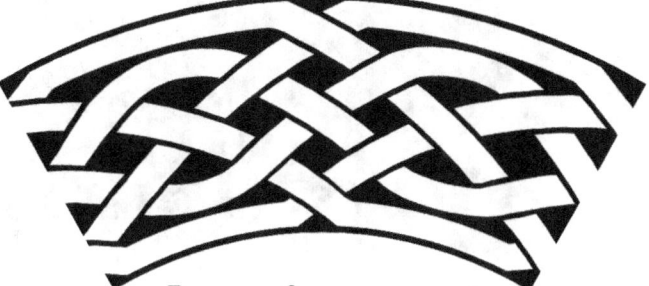

Repeats 6 times around
a 7" circle (o.d.)

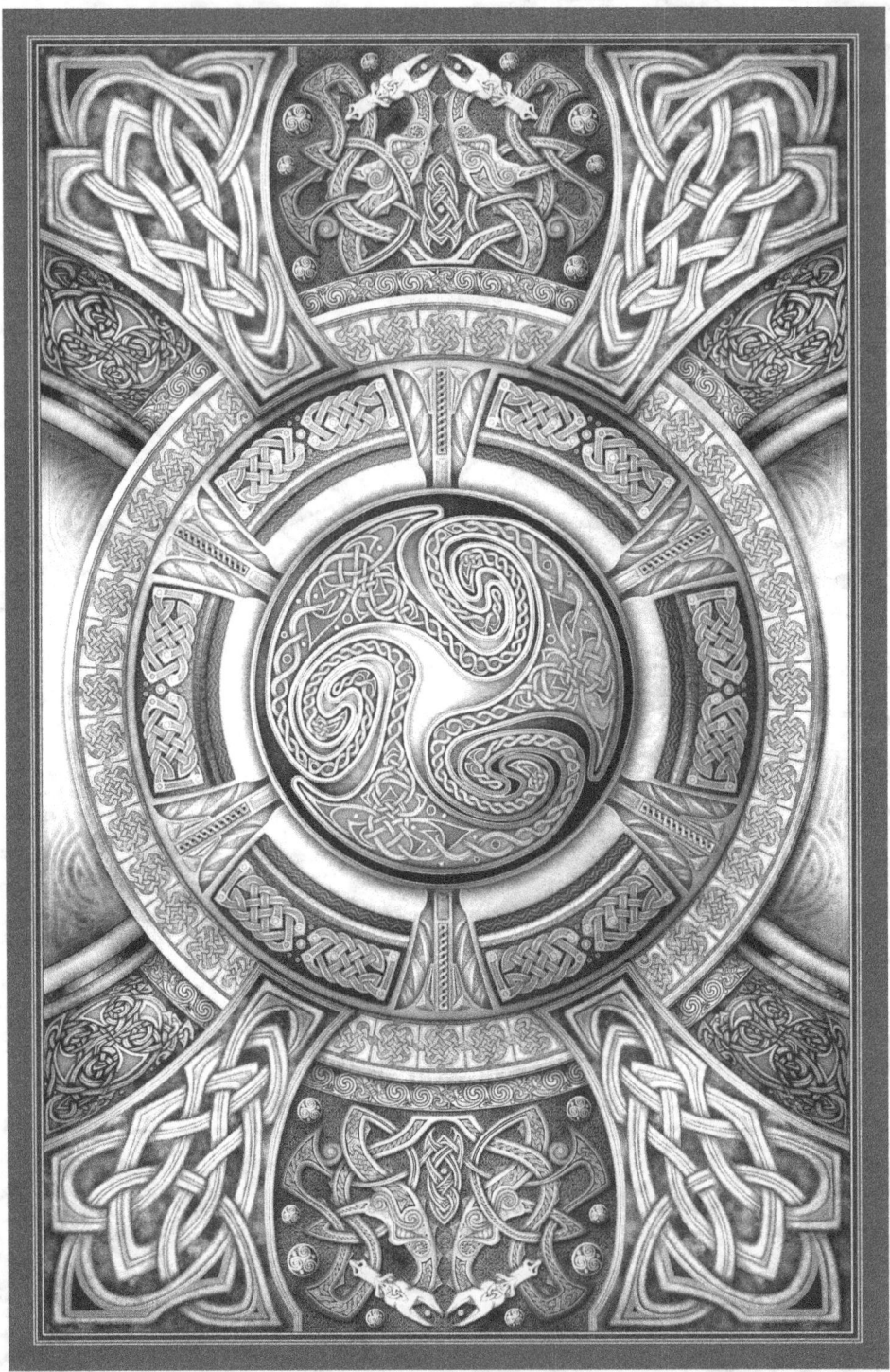

Triskelion Mandala

About the author

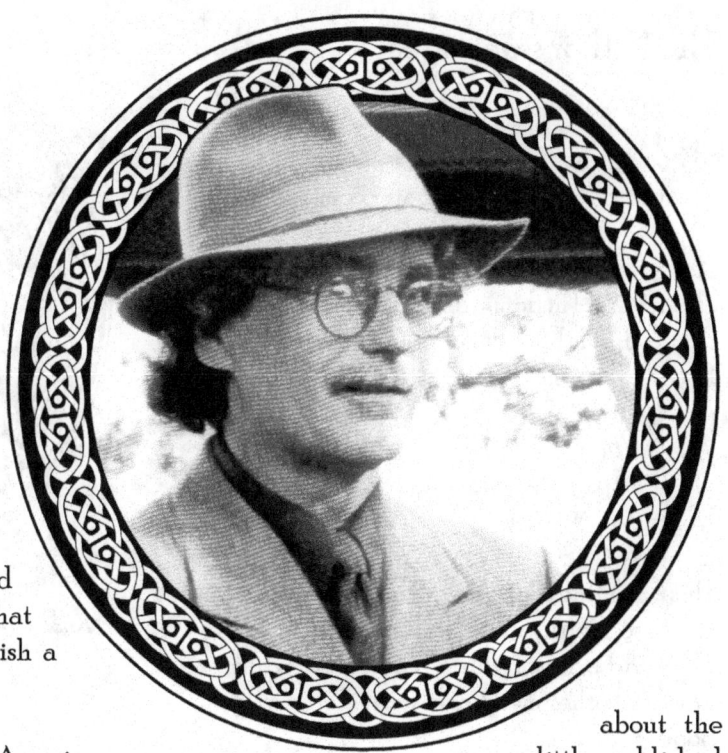

Bradley W. Schenck was born in California; but he's recently been caught up in an eastbound migration that's finally landed him in northeastern Ohio.

His intimidating last name is originally Dutch. His ancestors settled in New England when it was still called New Holland, and they remained mad enough about the name change that they fought a war against the English a hundred and forty years later.

It may be because of his two Irish American grandmothers that he wandered into Celtic art; already working as an artist by 1979, he ran across a copy of George Bain's *Celtic Art: The Methods of Construction* and began to explore traditional and Celtic Revival styles in his own work. At that time, this was all in ink and watercolor.

While Bain was seminal, Bradley gives perhaps even more credit to John G. Merne's *A Handbook of Celtic Ornament* in forming his own take on Celtic design. Merne's Celtic Revival style adopts some features of the Art Nouveau and Arts and Crafts movements in a very natural way and the nature of that (brief) book is less inclined to mathematical diagrams, and more to giving an artist ideas about how to fill spaces with original knotwork.

But ask him who his favorite artist is, in the Celtic vein, and he'll sit you down and tell you about the little-published Art O'Murnaghan (Brian Kells), who worked on a modern day illuminated manuscript in the early 20th century and whose work, housed now in the National Museum of Ireland, seems to make Bradley glow. He hopes to see it first hand one day.

Bradley's had a varied career, as many creative people do, with jobs as a draftsman and sign painter, at a retail window design company, and then seventeen years in the computer games industry as an artist, game designer, and art director.

Today, he says, he lives by his wits. This seems to involve selling his own work online and the occasional freelance commission.

(This article was originally published at celtic-tshirts.com.)

About the author

The author's web sites

Webomator Blog
   ...at http://www.webomator.com

Here's where I post notes, updates and excuses about what I'm doing, along with links to other things that I think somebody ought to be looking at. Like you, for example.

The Celtic Art Works
   ... at http://shop.webomator.com/celtic-art-works

This an online shop where I hawk my wares: in this case, Celtic art designs on posters and archival art prints, T-shirts, blank books, calendars, and other merchandise... including this book.

Retropolis: The Art of the Future That Never Was
   ... at http://shop.webomator.com/retropolis

But my brain is just so much stranger than that, and here's the proof. The *Retropolis* site gathers together all of the work that the other side of my brain does; and that other side of my brain spends its days in the Future that people used to believe we'd be living in by now. It's that streamlined, Art Deco kind of future that's full of rocket ships, faithful robot companions, and the occasional big green thing with an unfortunate number of eyes.

Like *The Celtic Art Works*, *Retropolis* offers that art on posters and archival prints, calendars, blank books, T-shirts, and loads of other merchandise.

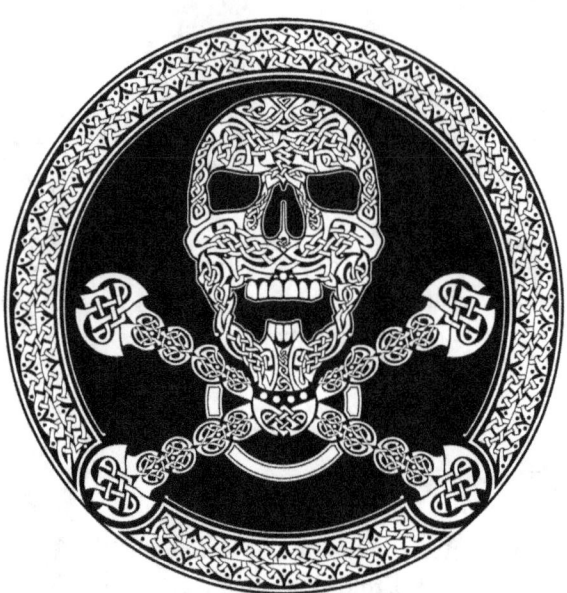

Knotwork Skull and Crossbones ~ from The Celtic Art Works; all rights reserved

Thrilling Tales of the Downright Unusual
   ... at http://thrilling-tales.webomator.com

And the *Thrilling Tales* site continues that theme with illustrated stories (some interactive, some published as weekly serials) from Retropolis, the World of Tomorrow. The stories are free on the web site but they're also available in print.

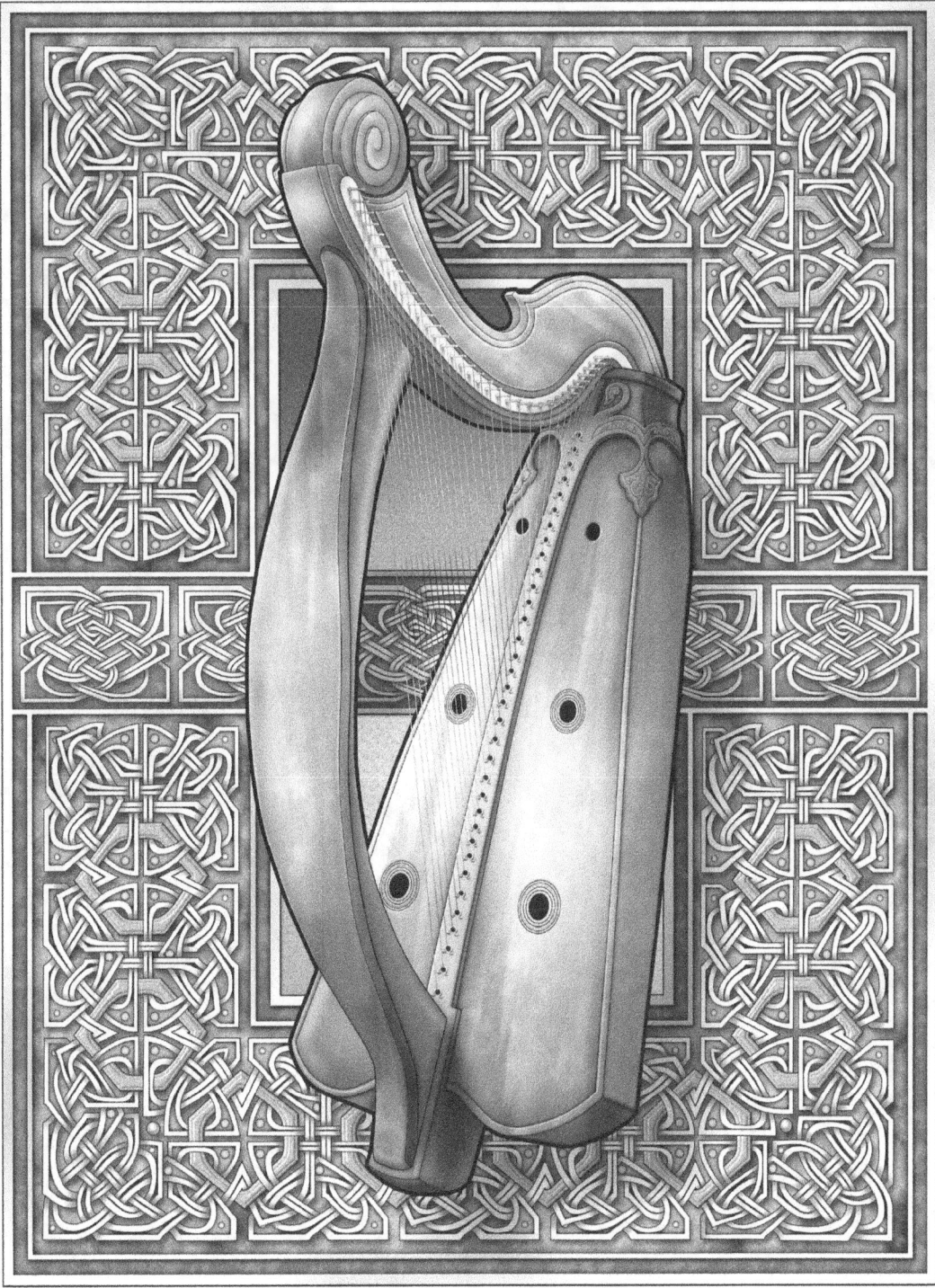

The O'Hogerty Harp